Beyond Pain and Suffering
Adapting to adversity and life challenges

By Tom Seaman

Author of: *Diagnosis Dystonia: Navigating the Journey*

www.tomseamancoaching.com
www.beyondpainandsuffering.com

Shadow Panther Press

Wilmington, NC

Disclaimer

This book is intended as an educational volume only; not as a medical or treatment manual. The information contained herein is not intended to take the place of professional medical care; it is not to be used for diagnosing or treating disease; it is not intended to dictate what constitutes reasonable, appropriate or best care for any given health issue; nor is it intended to be used as a substitute for any treatment that may have been prescribed by your doctor. If you have questions regarding a medical condition, always seek the advice of your physician or other qualified health professional.

The reader assumes all responsibility and risk for the use of the information in this book. Under no circumstances shall the author be held liable for any damage resulting directly or indirectly from the information contained herein.

Reference to any products, services, internet links to third parties or other information by trade name, trademark, suppliers, or otherwise does not constitute or imply its endorsement, sponsorship, or recommendation by the author.

Cover design by: www.100covers.com

ISBN: 979-8657480474

Table of Contents

About the Author

Tom Seaman earned his bachelor's degree in education and psychology in 1994, after which he partnered in private business ventures in health education. In 2001, he returned to school to obtain his master's degree in counseling. During his first semester he developed dystonia, a painful neurological movement disorder. His symptoms became so severe that he was unable to complete his degree. After numerous ineffective treatments and years of physical and emotional pain, Tom learned and applied a combination of techniques that greatly improved his quality of life. In addition to better managing his dystonia, he lost 150 pounds he gained due to his sedentary lifestyle with chronic pain.

In 2012, Tom became certified as a professional life coach and has continued this passion ever since. His focus is helping people better manage the challenges of various physical health conditions, stress, anxiety, depression, work/life balance, and relationships. Tom has had the pleasure of working with clients 11 to 78 years old in the US and all over the world, including Canada, the UK, Australia, New Zealand, Poland, Slovakia, Czech Republic, Portugal, India, Slovenia, South Africa, Lebanon, Spain, Switzerland, and China. Every day, he gets the opportunity to help others in life changing ways with his coaching/consulting practice.

In 2015, Tom wrote his first book, *Diagnosis Dystonia: Navigating the Journey*, which was recognized by the Michael J. Fox Foundation and added to their suggested list of resources. He has also written numerous articles about strategies for living with physical and emotional health conditions and other life challenges that have been published around the world. Tom has also been a guest on international radio shows and podcasts, and his work is featured in various magazines such as Brain and Life, Pain Free Living, and Pain Pathways. He was also the keynote speaker for the first ever National Dystonia Symposium in Canada.

Tom is also a health and wellness blogger, motivational speaker, volunteer for the Dystonia Medical Research Foundation as a support group leader, and is a member and writer for The Mighty, Patient Worthy, The Wellness Universe, and Chronic Illness Bloggers Network. To learn more about Tom, visit www.tomseamancoaching.com. You can follow him on Twitter and Instagram @CoachTom12 and @Dystoniabook1.

Why this book?

In 2015, I published my first book, *Diagnosis Dystonia: Navigating the Journey*. It is a combination autobiography, self-help, education book. It provides treatment options, coping strategies, skills for daily living, and tools for managing the physical and emotional challenges of life with a chronic health condition. I wrote this book for patients, caregivers, and doctors because I have lived with dystonia, a neurological movement disorder, for 20 years and there are very few resources available that address the totality of living with dystonia and other chronic health conditions above and beyond just physical symptoms. Not wanting others to go through the same intense suffering I did for years, I compiled a ton of strategies for dealing with the many challenges that dystonia and other health conditions present.

Ever since that book was published, many people told me I should write a second book because of how much the first one helped them. To my surprise, this was not just from people who have dystonia. I am often told by people who do not have dystonia how much that book helps, and if they replace the word "dystonia" with what they are dealing with in life, it would be as if it were written for them; and for many of them, it is not just a health condition they are talking about. It is about a multitude of everyday life challenges and various forms of adversity.

As I heard this more and more from people who were going through all sorts of things such as divorce and other relationship issues, difficulty with work or work-life balance, stress, life transitions, and of course health conditions such as chronic pain, cancer, heart disease, diabetes, anxiety, depression, Parkinson's disease, Meniere's disease, fibromyalgia, celiac disease, to name just a few, I knew I had to write this book. I wanted to reach the broader audience for whom much of the information was intended, with fresh, new information about what I have learned since my first publication.

In a nutshell, this book is about how to live as high a quality life as possible in the face of adversity, pain, and suffering that is part of everyone's life. More importantly, it provides strategies for how to make the very best of difficult life circumstances and situations. Pain and suffering accompany everyone in one way or another throughout life, and this book strives to provide you with tools to work through it all.

You could be the parent of a child who is being bullied and/or struggling to fit in socially. Perhaps you are painfully trying to determine the next step after high school and feel undue pressure to make the "right" decision. Or finishing college without a clue what to do with your life. Or a 30, 40, or 50+ year-old who feels the same way. Perhaps you are transitioning from a working career into retirement or other life transition and struggling with this new direction.

You could be someone like me who is trying to make ends meet while battling a health condition with chronic pain; or someone who is living with a life-threatening health condition; or a family member or friend of that person, losing sleep trying to come to terms with their pain and suffering as well as your own. You might be in a difficult marriage and can't find a way to get out. Perhaps you have gone through a traumatic natural disaster, struggling financially, fearful of the uncertain world in which we live, recently experienced the loss of a loved one, dealing with a difficult boss and/or co-workers, managing unexpected home repairs, or simply tired of the daily grind and feeling overwhelmed and overburdened.

The point is that there are many forms of suffering we can experience in life, no matter who you are and no matter what age. These few examples are just the tip of the iceberg and utilizing the tools in this book will help you cope daily and grow beyond these and other stressors in your life. Learning how to adapt to adversity helps us come to terms with our pain and suffering so we can live beyond it, meaning that our challenges are not the main focus of our lives. If you read my first book, you will notice some chapters overlap, but most of the material is new and updated and shared in a different context.

I want to share something that one of my teachers from years ago told me. He said that the quote, "knowledge is power," is a myth. It is the *application of knowledge* that is power. This is an absolutely true statement because we can be the most knowledgeable person in the world and/or have the most amazing skill set in a particular area, but if we don't apply our knowledge or skill set then what's the point? The same holds true for this book. There are many tools, tips, pieces of advice, and strategies for living a better life, but if we don't apply them and make them a consistent part of our life, they are of no use. We have to put them to practice if we want to effectively cope with and hopefully overcome the many challenges we encounter.

Introduction

"Life is difficult. This is a great truth, one of the greatest truths. It is a great truth because once we truly see this truth, we transcend it. Once we truly know that life is difficult - once we truly understand and accept it, then life is no longer difficult. Because once it is accepted, the fact that life is difficult no longer matters."

This is the opening paragraph in *The Road Less Traveled*, by M. Scott Peck, one of the most popular self-help books ever written. This very powerful assertion is simply stated, yet much more difficult to apply. This being the case, I encourage you to put it to memory and really think about it every day. By doing this, the more it resonates with us and we understand that when we better come to terms with the challenges of life and accept things just as they are without resistance, we learn to work with them and not against them. This helps us rise above the pain and suffering in our lives. In other words, we transcend whatever obstacle stands before us.

To move beyond pain and suffering does not necessarily mean to be without pain and suffering. It means learning how to work with physical and/or emotional pain so that we can keep it from being the most dominant force in our lives. The first step in getting beyond pain and suffering is to acknowledge that we are in pain and/or struggling. We then need to understand why it causes us to suffer and learn how to implement strategies to minimize despair.

Life comes at us quickly, so it is of great help to have tools in place for difficulties we are experiencing in the moment, and for the unpredictable stressors in life, such as financial distress, trauma, pain, diseases and other illnesses, relationship issues, fear, depression, anxiety, and grief, to name just a few. This book provides tools and strategies for how to cope and manage these situations and move beyond the pain and suffering they bring, be it physical, emotional, or both. It teaches how to not make the most difficult parts of our lives the most significant part of our lives.

As you will read in Chapter 2, we must learn to handle adversity differently than we have been conditioned throughout life. Anytime we are faced with an undesirable situation or circumstance, if we run from it or fight against it, it strengthens its power over us. If we deny it, it rears its ugly head in other areas of our lives which not only impacts us, but others as well.

We have to change habits of thinking and behavior taught to us by instinct, society, and culture to run from or fight against what we don't like, if we want to be healthy and create real change. This book will teach you how to manage adverse conditions and circumstances, and how to flow with the up and down rollercoaster that life can be, so you can reduce your pain and suffering.

I have come to learn an important truth about life...we are very much the same in many respects. We feel many of the same emotions and have the same fears, worries, anxieties, etc., even if our circumstances in life are totally different. Whether you are living with depression because of a tough relationship, stressed out because of a financial debacle, deflated and angered because of a life changing health condition, or anything else, everyone experiences very similar feelings. However, we often feel alone when we are going through a painful life experience because we can't imagine anyone else could possibly understand us. This is far from the truth as will be evident the more you read.

This book is an honest account of many life challenges that may be similar to the ones you face each day. It addresses the light and dark side of adversity in an honest manner, with the intent to acknowledge you, offer understanding, provide hope, and help you find meaning in your life that transcends your suffering. If we stand tall in our pain and suffering, this is how we get through it, and this book will guide you along the way.

Please take special note of my story in Chapter 1. This is the foundation from which I write all of the following chapters. It is very important to see what I have been through that prompted me to share the concepts and strategies in this book for effectively coping with different challenges in life. I think you will find some common themes that parallel your life.

I believe it is important to know where a person comes from to understand their perspective, as well as their credibility. People who have been through it, so to speak, and are open to being vulnerable, can offer insight and comfort to others. This is what I do as a life coach and health consultant. Many of my clients are exposed to a database of information that is based on great personal suffering (and triumphs!), and how to reach the pinnacle of success in their lives. My goal is to provide you with a good taste of that in this book.

Chapter 1
Rising from the depths of brutal pain and despair

In 1994, I graduated from college with a degree in education and psychology. I then went to work in a health education business. More specifically, it was a chiropractic and nutrition patient education business. Over the next five years, my partners and I developed other companies and services; a golf training and rehabilitation facility/seminar business; a nutritional analysis service; and a fitness center. Needless to say, I was very busy. The work was fun, but I needed a change.

In August 2001 at the age of 30, I returned to school for my master's degree in counseling. The year prior to starting graduate school, I took a job as a project manager at a new water park and family fun center on a lake in the town where I lived.

I worked very long hours every day, but it was great being active and outdoors versus stuck in an office or travelling the country to conferences. It was one of the most enjoyable years of my life. Little did I know, it would soon be followed by some of the worst years of my life.

Shortly before I was to move into my new university apartment and start graduate school, I noticed that my neck movements were a little restricted. More specifically, turning to the left was slightly difficult. I remember the first time I noticed it. I was walking past the lake where I worked on my way to lunch. When I turned to look at the lake on my left it took effort. I didn't have full range of motion and it was difficult to keep my head turned to the left. I felt it pulling back to center on its own. I assumed I was stressed and tight from working a lot or sleeping in a bad position, but the tightness never went away.

Within about a week or two, I started to feel a slight, involuntary muscle pull to the right as if someone were pushing or pulling my head. Some days I felt fine so the pulling never lingered on my mind as being a problem. I chalked it up to the wear and tear of working long hours and several five-hour car trips moving into my new apartment.

I never had much of a break between working, packing, and driving. I wasn't sleeping much either. I also had a recent fall from a bicycle and a few hard wipeouts while water skiing, so there were plausible reasons for my stiff neck.

During one of those long car trips to move my belongings, it felt like my head was tilting to the right (right ear towards my right shoulder). I turned the visor mirror down so I could look. My head was in fact ever so slightly tilting to the right. Again, I chalked it up to the stress of moving and school preparations. I figured it would resolve itself. I was also too busy to think too much about it.

When graduate school began in the Fall of 2001, I noticed that my neck was turning on its own to the right a little more, especially when I walked. It "flopped" back and forth as if my neck muscles had weakened. I couldn't keep my head straight without holding it with my hand. While sitting in class and at work, I often found myself cupping my chin in my hand to keep my head straight.

I was not in any pain and I didn't look any different to other people unless I pointed it out, but to me it seemed obvious that my head was turned. I soon became a little self-conscious in public. I began having a little anxiety about it which exacerbated my symptoms.

A few weeks into the school semester, I decided it was time to see a doctor before it got worse. Assuming it was a musculoskeletal problem, I went to a chiropractor. Logically this seemed like the right person to see. I had been around chiropractic most of my life and it was helpful for many other problems, so it seemed like the right kind of doctor given my symptoms. I wholeheartedly endorse the benefits of all chiropractic, but only when a patient has a problem within the scope of knowledge and practice of that particular doctor; this goes for any type of doctor.

The initial exam consisted of x-rays and postural tests. The doctor determined that I had restricted joint movement, thoracic and cervical posture issues, and a flat spinal curve in my neck. I was never given any diagnosis with a name; just a description of what he saw.

Treatment consisted of neck and back adjustments 3 times a week. Within about 3-4 weeks, the doctor started me on extension traction. I would sit upright in a wooden chair and lean my head back so I was looking at the ceiling. He then put a strap around my forehead with weights on the end to pull my head back even further. This is done in some chiropractic techniques to try and restore the curve in people with a flat or reverse cervical spine.

This forced hyperextension caused pain in my neck and back that did not previously exist. It was so uncomfortable that I told the doctor that I no longer wanted to do the traction and instead just stick to the adjustments. To his credit, he went against normal treatment protocol and obliged. The involuntary neck turning didn't disappear, but the pain subsided a little.

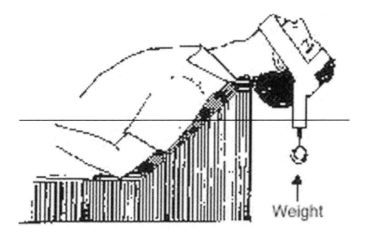

Barrett, S. A Skeptical Look at Chiropractic BioPhysics (CBP). www.Chirobase.org. Retrieved July 3, 2013 from: http://www.chirobase.org/06DD/cbp.html

As the first semester wore on, my symptoms ebbed and flowed. I would get a little better for brief moments and then worse again. Sometimes I thought I needed to get adjusted more and then sometimes less. I couldn't figure out what was causing the inconsistency in my symptoms. That being the case, I decided to stick to a regimen of 3 adjustments per week and just play out what I still thought was a temporary problem.

I began wearing a soft collar neck brace on occasion to reduce the uncontrollable spasms and head turning/pulling. The collar helped me do some activities with more ease, but I always felt worse when I took it off. My muscles felt weaker and my head turned more. I was also starting to have pain again, and this time it didn't go away.

Nearing the end of the semester, my symptoms were worse than they had ever been. I assumed it was because of the stress of final exams and all the papers and presentations I had to do. I was spending countless hours with my nose in a book or on the computer, so it seemed logical that this was why my neck was pulling to the right a bit more than usual and why I had some minor pain.

It was tolerable. I just had a neck that turned away from center a small amount and "flopped" a little when I walked. Granted, my symptoms had gotten worse over the past four months and my neck was starting to hurt, but I could still manage all of my activities. Looking back, I think I was in denial about how bad it had become, but I was still completely functional so I didn't give it the attention it deserved. Hindsight of course being 20/20, because there was obviously nothing normal about it.

After I took my last final exam, which was essay in format, my neck felt the best it had the entire semester. As silly as it sounds, I thought the way I sat while writing for three hours corrected the problem. Recall that I thought one of the reasons for it happening in the first place was from sleeping in a bad position so it seemed logical for me to think this other position might have corrected it. The relief I had from being done with the semester factored in my mind as well.

I was symptom free for a couple days and rejoiced by telling my family and friends that I was all better, a logical conclusion at the time since it was the longest I had gone without any symptoms.

During the Christmas break I visited family and friends. As the days progressed my symptoms started again. I was having more pain and involuntary muscle contractions than ever before. It forced me to lie down often, but it was still pretty minor relative to how things would become. I decided to go to a sports medicine doctor in my hometown and while I was having x-rays taken, the technician impatiently kept telling me to keep my head straight. I told her, "I can't. This is why I am here." Even the doctor was indifferent, to put it mildly. He never even put his hands on my neck or shoulders to see how my neck was involuntarily trembling. I had to ask him! He just looked at me and said I had spinal stenosis, which was not at all what was wrong. The frustrating journey with doctors was just beginning...

The night I returned to school for the next semester is when things began to go downhill very quickly. I recall feeling a combination of a spasm and an itch in the middle of my back next to my right shoulder blade. I reached my arm back to scratch it and I felt an unfamiliar yank in my neck. Instantly my head/neck began to involuntarily pull to the right harder than it ever had before. I was terrified. Adrenaline pumped through me. I had no idea what was going on.

I managed to get to sleep and the next morning I went to my chiropractor. He did his normal adjustment and there was no change. I went back almost every day the next two weeks. During those two weeks, I also saw a physical therapist and a medical doctor at the college health center. All in all, within the first 6 months, I saw a total of 15 doctors who specialized in different areas. None of them had any idea what was wrong and pretty much dismissed me because they didn't know what to do.

Not knowing where else to turn, I continued going to the chiropractor. Nothing he did helped, so he referred me to another chiropractor in town who used a different, yet similar technique that was designed to specifically rehabilitate your spine and correct your posture. The approach was a little more intensive, but my referring doctor felt this would be best based on my worsening symptoms. He made me feel confident that this new doctor would fix my problem. I was all for it because I was getting desperate.

My neck and back were in so much pain and my head was not only pulling and turning to the right, it started to lock in that position. This made it very difficult to work and go to class, let alone concentrate when I was there. I could barely hold up my head without using my hand, so I was game for anything.

I saw the new chiropractor the following week. When I was in the waiting room, my neck muscles were involuntarily contracting, pulling my head towards my right shoulder. A patient sitting across from me who looked perfectly normal said, "I looked just like you two weeks ago and the doctor fixed me right up!"

This was the most reassuring thing I heard since my symptoms started 6 months earlier. I was so relieved and excited. I thought I finally found the doctor who was the answer to my problem. Little did I know that his treatments would be the beginning of the worst nightmare I ever experienced.

They took a series of X-rays and while I was still not given a diagnosis, the doctor determined that I would need a minimum of 6 weeks of treatments 3-4 days a week, with exercises at home as well. Believing wholeheartedly that it would help from the glowing referral and patient testimonial, I gladly signed on to my only known option at the time. Recall that I still had no diagnosis. We had the internet to search for things, but nothing like the resource it is today to more easily narrow down problems.

Treatments consisted of over-the-door cervical traction, a head and shoulder harness with weights, and neck adjustments. I was also instructed to do over-the-door cervical traction at home and wear the weighted head harness a few times a day.

This chiropractor gave me the most violent adjustments I ever had in my life, and I had been to numerous chiropractors since I was a kid. Since my neck muscles were so strongly pulling my head to the right, he literally had to put me in a headlock to be able to adjust my neck. I saw him adjust other patients and knew this was not his standard neck adjustment technique. He adjusted me this way because he needed extra leverage to fight the muscles that were forcefully pulling the opposite direction he wanted to move my head.

When I think back to allowing him to do this to me, I cringe, but I was so deeply suffering with no other answers, I let it happen. I don't beat myself up over it, because I did the best I could with what I knew at the time.

I could barely get out of bed after a few treatments. I had pain in my back, shoulders, and neck unlike anything I ever experienced before. The pain to lift my head off my pillow was the worst I ever had in my life. Naively, I figured this was no different than any other kind of exercise I had done in the past where I felt pain the next day, but this was extreme.

I managed to get to the doctor later that morning and he told me it was normal to feel this way. Trusting him, because I was desperate, I continued with treatments. Each day over the next two weeks I got worse. My neck was turned and now locked to the right. I could barely move. I also had forceful muscle spasms that pulled my right ear towards my now raised shoulder (about 4-6 inches higher than my left shoulder). I was unable to sit or stand without holding my head to relieve the brutal pain. I was again told it was normal and would subside. How could this be normal? I was basically in tears all day from the pain, and I knew pain! I had plenty of it with numerous sports injuries. This was an entirely different world of pain.

One day my parents were visiting so they drove me to the doctor. On the way to the appointment, my head involuntarily jerked and slammed into the passenger side window. I hit it so hard that it felt like I had cracked my head and/or the window. There was no damage other than a big lump on my head. My parents were taken aback at how much I had declined so quickly.

After going downhill like a runaway train, I searched the internet harder than before for answers. I was barely able to fight back tears from the pain as I sat at my computer pushing my head with one hand while typing with the other. I could only handle sitting for 10-minute intervals. There was a red welt on my chin from pushing so hard to try and keep my head straight.

During one of my internet searches, I came across "torticollis." Torticollis literally means "twisted neck" and is usually an acute condition that can be resolved in a short period of time. It is when a muscle, joint, or ligament in the neck is irritated. It is often referred to as "wry neck."

"Acute" means that the symptoms developed quickly, over a period of hours, or overnight. This is what I think the girl in the waiting room had wrong with her and why she got better so quickly.

I then came across "spasmodic torticollis (ST)." Spasmodic torticollis, better known as cervical dystonia, is a problem within structures of the brain. It is a very different condition and in most cases should not be treated the same as acute torticollis (even though they might look similar), which is a problem with joints/vertebrae. Cervical dystonia is a brain based, neurological movement disorder and there is no known cause in most cases and treatment efficacy is highly variable.

Dystonia is the third most common neurological movement disorder after Essential tremor and Parkinson's disease. It is characterized by uncontrollable, involuntary muscle spasms and contractions (often persistent), causing repetitive movements, twisting, and/or abnormal postures. It can impact any part of the body. In the case of cervical dystonia, the neck muscles contract involuntarily, causing the head to twist or turn to one side, or forward or backward. EXACTLY what I was experiencing!

Needless to say, when I read about spasmodic torticollis/cervical dystonia, I finally knew what was wrong. The page could have literally been written by me. I told my doctor the next day what I found, and he agreed that this was probably what I had. He wasn't entirely sure, but it sounded pretty close. Not knowing a lot about it, he continued with the status quo of treatments. I continued to get worse, so I told him I was not coming back anymore. I wish I had done that much sooner. The course of my life might have been much different. There might not have been decades of painful suffering.

I then sent out a blanket email to every doctor, nurse, and medical student at the university asking for treatment suggestions. Most who responded said I should get Botox. Others suggested physical therapy, medications, and chiropractic.

I read up on Botox and although it is one of the most common treatments for dystonia, along with oral medications (muscle relaxers in most cases), I was not comfortable putting a neurotoxin in my body. I hoped to find another option. However, I did follow a suggestion to go to Duke University for a neurologist's opinion (it never even dawned on me to see a neurologist and no one ever suggested it prior to my blanket email). The doctor confirmed my diagnosis as cervical dystonia and also suggested Botox injections. I was still leery about it so I declined, but finally getting an official diagnosis was a relief.

I continued to search the internet for alternative options to medication. I came across the ST Recovery Clinic in New Mexico (ST standing for Spasmodic Torticollis). It offers a natural approach to symptom management which includes things like stretching, exercise, massage, and nutrition. Everything I read and from everything the director told me over the phone made perfect sense, so I decided that this was what I wanted to do. I was able to get into the clinic a month later.

In the meantime, I spent my day on the floor rolling around in pain beyond words. Literally, that was my entire day. The pain had become that bad. Even having lived through it, I still find it hard to fathom.

One day I couldn't take the pain anymore, so I went around the corner to a 24-hour medical facility for medication. I had to find some relief. I truly wanted to die. I never even liked taking over the counter medicine, so this was a major thing for me to do.

In tears, I begged the doctor for the strongest drugs he could legally prescribe. I don't recall what I was given, but it took a lot of the pain away and I was able to go to sleep pretty easily for the first time in months. Unfortunately, I woke up having hallucinations, cold sweats, and unshakable fear. Thankfully, this all dissipated in a few hours, but the pain returned. I never took those medications again. It was terrifying.

You might be thinking to yourself as you read this: why did you go to all these doctors who didn't help? Why don't you remember what medications you took? Why didn't you go back and tell the doctor what the medications did to you? Years later, I asked myself these same questions. The simple answer is that the pain was such that I could not think clearly, I had no diagnosis and was clinging to a miracle, and I felt I had to do anything at all to find some kind of relief and didn't know where else to turn. I didn't care about anything other than how to end the pain or end my life. This is the reality of intense suffering and misery.

When someone is in this state of mind, not a whole lot of rational thought takes place. I had never experienced anything like this before. It was far worse than any broken bone or other injury I had incurred prior to this point in my life. I was in unchartered territory that I was unprepared to handle, as was the case for my family and friends. None of us knew what the best thing was to do.

My neck was now locked to the right and the muscle contractions/pulling significantly worsened with any type of movement. The intense spasms felt like a freight train was pulling me over. It was a miserable existence. It felt like I was simultaneously being beaten by a baseball bat while a drill penetrated the back of my neck and skull.

I began to have suicidal ideations, but loving life as I do, I couldn't and wouldn't give up. I believed there was an answer out there for me, but I was very lonely with bizarre symptoms no one really understood. For example, I showed someone close to me how my neck snapped to the right when I took my supporting hand off my face. They said "ewww" and looked away. Still looking for compassion, I showed them again what I was living with and they said I looked gross and asked me to never show them again. They meant no harm because they didn't understand the seriousness of it, but hearing this made me feel even more alone.

During the month of February 2002 while waiting to go to the ST Clinic, I spent the day as follows: wake up, eat breakfast, lie on the floor, eat lunch, lie on the floor, eat dinner, lie on the floor, and then go to bed and try to fall asleep. In fact, I also ate meals lying on the floor. I would lie on my side and slide food from the plate into my mouth. The only time I got up was to go to the bathroom or get something to eat. I spent about 14-16 hours a day in a fetal position on my floor in tears most of the time.

I became almost totally dependent on the help of others. Everything I could do, or had to do, was with one hand because the other hand was constantly supporting my head and neck to try and alleviate some of the unbearable pain and muscle pulling.

Every week, my parents drove over two hours to stay with me for a couple of days to do my laundry, go food shopping, clean my apartment, and just be there with me. I was useless. I can't imagine how they felt seeing their son suffering so intensely with no idea how to help. None of us had any idea what to do.

At the end of February, I made the trip to the ST Clinic in New Mexico with my father's help. To this day I am still surprised I was able to do it considering my symptoms. It was sheer will power and determination. I had to fight through the relentless pain every minute of the trip.

I took any chance I could to lie down in airports, restaurants, and rental car agencies. I didn't care what people thought. I had to find a way to make it there as comfortably as possible. The hardest part was sitting upright on the plane. I can only imagine what people thought was wrong with me as they watched my neck twist and turn while I squirmed around trying to get comfortable.

When I got back from the clinic, I returned to the floor for most of the day. Occasionally, I would attempt a stretch or two I had learned, but that was all I could muster up the strength to do. Everything I did caused screaming pain. Anytime I got up to eat or go to the bathroom, I would be wiped out until I had to get up again to eat or go back to the bathroom. These were literally my only activities. I didn't do anything unless I had to. I couldn't tolerate the pain.

Things like shaving and showering for me were the equivalent of working out with weights or doing high impact aerobics for an hour. Let that marinate for a moment; the strength it took to merely shave my face or shower was as physically demanding (and far more painful), than heavy exercise. This speaks volumes about how torturous dystonia can be. Please check out the photos below which show me trying to simply peel a banana. The muscles in my entire upper torso were simultaneously contracting.

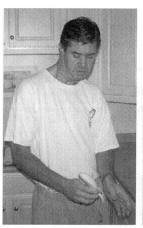 

Although these are still photos, you can tell that it was brutally difficult to move properly due to the forceful muscle contractions. For those of you who experience symptoms to this degree, you know what I am talking about. You are not alone and you are not without hope. Things can get better, and I will soon get to the good part of my story where I talk about how I began to improve.

A few more weeks passed with no relief. As much as I wanted and tried to stay on my own, I couldn't live like this anymore. I needed significant help. I gave in to pleading from friends and family to move in with my parents. I still remember the day I called to tell them I accepted their offer to live with them because I couldn't carry on by myself any longer. A week later I was living in their guest bedroom. It was a very humbling experience to give up my independence.

March 9, 2002, the day my Mom drove me to their home (a 2 1/2 hour ride), is clearly etched in my mind. Within about a mile from my apartment, I was in so much pain that I begged my Mom to take me back. The spasms, pulling, and pain were so intense that I could not keep from crying, screaming, and thrashing around trying to find some level of comfort to handle the ride.

I didn't think I could make the trip. My poor Mom helplessly watched as she drove. The person next to her was being tortured by an invisible force and she couldn't do anything to stop it.

My father was in his van ahead of us with all my belongings. We thought about calling him to tell him we were turning back, but never did. Somehow, I was able to grind it out, mainly with my Mom's help. She kept reassuring me that things would be okay.

I still remember her repeatedly saying, "we have to keep going. The sooner we get there, the better it will be. Hang in there. Everything will be better in a couple hours." I knew she was right, so I pleaded with her to drive as fast as she could. She never breaks the speed limit, but this day she put more pedal to the metal than I ever saw before. My pain trumped the risk of a speeding ticket.

When I got to their house, I was met by several family members. Neighbors also came by throughout the day and brought food. It was really strange; as if someone just died. I don't think anyone knew what to do other than just be there for me, for which I was very grateful.

Everyone thought this was going to be a temporary problem and they would be there to help me out for the next month or so while I "recovered." People looked at it no differently than recovering from surgery or an injury that required me to get a little rest and relaxation. I was pretty much thinking the same thing.

In the following months and years when no recovery took place, it changed some of my relationships. There was an expectation from others that was not realized. The fact that I had a chronic condition that might never go away was not something people were able to embrace. It was not something I was able to embrace for a while, so I couldn't expect them to either.

Some of my friends came down hard on me. The expected me to do more than I was. No matter what I told them about how I felt or how challenging it was to just get through the day doing menial tasks, it was never good enough. I felt so misunderstood and nothing I said or did changed their opinion. I was heavily judged and ridiculed by some people.

As the weeks went by, I slowly began following parts of the movement therapy program I learned at the clinic in New Mexico. It was extremely hard because I was in so much pain, but I pushed through believing it would help.

Easter arrived and I went to my aunt's house a couple miles away to be with the family. My Mom had to get a plate of food for me because I needed my hands to support my head from the unrelenting muscle contractions in my neck. Within about an hour, my pain climbed to a level where I had to leave. When I got back to my parent's house (thankfully just around the corner), I lied down on the floor to try and reduce the pain. I was crying uncontrollably. The physical pain was brutal and the mental pain of not being able to sit and enjoy a holiday meal with my family was very sad.

Not being able to handle something as simple as eating a meal at the table was very hard for me to grasp. Less than a year prior, I was able to do what I wanted, when I wanted, and how I wanted without a second thought. Now I could barely do anything without screaming pain. It was at this moment that it hit me that I had something seriously wrong with me that may never get better. Reality hit me like a ton of bricks and I was terrified.

A couple days went by and I decided I wanted to go on medication. I needed some relief. Imagine the pain I was in to get to this point after the earlier episode when I took medication that I thought was going to kill me.

There are no drugs specifically for dystonia, but I read up on those that might be effective for my condition. In other words, they are used "off label," meaning that they are designed for another condition but have been found helpful for something else. The one I chose was klonopin (clonazepam), which is a benzodiazepine. From what I researched, it seemed like an effective and commonly used drug for dystonia. It seemed like the best option for me.

I went to see a doctor that week. He was an internist who knew very little about dystonia, but he was the only doctor in town my family went to and trusted. We went over the literature on medications used for dystonia. I told him I wanted klonopin and he agreed. Within about a week or two, my pain subsided a little because the medication helped reduce the muscle contractions. My adrenaline that was fired up from the pain also mildly subsided.

This minor relief made it so I could function with a little more comfort. I began to drive a little and started going to my sister's house a couple miles away to go in her family's pool. I found that submerging my body in water reduced my symptoms a little, so I was there almost every day for about an hour.

The sunshine also helped me feel better, as I previously locked myself in the house all day long. My Mom expressed concern about me being such a hermit and suggested I sit in the sun a little each day. She was right and I made a point of reaping the healthy benefits of fresh air and daily sun exposure as often as I could. However, after only an hour (often less) I would have to lie in bed for several hours, if not the rest of the day on some occasions. This minimal activity wore me out because the pain would set in very quickly and render me almost useless.

I continued with the program I learned at the New Mexico clinic and began to notice I was getting a little more control of my neck and I felt very slightly less twisted. Pictures proved otherwise, but I was feeling a little better because I had a little less pain. I began to spend a little more time outside of the house. It felt good to be out and about a little more, but the increased activity caused more pain and spasms. Finding a balance between rest and activity was tricky.

To clarify, my "outside of the house" activities consisted of maybe attending a school event for one of my nieces or nephews once in a while, hanging out at the pool for an hour or two, and slowly walking around the yard. Anything beyond that was far too painful. I had no social life and wouldn't even entertain the idea of eating out, catching a movie, concert, or sporting event, etc. Basic tasks around the house were still a heavy chore.

A few months passed and it felt like my medication was not as effective as it once was so my doctor doubled my dose. For several months I was on a good program. I did my stretching and exercising every evening, took an Epsom salt bath, and then got a back rub from my father before I went to bed. I began to notice small positive changes. However, I was becoming very impatient. I was not getting better as quickly as I would have liked. Not being a patient person, this didn't sit well with me. I wanted faster results. I did so much and got so little out of it.

One day I was offered a beer. I was fearful of drinking alcohol while on klonopin, unsure of how they would mix. The person who offered it to me said not to worry because if anything, it might just increase the effect of the medication. Since the medication was helping a little, I thought some added benefit would be great. I was also pretty miserable and didn't have a whole lot of regard for my body and life at that time.

As it turned out, the alcohol did enhance the benefit and I had no side effects. So, from time to time I had a drink or two. Little did I know that this would lead to a lot more than just one or two drinks within a couple months.

My daily regimen of stretching/exercising, Epsom salt baths, and massage began to change. I grew tired of the routine and I liked the benefit of alcohol. I started to have a glass or two of wine in the late afternoon and then do my neck stretching and exercising before dinner. I found that the alcohol loosened me up and I was able to do my stretches with greater ease.

I was seeing a psychologist during this time (I had to lay on his floor during sessions so I was comfortable) and I told him about my routine. He didn't see any harm in me having a couple drinks if it loosened me up to help me stretch. His approval was surprising to me, but I welcomed it because it gave me permission to do something I knew was probably not a good idea.

After a few weeks on this routine, I found that I needed more alcohol to assist me with my stretching. Eventually, I found much more relief from drinking alcohol than stretching, but it was not long lasting.

After about a 6-pack or half bottle/bottle of wine, my neck was more relaxed and I was in less pain. My improvement was apparent to my parents and anyone else in the house. They thought my neck was better from the exercises. Little did they know that I was not exercising much, if at all. It was the alcohol that was really helping my muscles relax.

I pretty much replaced alcohol for exercise and deceived the people who loved me most. I felt guilty every single day, but obviously not guilty enough because all I did for my symptoms over the next four years was drink every day. It was the most desperate and alone I ever felt in my entire life.

Looking back, I completely understand why I did all of it. I was deeply suffering and desperately trying to find anything that would give me relief, even if just for a short moment. When a person is in this state of mind where it feels like life is over, but you wrestle with not wanting… and then sometimes wanting… to end your life, you do things to cope that are often very out of character.

I don't think anyone can truly understand the mindless desire to self-medicate with alcohol and drugs unless they have experienced such miserable pain. It's no excuse, but desperation can make a person do most anything.

Pretty soon I began to put on a lot of weight from drinking. I was also eating a very poor, high calorie diet that greatly contributed to the weight gain. My Dad tried to talk to me about my diet, but I didn't want to hear it. I didn't want to tell him the truth about my drinking. I was embarrassed and ashamed. I also knew that if I told him he would have found a way to get me to stop, and that scared me because alcohol was the only thing that gave my body any pain relief.

It was a terribly scary and lonely place to be. It got to the point that every day was pretty much a daze, except for the daily wake up vomit or dry heaves, accompanied with ridiculous pain during the day until I started drinking again.

Minimal activity caused horrible pain. For example, I only shaved once every week or two because it was too difficult. As for haircuts, it was too painful to sit upright to have it cut; nor could I groom it, so my Dad gave me crew cuts. I stood outside on the back porch and leaned over as he shaved my head.

I would beg him to go faster because my head and neck hurt so much. He did the best he could to get it done quickly, but I know I drove him nuts rushing him. When he was done, I would lie down the rest of the day. I didn't care how it looked. I just wanted it short. The less grooming the better because it hurt too much to raise my arms to my head. Please think about that. Just getting a 10-minute buzz cut knocked me out for an entire day! It's amazing the number of things most of us take for granted that we can do without a second thought. I don't mean for that to sound judgmental because I also took SO much of my life for granted before all of this happened. I don't think we can really appreciate what we have until it is gone.

I spent most of my time alone in my bedroom. I didn't like who I had become. I was miserable. I stopped calling and visiting people, and they stopped as well. Pretty soon the phone never rang.

I know I said this earlier, but I promise I am getting to the good part of the story! There is a happy ending.

I never went to any family functions or holiday gatherings for several years, unless they were at my parent's house. I lived there so I couldn't avoid them. I would have left if I had somewhere else to go because I didn't want to be around anyone. I was too riddled with pain and depression, as well as embarrassment about my weight and my crooked neck.

I was also experiencing significant anxiety, so being around a lot of people was uncomfortable. I also had no friends because I didn't know anyone in town other than my family and I was in too much pain to get out and meet people. Dystonia relocated me to a town where I had no social or vocational connections, and I didn't feel well enough to get out and grow some roots. It was very lonely and I lost a lot of self-confidence. Around this time, I began having panic attacks and was often afraid to leave the house, except when I absolutely had to. It was the most horrible time in my life.

My panic attacks were such that I would get very dizzy and weak when I was in public. My legs, arms, and head would shake, my palms would sweat, my heart would beat rapidly, my vision would get cloudy, and I would lose all sense of where I was. My mind would go blank and I couldn't think clearly. I feared passing out. When in a grocery store, the shiny floors looked and felt like ice. The fluorescent lights also seemed to drain me of every ounce of energy.

I was also self-conscious about how I looked. Having always been thin and athletic, it was a different life being overweight. It felt like all eyes were on me. My twisted neck added to my embarrassment and shame.

When I hit around 240 pounds, my doctor put me on blood pressure medication. This was mind boggling to me. Never in my life did I have trouble with my blood pressure. What in the world was I doing to myself?

One might think this would deter me from my unhealthy lifestyle, but the pain was still too much to handle so food and beer remained my drugs of choice, along with my prescription medications. I'm lucky to be alive considering what I was putting in my body.

When my weight reached 310 pounds, I stopped getting on the scale. I refused to look anymore. I couldn't even watch shows like *The Biggest Loser* (a weight loss show) because I felt so guilty seeing others face their weight problem while I continued to gain weight. I tried to ignore my guilt and shame as much as I could.

I used to run from the camera. I regret it now because I don't have many pictures to compare with how I look now, but I didn't even want to look in the mirror let alone have a picture taken. On Christmas 2005, my niece and nephew stood behind me as I opened a gift from them. Before I knew what happened, my sister-in-law took a picture of the three of us (next page). I was upset for a moment and then forgot about it.

A month went by and it was my birthday. My niece and nephew gave me a birthday card with a picture on the front of the envelope. It was a picture of them with a man I didn't recognize. I stared at the picture for a while wondering why they would give me a picture of them with someone I didn't know. Then it hit me. It was me!! I was shocked. You might think this would have turned my unhealthy lifestyle around, but it didn't. I kept drinking and eating poorly for another year.

A few weeks prior to Christmas 2006, at around 330-350 pounds (I am not entirely sure because I stopped weighing myself a year earlier at 310 pounds), I came down with a stomach virus and was too sick to eat or drink anything. I spent most of the time in the bathroom with diarrhea. The rest of the time I was in bed. I didn't have any solid food for over a week and all I drank was water and ginger ale.

Of course I couldn't drink alcohol. This concerned me because I thought I would need it to curb the pain. Thankfully, this was not the case. My neck felt pretty good, all things considered, and I have found in the years since then that when I get sick, my dystonia and pain tend to decrease a little. Almost as if my body is too weak for the muscles to contract. My neck was still turned and off center, but I was not in as much pain. All the resting was very helpful in that regard.

I also feared I had become addicted to alcohol to the point of facing difficult withdrawal. Luckily, perhaps even miraculously, I didn't have any at all and my drinking days were over. It was like turning off a light switch. I realized drinking would eventually kill me and made the conscious decision to stop. I have never looked back. I am deeply grateful that my problems with alcohol went no further.

Getting sick with the stomach virus was the best thing that could have happened to me. Those two weeks of being idle gave me time to rest my body and think about my life and what I was doing to myself. After a lot of reflection, I made the decision that I had better change my lifestyle or I might soon be dead.

It was such a relief to finally let go of that chapter of my life. It was an even bigger relief when I eventually told my parents about my drinking habits and why it had dominated my life. Being the saints they are, they listened and didn't judge me. They understood why I did it and felt sad that I was in bad enough shape to do that to myself. They were mostly proud of me for having the strength to overcome it.

All along, I knew what I had to do to improve myself, but I was afraid of making changes because I wasn't sure if the changes would make a difference (which was delusional because deep down I knew they would), but more than anything, I had become comfortable in my misery. I had to make the tough decision to dedicate myself to learning how to become comfortable with doing new things that were not at the moment comfortable, in order to improve upon my situation in life. This is not uncommon for a lot of people. We are creatures of habit and comfort, not often liking change, so we might remain in a dreary place because it is what we have come to know and trust, despite the pain and suffering.

I lost about 10-15 pounds while I was sick and when I was well enough to get out of bed and eat solid food again, I went back to my healthy eating habits (see Chapter 15). My parents also encouraged me to begin walking a little each day. I was still over 300 pounds and could only walk about 50 feet, but I was determined to change my life. I made it a daily practice to walk to the end of my driveway and back. That grew to walking to the end of my street and back. My parents came with me most times to make sure I didn't fall. I was dizzy, anxious, and unstable from the weight and my tight neck. I also quickly ran out of breath.

In about two weeks I was confident enough to walk by myself. It felt great. I was so excited. I remember coming in the house one day after a short walk and saying to my parents, "that felt so good! I'm going to do it again!" That day was the start of my weight loss journey. I got the fever to be healthy again and I never looked back.

Further into the book in the nutrition section, you can read how I lost all the weight (with photos), but to summarize, I went from well over 300 pounds to 180 pounds in less than a year. I completely dedicated myself to changing my lifestyle to get healthy again. In the process, my dystonia symptoms also improved, which I attribute to better nutrition, stress reduction, and faithfully incorporating a very targeted exercise routine into my lifestyle. I also began to work more on the emotional/mental side of this health condition, much of which is covered in this book. I discuss additional things I do to manage my symptoms throughout the book, with a specific list in the pain management section of Chapter 13.

Unfortunately, my desire to lose all the weight pushed me past my limits. I walked too much which made my neck muscles pull hard to the right again, causing pain in my mid back. I started walking less, but the pain was too much so I had to stop walking entirely. Thankfully, I continued to lose weight and keep it off by eating properly. Below is a weight loss photo of me with my nephew, taken 10 years apart.

I began doing the program I learned from the ST Clinic (my second attempt), which consists of specific stretches, exercises, and lifestyle habits, all for the purpose of lengthening and strengthening muscles, and reprogramming motor areas of the brain responsible for movement. I did other exercising as well, primarily for strengthening my core and improving my balance. I went about the program in a much different way this time, with far more patience and understanding of the process. I was also still taking medication, but the ST Clinic program was the foundation for my improvement, along with proper nutrition and stress management.

I also received acupuncture treatments every two weeks and massages as often as possible. I also used various trigger point tools to relieve pain and relax tight muscles. I rested and used heat and ice as needed. I also prayed, meditated, and did relaxation breathing exercises combined with visualization techniques. These are all things I still do to this day.

Each time I went to the doctor (about every 2 months) he couldn't believe how much I changed. Everyone in the office also took notice. Most people commented on the weight loss versus the change in my dystonia. That was understandable because losing 100 plus pounds was far more obvious, but dystonia symptom reduction was my main focus.

In the Fall of 2007, my doctor and I discussed reducing my medications. Considering how much my symptoms had improved, we both felt they were no longer necessary. I was already off the blood pressure medication. Now I wanted to get off klonopin, as well as baclofen and restoril I had also been taking, so he started to taper me down.

Unfortunately, my taper plan was far too much medication way too fast. Within a couple weeks, I began having bizarre symptoms that introduced a whole new level of horror. This was a major kick in the gut. I had worked so hard to get to where I was, only to have a new problem with which to contend. Life was flipped on me again.

In brief, I became very weak and dizzy, among many other symptoms that included extreme anxiety, depersonalization, and auditory and visual hallucinations. I was so weak and off balance that I did not know how I was able to stand most the time. A small bottle of water felt like a 10-pound weight. I tried getting stronger using weights, but they were too much for me. I had to use soup cans to exercise and even they felt heavy.

My muscles began to atrophy and I became skinny and frail. It was very disappointing. I went from fit and athletic, to weighing well over 300 pounds, to almost sickly thin.

I became extremely sensitive to all sorts of visual and auditory stimuli, and it felt like my skin was dripping off my body. When I drove in a car it felt like I was floating on top of the seat and wasn't aware that I was even touching the steering wheel because my sense of touch was altered. In the morning and evening I also experienced full body spasticity where I could barely move.

My doctor thought all of my symptoms were side effects of the medications (he thought I was taking too much for my new body weight), as did other people, so he tapered me off even more! This made my symptoms worse, so I started talking to other people and reading about benzodiazepines, the class of drugs home to klonopin and restoril. After living in confusion about my symptoms for over a year, my search was over. I discovered I was in severe benzodiazepine withdrawal.

Over time, the brain develops tolerance to certain medications. This can happen even when taking the prescribed dose, as was the case with me. When they are decreased in large amounts or when they are reduced (usually abruptly), the brain can go into withdrawal, potentially causing hundreds of strange symptoms. The drugs take the place of natural neurotransmitter production, so when they are removed there can be significant communication failures in the brain which cause many uncomfortable symptoms. For me, in many ways, it was worse than dystonia and pain.

I sought out a doctor who specializes in helping people with medication addiction. I was not an addict in the sense that most people think. I was what is called an "accidental addict" by virtue of my brain developing tolerance to a prescribed medication. This is extremely common all over the world. Over the course of a year, this doctor helped me reduce my withdrawal symptoms by changing my medication and taper regimen.

When I was better stabilized with my medication, I had more energy which enabled me to establish an exercise routine again so I could focus on improving my dystonia symptoms. After a few years of hard work following my personalized dystonia movement therapy program, I was able to do some very light biking and swimming a couple times a week. I was also able to lift light weights, do squats, lunges, and modified pushups. I also became very flexible from stretching. The strength training and flexibility work proved to be beneficial in helping manage my symptoms.

As you can see in the photos at the end of this chapter (ranging from 2002 to 2020), I have made significant progress. My dystonia has greatly improved and my body is much more balanced and relaxed. The biggest change, which you can't see in the photos, is how I feel on the inside. I felt SO much better! However, I was and am not without challenges.

While my neck and body appear straight, my cervical spine actually angles to the left and I tilt and pull to the right, particularly when I stand or walk. C1 is apparently rotated about 10 degrees from center and I also have scoliosis. I feel as unstable as a half-played game of Jenga.

I do exercises that specifically target the muscles that keep my neck and back as straight as possible. Some days, depending on the rigors of the day and other stressors, these muscles need to work harder than other days to compensate for the imbalances. This can cause pain, instability, and fatigue, so I do my best to balance my daily activities to minimize these symptoms. I consistently use massage machines and trigger point tools, ice, heat, topical lotions, follow good nutrition protocols, and I practice mind calming activities and stress management.

On occasion, I have mild anxiety because I never know how my body is going to behave. I can get dizzy and have muscle contractions that come out of the blue, making me apprehensive about being in certain environments. However, as you will read in upcoming chapters, this has been significantly reduced by following the strategies that I provide.

Apprehension and fear are common for people with movement disorders because we often don't know how our bodies will cooperate. Since these distressing emotional symptoms often go unnoticed, many of us are a good example of the saying, "don't judge a book by its cover."

My visible dystonic movements are now more task-dependent, versus years ago when they were present no matter what I did. For example, my neck pulls off center when I walk, eat, shave, brush my teeth, and if I sit or stand for too long. My current symptoms are similar to when mild manifestations of dystonia began back in 2001, but my body is different.

The years of physical wear and tear, medications, medication withdrawal, scoliosis, compensatory muscle activity, and changes to the joints and discs in my spine, make me less functional than I was when my symptoms first started. The difference now is that I better understand my symptoms and how to do things to manage them and live my life within my boundaries. To learn more about the specifics of what I have done the past 20 years to help manage my dystonia and other symptoms, this is explained in detail in my other book, *Diagnosis Dystonia: Navigating the Journey*. I also provide a brief list of my symptom management tools in Chapter 13 of this book.

To maintain balance in my life, it is important for me to address my physical, mental, social, emotional, and spiritual needs. I exercise my body and eat healthy foods, I involve myself with positive people, I challenge my mind by learning new things, and I spend time in meditation and prayer. These all help keep any problem, health or otherwise, from being the dominant force in my life.

I have learned to work with my challenges rather than fight against them. I have had to learn to accept that life is different than it once was and most of the time I am okay with this. Adapting to change is a key component to any healthy life. Please see upcoming chapters for more specific details about this.

Of course, I experience frustration not being able to do some of the things I love so much, but considering how sick I once was where I couldn't do anything, I am doing great! I am a better person in so many ways and my life is filled with new and exciting things that were non-existent for years.

Instead of living as a victim by focusing on my limitations and how life was before dystonia, I look at the obstacles I overcome every day and build on those accomplishments. I don't measure myself with who I was before dystonia. I measure my growth from my darkest days. I am grateful for everything I can do now, which is a big part of my ability to cope. Every day when I wake up, the very first thing I do before my feet hit the ground is say, "thank you." Despite many challenges, I have a boatload of things and people and experiences for which to be grateful.

I dedicate myself to a healthy lifestyle, body and mind. I avoid toxic food, toxic people, and unhealthy relationships. I frequently remind myself how horrible my pain and debilitation used to be and live in gratitude for everything that now occupies my life. I choose to not let adversity get the best of me and I don't feel sorry for myself. I keep looking for solutions to challenges and new ways of doing things.

I do my best to vary my days to keep life fresh, even if I only make one small change. On difficult days, which I still have, I don't fight it. Fighting makes it worse. I do my best to listen to my body. When it says rest, I rest. When it tells me to be active, I'm active. I try to not beat myself up when I make mistakes or have a challenging day. I do my best to put my ego aside and take baby steps towards a better tomorrow. When I try to solve everything at once, I make life more difficult.

I don't think too much about how my life once was. I can't change the past. Now is the only moment I have. No dwelling. No regrets. I've learned and grown from it all. I value whatever is happening right now because I believe everything is a lesson. This is easier now because I feel better and my mind is in a better place, but I still have to remain disciplined. I can easily get lazy and fall into negative patterns of thought and behavior.

One of my biggest challenges was learning to not feeling guilty for having a debilitating illness. For years, I felt like a failure not being able do more for myself and live a "normal" life. I also felt guilty that people sacrificed so much to help me. I have now learned to accept help with less guilt. I let people who love me love me more, and I do the same in return. I also give myself and others more credit that we are handling things quite well despite all of our challenges.

Everyone does what they feel they can to help me and if the roles were reversed, I would do the very same for them. We all have challenges and need help from others. Accepting help and providing help to others are important parts of any healing process. Put your ego aside.

People often ask me what prompted me to change my lifestyle to get to where I am now and how I stay motivated every day. The short answer is that I love life and want to make the biggest impact I can on the lives of others for as long as I can. I want to motivate people to grow and make positive changes. I can't do that very well if I am sick. Plus, the bottom line is that feeling sick all the time stinks!

2002

2007

2014

2020

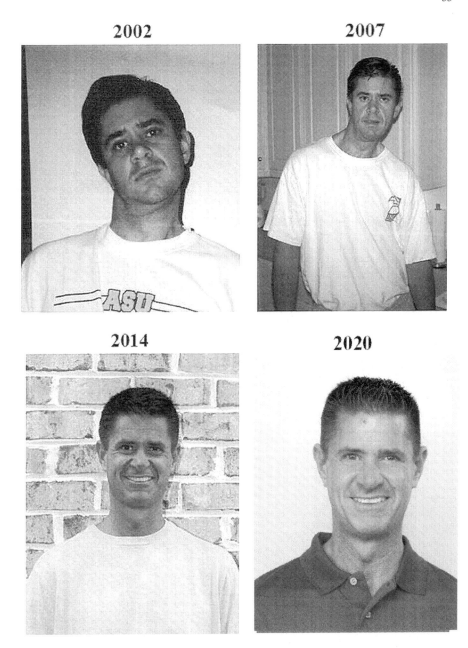

In 2012, I became certified as a professional life coach to help others who live with similar challenges. My main focus is health and wellness, primarily working with people who have chronic health conditions, weight loss issues, pain, anxiety, depression, and those needing help making lifestyle changes. This has grown into working with people who have anger issues, relationship challenges, and work/life balance. Living with dystonia and pain have taught me valuable lessons that provide me with opportunities to help others in meaningful ways. What a gift!

While I would never choose to go through all I have, many positive things have come from it and I am extremely grateful. I believed this even on those dark days when I thought about taking my life. Maybe that is one of the reasons I never did. I knew there was meaning in all of it. Along with my love for life and the people in my life, this is what keeps me going. I believe everything happens for a good reason, even when it causes pain and suffering, and I am staying around as long as possible to learn all I can.

Sometimes it is in our pain and suffering when the greatest growth occurs, which is one of the reasons I chose the title, *Beyond Pain and Suffering*, for this book. Adapting to adversity helps us come to terms with our pain and suffering so we can live beyond it, meaning that our challenges are not the main focus of our life. Instead, they become fuel for making us stronger and connecting to ourselves and the world in different, and hopefully, more meaningful and profound way.

Chapter 2
Adapting to adversity

What is adversity?

When you look up the word adversity, these are some of the many synonyms:

difficulty, pain, hardship, suffering, trauma, sorrow, misery, heartbreak, distress, disaster, opposition, misfortune, setback, crisis, tragedy, burden, torment, hard times, trials and tribulations

All of these words fit the bill very well for adversity, but they are just words. They mean very little until we are actually faced with adversity and are forced to live these words and the feelings that come with these words. The reality of suffering they produce can infiltrate practically every aspect of one's life.

Adversity can come at any time. It is neither fair nor unfair. It simply is. The question of course becomes, what do we do when adversity strikes? There are many answers and strategies, as outlined in this book, but let's begin with something small for starters. It's all about mindset and whether or not we respond or react to the event or situation.

Responding to something is a thought-out activity and a reaction is usually quick, emotional, impulsive, and often irrational. I make this distinction because how we respond or react can determine how much of an impact the event or situation will have on us. Responding is taking a step back, letting it set in, finding perspective, and then acting with a rational mindset. Reacting is immediate (visceral/gut) and often fueled by emotions. There is nothing right or wrong with responding or reacting. What matters most is when and to what we respond or react.

In my opinion, when we are initially faced with adversity and/or trauma, reacting is the natural response, but responding is the healthier response for many reasons. The main reason being that we want to bring as little emotion to something that might already be serious, tense, and dramatic. The more emotional we are, the less able we are to think clearly to have the necessary perspective to find answers or solutions.

I try to remain in a response mode when tough times happen. To help me with this, my working phrase is, "making the best of a difficult situation" or "how do I make the best of a difficult situation?" This removes drama and reactionary, emotional thinking, and puts me in an objective, proactive mindset immediately. The alternative is becoming a victim of circumstance and playing the "why me?" game, which makes us suffer much more than necessary.

Making the best of difficult situations is something I have had to do all my life, as we all have, but none more intensely and focused than the past 20 years. It was the summer of 2001 when I began to have the first symptoms of my lifelong companion: chronic pain from dystonia which totally changed my world in every possible way as I discussed in Chapter 1. I lived with intense physical and emotional pain, anxiety, fear, isolation, and depression. It was so intense and scary that I retreated from the world as much as I could. I have worked many years to find tools and techniques to work through all of this and "make the best of a difficult situation," which is what this book is all about.

Adversity comes in all shapes and sizes, and in so many different ways depending on the person, depending on the day. It can come on slowly or hit us out of nowhere. No matter how it arrived, the most important thing is not the adversity. The most important thing is how we respond to the adversity. By using the tools in this book to face your adversity in a practical, non-threatening way, it will help reduce any form of suffering you or a loved one may be experiencing.

Despite the challenges we all face, the biggest and most complex obstacle we will ever have to personally overcome is our own mind. We are not responsible for everything that happens in life, but we are responsible for the self-defeating thinking patterns undesirable experiences might create.

Life always throws us curveballs, so we must learn to adapt to changes. This is often when the greatest learning in our lives takes place. We can look for this opportunity in the challenge or we can close our eyes and be angry, keeping us imprisoned.

When we are not able to change a situation or the broken world around us, we are challenged to change ourselves. If we don't, we keep playing the same record over and over in our minds, viewing life from the same foggy perspective and judgment that is filled with justification for why things are so hard.

The key is learning to become resilient when confronted with adversity. Marcus Aurelius, Roman Emperor from 161-180 A.D, defined flexibility and resilience as the ability to look a situation in the face and say, "you're just what I was looking for." His belief was that the formula for greatness was the ability to turn obstacles into fuel.

What does it mean to adapt?
Adapt is defined as, "make something suitable for a new use or purpose." Synonyms for adapt include modify, alter, change, adjust, transform, redesign, restyle, refashion, remodel, reshape, revamp, rework, reconstruct, reorganize, accommodate, habituate.

Anytime we experience something unplanned or unexpected, we have to adjust our sails and do everything mentioned in the last paragraph if we want to flow through or with things smoothly to avoid a surge of stress and calamity on our minds and bodies.

Change and adaptation can be hard. I am not challenging that. What I do want to challenge is why? Why does it have to be hard, or at least as hard as we often allow? Why are we conditioned to immediately say that change is hard? The simple answer is that we are creatures of habit and most of us have probably been trained to think this way ("change is hard") our entire lives. Also, the unknown for many is scary. But the unknown can also be exciting, and this is how we turn the tables on anything and use it to our advantage; by challenging our long-held beliefs and flipping them around.

There are 3 simple phrases to practice whenever faced with change, a task you have to do that you don't like, or work through something difficult that pops up unexpectedly and seems threatening:

I will
It's easy
It's fun

These three phrases go against *everything* we are told about change, but the only way to reprogram the mind is to practice a new dialogue. If we want to change patterns of behavior, we must change patterns of thought. As the late Wayne Dyer said, "peace is the result of retraining your mind to process life as it is, rather than as you think it should be." Rather than resist the flow of life, we need to learn to become part of the flow of life as it is.

When I hit rock bottom with my health and finances to where I was unable to physically live on my own because of the severity of my dystonia and financially unable to support myself, I had to move in with my retired parents. This is not at all what I wanted or expected at the age of 30 (nor did they), but I had no other choice. As much as I love them, I resisted living with them because in my mind it meant I was giving up all independence and everything I worked so hard for. Ironically, this living situation provided me with the opportunity to work hard for some of the most meaningful things I have ever done in my life. Instead of the three phrases above, mine were: "I won't," "It's hard," and "I hate it."

When I reframed my thoughts from "I am a failure" to "I need help and thank God they are here and willing to help me get back on my feet," I was more proactive in my efforts to get back to being more independent. I used the phrases above (I will, it's easy, and it's fun) to change my experience of living in that environment to make it easier for me to cope every day and find solutions rather than being so focused on self-shaming thoughts for having to take what felt like a major step back in my life. When I changed my inner dialogue on a regular basis, the circumstances were no longer controlling my emotions/feelings. I was now in control of how I felt about my situation at the time. This is when I began taking steps to getting back on my own again.

Turning suffering upside down
Most great things in life don't happen by chance. Most things happen by choice. For me, it is not so much about accepting hardship or resigning myself to it. Rather, it is a matter of agreeing to work with it. To decide to make the most of it. To see hardship as an opportunity, not an obstacle. This allows me to see options, and this remains my key to achieving and maintaining good health and joy in my life. Regarding chance, there is a popular saying that I believe to be true: "chance favors the prepared mind." However, having a prepared mind is a choice based on behaviors we adopt.

Happiness is not the absence of problems, but the ability to deal with them. If you are struggling with something, it doesn't mean you're failing. Almost every great success requires some kind of worthy struggle to get there. Be grateful when tough things happen because you plan to use the experience for good; for personal growth and/or teaching others, be it your children, family, or friends, sometimes just by modeling strong, positive, virtuous behaviors.

Tough things in life prepare us for greater things. They also help us much better appreciate all that we may take for granted in our lives. We gain greater perspective when the chips are down. When life is easy, we rarely learn or grow. We are not put in a position to adapt, so we can lose perspective about what is most important and what to appreciate about life.

Most suffering comes from expectation. Most of us have a blueprint for how life should be and when it isn't how we planned, it can cause sadness and even depression. We must understand that things happen that we will not always understand, but maybe we are not supposed to understand everything. Maybe we are supposed to let go, accept it, trust and have faith that everything will work out (which it almost always does), and let it happen without resistance. Resistance to any adverse circumstance increases its power over us.

Suffering also comes from wanting the world or people or things to be different than they are. It's okay to want things, but to need something different than it is or can be creates pain and suffering. Instead, love people and things for who and what they are. Not for who and what you want them to be.

We often learn the hard way that our world is ruled by external factors. We do not always get what we feel is rightfully ours, even if we've earned it. Not everything is as clean and straightforward as we plan for in our minds. Psychologically, we must prepare ourselves for this fact. It is far better to prepare for all the ups and downs rather than be blindsided or caught off guard. Realistically, a pleasant surprise is a lot better than an unpleasant one. We are always prepared when things go right. It is when things go wrong that we are usually not ready.

This being said, be careful about getting caught up in always preparing for the worst. This is not exactly what is meant by prepare. It means being honest that life is difficult and doesn't always go our way. Be a realist and don't look back in despair. Instead, look forward and prepare.

Life can unexpectedly bounce us around like a pinball machine. There is no way around this. Accepting this reality is the first step. If we resist, we do not adapt. When we flow with life, we can find peace and stillness. In this peace and stillness, we give ourselves a break from the blaring noise of the world around us, which gives us space to do some critical thinking; something very much needed by all of us. If we are filled with anxiety, stress, anger, or distraction, it is very hard to develop the insights required to solve difficult problems.

We may not be able to control all the things that happen in life or what people say and do to us, but we can decide not to be reduced by them. There is an incredible amount of inner freedom that comes with detaching from the things over which we have little to no control.

Embrace the suck of life

Most of us are familiar with the Latin term, carpe diem, which means "seize the day." This phrase became especially popular in the movie, *Dead Poets Society*, with the late Robin Williams, where he quoted Henry David Thoreau and talked about sucking the marrow out of life.

I love this line and way of thinking. However, when you are deeply suffering with anything in life, as I did for years with dystonia that was life changing and ridiculously painful, this means little. During my deepest suffering and feelings of helplessness, in my eyes there was no life left from which to suck the marrow. I lost everything so I had to embrace a new concept, which took me years to understand, a learning journey I am still on and will be for the rest of my life, as will you. I had to embrace what I call the "suck of life" and use my suffering as a tool to rebuild my life and reduce the suck of it all. This is actually very similar to carpe diem as you will see in upcoming paragraphs.

Before I continue, please forgive me for anyone I offend by using the word suck, my Mom being one of those people (sorry Mom). In my house growing up, we were not allowed to use this word or else we would be in trouble. It was considered as bad as any curse word. However, for the purposes of this topic and section, suck is the best word to use.

What does it mean to "embrace the suck of life?" In a nutshell, it means radical acceptance; acknowledging that life is hard and filled with pitfalls, and tough times are not to be ignored, denied, covered up, or masked with drugs, alcohol, food, poor relationships, and behaviors where we deal with the suck of life in an emotionally reactive fashion.

I didn't do any of this for the first 5 of my ongoing 20 years living with dystonia. I turned to food, alcohol, and isolation to try and hide from my physical and emotional pain. I also had to deal with morbid obesity after gaining 150 pounds from living this lifestyle. I didn't know back then how to embrace the suck of it all, so I embraced pain, anxiety, depression, and avoidance instead, as well as intense anger and resentment. Learning to reframe and restructure my perspective about my personal suck of life issues has put my life on a much better course.

When we deny what reality is giving us, what is really happening, then we create suffering; exactly what I did that increased the suffering I was experiencing. Life is a dance between minimizing expectations and surrendering to what our lives actually reveal to us. By embracing our lives totally (even the stuff that sucks), we better manage tough times.

"Embrace the suck" is a widely used military term (I did not know this until months after I wrote this section). In military jargon, this means to consciously accept or appreciate something that is extremely unpleasant but unavoidable.[1] The armed forces have no other choice. For example, if they are in the Iraqi desert or in the mountains of Afghanistan, the only way they're going to get through those challenging experiences is by embracing (rather than denying or ignoring) them.[2] Another way of saying this is, "be comfortable being uncomfortable." I talk more about this in a section of Chapter 21 called, *Learning to be okay with what we view as not okay.*

For most of my life, everything pretty much came easy for me. When I hit the age of 30 and was stricken with chronic pain from dystonia, everything changed and nothing was easy. In the last 20 years, I have found ways to improve upon my symptoms, but my life is nothing like it once was. I am not involved in many activities that I once loved or the same social and business circles. My body can't handle it like it once could. Along with many time-consuming self-care activities, treatments, and therapies I would prefer not do, I have to carefully plan my day so the activities of the day do not cause an aggravation of symptoms.

I could very easily look at my life right now and the physical challenges I have and get totally lost in the depressing suck of it all by focusing on all I have lost. If I do this, I will be in a frozen state where I do not see options and opportunities for how to make the most of my life, exactly as it is right now. In order to move on, I have to embrace the suck of this part of my life so I can make the best version of me that I can, right now, in this moment. The more I practice this, the more joy, meaning, and purpose I experience. Despite daily challenges, I love my life.

I totally understand that this is a process for all of us and happens in our own time, so let it happen. Don't resist or force the process. The first step towards this is acknowledging that acceptance is the way to reduce the suck of life. It doesn't mean giving up, not dealing with problems, or not fighting. It means fighting in a productive way. It means, "I understand that this is what is happening and I accept that this is reality." Not "why me?" thinking. It is an acknowledgement of reality and finding ways to make the best of it.

Because my life is different now, I have replaced the things I used to do with new things and experience the same joy that was missing for so long when I got lost in the suck of life and resisted the change in my life that I hated so much (you can read more about replacement activities in Chapter 21). For people who do not have a persistent/chronic health condition, they have their own "suck of life" issues, so no one has it better or worse; we just have different things to deal with, so "embracing the suck of life" applies to everyone.

In a wonderful book called, *The Obstacle is the Way*, by Ryan Holiday, it teaches us that whatever impedes us can empower us. In other words, what stands in the way becomes the way. It is an art known as "turning things upside down" or "flipping the script," meaning the key to handling suffering and hardship of any kind is the belief that in all of life's obstacles is an opportunity to practice virtue, patience, courage, humility, resourcefulness, reason, justice, and creativity. When we recognize that something could not have been otherwise and learn to accept it with dignity, everything that was once dreadfully painful will lose its power.

I recognize that some people are not in a place to embrace their "suck of life" and that's okay! When ready, it is important we understand that the way to dig ourselves out of any hole is to first get in the hole. Not deny that we are in the hole, despite seeing darkness all around. We need to allow ourselves to see the darkness, feel it, touch it, and ultimately come to terms with it so we can grab a shovel and start digging... because it is only when we embrace the suck of life that the things that suck no longer matter. If we learn to use suffering and adversity correctly, it will buy us a ticket to a place that we could not have gotten any other way.

Radical acceptance

Take on everything in your life (good and bad) as if you chose it. Take full responsibility for literally everything. Whether or not you are completely responsible for something, act as if you are completely responsible for it. This mindset is very powerful when put to practice. It eliminates the ego's desire to blame outside influence and project our problems. It is the only way we can ever really truly find peace and freedom and control over our lives. When we assume responsibility for everything, we discipline the mind to shut out external noise from the world and find inner strength, peace, and humility.

Realistically speaking, even if something happened that you did not choose, such as the death of a loved one, losing your job, a catastrophic natural disaster that destroyed your home, etc., the choice we have in those circumstances is how we respond to what happened. So, with this in mind, we truly can look at everything in life as a choice. Please try it and see if it offers you a new perspective on things.

As a real-life example, in the Summer of 2020 we had a hurricane and at 11:00pm, a tree limb fell and landed on my car which I only had for a year and was in great condition. I heard the crash and went numb. After the initial shock, I knew the next day would involve a lot of cleanup and dealing with my insurance company, so I somehow had to get some sleep. The way that I did it, as silly as it may sound, is I said thank you because once again I was being challenged by something in my life that I had to deal with that I did not want to and find a way through it. It was another lesson in adversity, acceptance, persistence, and growth.

What really helped talk me down so I could fall asleep was telling myself that I was responsible. I bought the car, I chose where I live which is a place that does not have a garage, and I chose to leave my car in my driveway with unstable trees surrounding it during a hurricane, so I had to assume full responsibility. By taking that position, I was able to calm myself enough to fall asleep. I woke the next day prepared to get the car cleaned up and ready to go to the collision center for repairs. I decided to take full responsibility for everything related to the accident, and I am convinced that is what got me through the ordeal.

Acceptance doesn't mean resignation. It means understanding that something is what it is and there's got to be a way through it.
- Michael J. Fox –

Non-resistance

If you have not seen the movie *Shawshank Redemption* and want to, please do not read this section because I am going to give away the story. The main character, Andy Dufresne, was wrongly accused of murdering his wife and incarcerated. He didn't fight the incarceration. He embraced the life of a prisoner, without becoming a resigned victim, and in the end, found a way to escape his captives after 19 years of a life sentence.

If he fought against the powers that be and tried to prove his innocence to people who refused to hear his side of the story, his incarceration would have lasted even longer and been riddled with far more painful torture from the spiteful warden and guards. He chose to "play the game," so to speak, and was better for it in the end. On the few occasions he fought it, he was brutally punished.

In a real-world scenario, consider the peaceful nature and perspective of Nelson Mandela who was incarcerated for 27 years. In his efforts to bring peace to his nation, he was quoted as saying, "if you want to make peace with your enemy, you have to work with your enemy. Then he becomes your partner." This is such an astonishing and humble response to years of injustice imposed upon him.

I have no doubt that some people will think that embracing the suck of life is a negative perspective. On the contrary, if we do not acknowledge the difficult times in life and find ways to work through them, we deny their existence and don't look for solutions, which will only increase our suffering. Too often, we resist allowing ourselves to feel things that hurt, which distorts our reality and our identity, and plunges us further into despair.

If we want to transcend any state of suck, we have to change the way most of us have been conditioned to run from pain and instead, feel it, own it, live it, and face up to it. Denial of it will worsen it and prolong it. We must embrace it to face it to erase it.

Life is a series of natural and spontaneous changes.
Don't resist them; that only creates sorrow. Let reality be reality.
Let things flow naturally forward in whatever way they like.
- Lao Tzu -

References
1. www.developgoodhabits.com, Embrace the suck meaning and 8 lessons to use in your life. Retrieved on September 12, 2020 from: https://www.developgoodhabits.com/embrace-suck/
2. www.careershifters.org, Why embracing 'the suck' is the key to setting yourself free. Retrieved on September 12, 2020 from: https://www.careershifters.org/expert-advice/why-embracing-the-suck-is-the-key-to-setting-yourself-free#:~:text=There's%20a%20military%20saying%3A%20%E2%80%9CEmbrace,lives%20actually%20reveal%20to%20us

Chapter 3
The powerful mind/body connection

A common theme throughout much of this book is mind/body connection. This chapter focuses more on basic biochemistry of the mind, while other chapters discuss more about habits of thinking and behavior. See Chapter 16 for more on strategies for using the power of the mind.

The last chapter discussed adapting to adversity and how it is essential for us to change the way we think about life circumstances to change habits and patterns of behavior. Habits of thinking create behaviors and behaviors create outcomes. If we want to change outcomes, we must change behaviors, which means we must change habits of thinking. Doing this rewires the brain to produce different chemicals, which is discussed below. The basis for this is called neuroplasticity, which refers to the brain's ability to reorganize itself by forming new neural connections throughout life.

We all know that changing habits of behavior changes our life experiences, but putting this to practice is where a lot of us get stuck. Either we doubt our ability, we are not sure what to do, or we feel overwhelmed with the speed at which life moves and/or the chaos that seems to exist all around. Life these days is "loud," making it hard to be at peace to put in the work.

However, the work does not need to be done all at once. Just one step at a time. It took me years to write this book, a little at a time. I never could have done it in one sitting. Progress takes place in small chunks, but small chunks can lead to big things. If we take just one small step every day, before we know it, we have created something new or a new way of thinking. Too often, we think we have to do significant things to make progress. It is more often the other way around. With a few small changes or even just one small change a day, we can create something significant. There is no rush.

Think about this: if a pilot changes the course settings on the airplane's computer by just one degree, the plane will end up in an entirely different destination. That's how it is with us. Just one degree or 1% of 100 is all we need to make change. Please don't overwhelm yourself by doing too much.

Our mind is as powerful as any drug
We have chemicals in the brain as powerful as drugs for stress, pain, depression, anxiety, and other conditions. Among them are neurotransmitters called endorphins, serotonin, oxytocin, and dopamine,

which are often referred to as the "feel good" or "happy" chemicals. Let's play around with endorphins...the body's natural pain killer (our own private narcotic). Endorphins affect us like codeine and morphine by blocking a cell's transmission of pain signals, but without the addiction. The word endorphin derives from two words – endogenous (from within) and morphine.

In addition to decreased feelings of pain, secretion of endorphins leads to feelings of euphoria, modulation of appetite, enhancement of the immune response, and fewer negative effects of stress. Endorphins are popularly associated with "runner's high," but no need to worry if you don't run. There are numerous ways to increase production of these potent brain chemicals besides strenuous workouts. These include, but are not limited to, the items in Table 1.

Table 1 – How to increase endorphin production

Massage	Acupuncture
A good movie	Prayer
Positive thinking/affirmations	Physical exercise
Music and dancing	Regular sleep/wake cycle
Laughter. Even fake laughter does the trick! The brain doesn't know the difference between real or fake laughter. Even the anticipation of something funny releases endorphins	Fun hobbies (arts and crafts, photography, beadwork, quilting, cooking, nature walks)
Shopping	Quality time with family and friends
Reading a good book	Being around animals
Sauna/hot tub	Biofeedback
Sex (including cuddling, kissing, and holding hands)	Alcohol (light drinking; heavy drinking negates the effect)
Good deeds (the flood of endorphins and serotonin caused by being generous has been called "helper's high")	Meditation and controlled breathing exercises (breathe through your stomach; not your chest)
Nutrition (anti-inflammatory foods)	Sunlight

Practically all of these things are at our disposal, so we should try and take advantage of them as much as we can. Not all of them will be of help (or interest) to everyone, but I wanted to share many of the options available to us. I also recognize that when in pain and feeling mentally down (I have been there!), these things are not always easy to do or yield results the first or first few times doing them. If this is the case for you, maybe start with one thing you enjoy and do your best to make it part of your lifestyle. Please see more on this approach in Chapter 15.

Perhaps before starting there, practice the art of appreciation and gratitude (see more about this in Chapter 6). This is a great first step when we are suffering with anything. It helps take the focus off us and helps us better see more of the good things in our lives. Focus on something or someone you appreciate, list the reasons for why you are grateful, and then move forward with hopefully more peace in your heart. Anything that gets us looking outward and/or releasing pent-up feelings has the potential of helping.

People often ask me the different ways I manage my chronic pain associated with dystonia, and I usually list many of these things in Table 1. I cannot say for sure how much they play a role, but when I do not do them on a regular basis, pain is more severe. I also used to be depressed and full of anxiety, a far cry from the person I was pre-dystonia and a far cry from the person I am now, thanks to many of these things.

A fun fact to keep in mind is that neutral or positive sensory messages travel through the nervous system faster than painful messages. More specifically, soothing sensations travel up to seven times faster than sharp or burning pain. This means that if soothing sensations and painful sensations reach the "pain gate" to the brain at the same time, the pleasant sensations will prevail, blocking the slower, painful ones.[1] In other words, to reverse the course of pain and depression, it helps to do things that consistently provide reliable pleasant body experiences that compete successfully with pain (i.e., activities that produce endorphins, oxytocin, serotonin, and dopamine as listed in Table 1).

An easy way to remember how to harness the power of the brain's natural drugs is to live by the popular saying, "sing like no one is listening, dance like nobody's watching, love like you've never been hurt, and live like it's heaven on earth." In other words, have fun and do your best to not care so much what others think about you. Live your life on your terms. Never give up. Be patient with yourself. Never lose hope. Trust that everything will always work out. All of it is easier said than done, but when we get the "feel good" hormones flowing, nothing and no one can ever take away our peace of mind and body.

Trust in the power of your mind's natural ability to conquer anything and practice learning how to use it. If we don't look for ways to improve how we can better use our mind and how we choose to perceive the world, we can become victims of circumstance. If we live this way, we get caught in fight or flight mode (also called sympathetic dominant, referring to the sympathetic branch of the autonomic nervous system) and react to life rather than thoughtfully and mindfully being a part of the flow of life. There will be more on this in upcoming chapters.

References
1. Phillips, M. (2007) *Reversing Chronic Pain*. Berkeley, CA: North Atlantic Books

Chapter 4
Slowing down our rushed minds

If you are like most people, you probably do not allow yourself to flow with life and instead, rush through your day and all of the moments throughout the day. The problem is that we often give ourselves a big "to do list" while already being pulled in a lot of different directions with work, social media and just our regular social circles, and family, making it difficult to not feel rushed and be able to devote quality time to the people and things we love most. It feels like we don't have enough time for anything. As George Carlin said, "we've learned to rush, but not to wait."

This is something I struggle with and why I wrote this section, because I know I am not the only one. I often feel rushed no matter what it is that I am doing. The following example is one I often use because it is so incredibly illogical and a good example to illustrate my point.

I used to work a half hour from home and there were times when I was running late. I hadn't eaten yet, so I brought food to eat while I was driving. Because I was late and felt rushed, I felt like I had to eat quickly. Within the first five minutes of the half hour drive, whatever I was eating was gone because I wolfed it down. My mind tricked me into believing that I didn't have enough time to eat because I was late, yet I had a full 30 minutes to slowly eat my food. My adrenaline was pumping so everything seemed like it was moving faster, or needed to move faster, than it really was.

If this sounds like you, I bet you feel overwhelmed and exhausted. If so, I encourage you to look for opportunities each day to practice slowing down your mind. The saying, "take time out to smell the roses," is something we should apply to our lives as often as we can. In other words, find opportunities to practice slowing down.

For example, when you see a sunrise or a sunset, stop and take notice for a few moments...or many moments. Get lost in the sky. The next time you get caught at a traffic light or stuck in traffic, be grateful that you are going slower. Embrace what it feels like to move more slowly. Instead of getting angry at the driver in front of you who is going below the speed limit, thank that person for helping you slow down. Getting angry will not increase their speed. It will only increase your blood pressure.

Unless it is an emergency, don't answer every text message or email right away. Let time pass. If it is too hard at first, start by putting your phone in a different room. When you are watching a television program or listening to the radio and there are commercials, sit through the commercials without changing the station. Browse stores in the mall. Write a handwritten letter. Start journaling. When shopping, look for the longest line and get in it. Make a home cooked meal from a recipe book. And when you see a rose, STOP and smell it. The phrase, "take time to slow down" could not be more literally spot on. It's okay if you don't get to everything you feel you need to do in a day. It only matters as much as our mind tricks us into thinking it does. This goes back to habits of thinking and behaving that we discussed in the previous chapter.

Above are just a few examples of what we can do to train our racing mind to slooow dooown. We should practice more than most of us probably do. We have become prey to the fast moving, modern instant message world. There are studies to show that stress, anxiety, and depression are on the rise because of the way society is now, but we don't need the studies because most of us live it and feel it every day. *WE* are the walking, talking study.

Along with practicing things like meditation, breathing exercises, exercise itself, etc., we should be practicing mindfulness type behavior all day long using the things I mentioned. The more we practice doing this the more it becomes habit and we don't have to think about it anymore and purposely look for opportunities to slow down. We simply slow down because it becomes our nature... and when we slow down, we begin to see all that we have been missing in our lives and learn to appreciate things more. For more on this, see Chapter 16 about mindfulness.

What to do when you feel your mind racing out of control
How many of you feel as though you are in control of your life? I would guess probably not too many. However, I bet a great majority of us try to control as much of our lives and our surroundings as possible, to our stressful detriment. We have a big problem with stillness. This is especially true if you live with a chronic health condition like I do, because the health condition can often dictate each moment of each day depending on how we feel, keeping us on edge because we are anticipating pain or other uncomfortable symptoms.

The condition I have, called dystonia, is especially unique when it comes to control because it is a disorder where the main feature is involuntary muscle movements where one often feels like a marionette because the body is doing things the conscious brain is not telling it to do. Talk about feeling out of control!

For a lot of people with this condition and other movement disorders such as Parkinson's disease, essential tremor, ataxia, multiple system atrophy (MSA), Tourette syndrome, Huntington's disease, restless legs syndrome, among others, we try very hard to consciously control our movements. Doing this often causes us to become more physically rigid where we sometimes even forget to breathe. We try so hard to keep our bodies still that it can have the opposite effect, in that it can make the involuntary movements stronger and increase resting muscle tension.

Whether or not you have one of these health issues, if you are someone who does not allow for life to happen and you are not mindful of your emotional reaction to life events, it is probably because you are an over-controller. If so, I am going to guess that you are stressed out and life is rather exhausting and painful for you at times. It certainly is for me because I like control and routine, and I can be stubborn, so when things don't go as I would like, it can be tough on me. I have worked hard to be much better in these areas, but it comes with a lot of practice. There is nothing wrong with being stubborn. It can be a very good quality. Like all qualities, it is the way we apply them that can be to our benefit or detriment.

So, what does all of this mean? The bottom line is that there is very little that we control in life, and ironically, embracing this truth is the way to gain real control. Remember, the only thing we can control is how we respond to what happens in life. This is where we have power.

We heal by focusing on what we can control and by reframing our self-defeating thoughts. We also grow when we look for lessons and use them to prepare for the future. It is in this that "we become better because of what we went through; better than if we had resisted and never been broken in the first place," as Nassim Taleb said in his book, *Antifragile*.

If we resist the natural flow of life by trying to control that which we can't control, we suffer greatly. In other words, whatever we resist in life that is out of our control will begin to control our emotional health. Our stubbornness to want things a certain way, especially when things don't go our way, dramatically increases our level of stress. Like water, we need to take the path of least resistance and practice learning to flow with life no matter what is happening.

The idea is that flowing water never goes stale, so just keep on flowing.
- Bruce Lee -

This section of the book was prompted by a month where life basically beat me up. Without going into the particulars, one day after the next, a new problem would arise. Often, when the problem seemed like it was fixed, a twist in that problem occurred, which prolonged it, followed by a new one right on top of it; and they were not small problems. They were important, dangerous, serious, expensive, life changing issues that I was dealing with seemingly nonstop. I was so beaten down at the end of each day and I kept trying to figure out why it was all happening, which furthered my exhaustion.

I have no concrete answers without going into philosophical hypothesizing, but the main thing I finally had to do was throw up my hands, laugh, cry a little, and accept all the insanity as well as I could and not make it worse with anger and fear. I had NO other choice if I wanted to get through everything as unscathed as possible. NOTHING was in my control, except my response to what was happening.

This is an example of what is commonly called mindfulness, as I discuss in more detail in Chapter 16 along with mindfulness exercises. I had to be present and aware of what was happening in the moment and only deal with each challenge as it was happening. When I tried to figure out everything at once, nothing was getting solved and I was overwhelmed. I had to break down each event and do the best I could as each part of each challenge was presented.

Marcus Aurelius speaks of this in the context of reaching or achieving stillness. He writes about trying to be "like the rock that the waves keep crashing over"; the one that "stands unmoved and the raging of the sea falls still around it." Try to be the rock on the shore that the waves keep crashing over to find stillness in the calamity of life.

To remind me of this image and the feeling that comes with this image, I carry a polished stone in my pocket. Whenever I feel a lack of stillness or need to remind myself to be grounded and at ease, I hold onto it. Maybe this, or some other symbolic item, is a way for you to also connect to something of importance to you.

Whatever your belief system, a very important factor when you take your hands off the wheel and allow the flow of life to take its course without interfering, is to have faith in that belief system. Surrender to what you place your faith in and allow it to take care of you. Let go and allow. When we do this, which I know can be hard, and see that things much more often than not work out, we can begin to trust life and ourselves more, which reduces worry, fear, anxiety, and stress. It is a practice that I have to devote time to every single day of my life, and the more I do, the better I feel and the more at peace my life becomes, no matter what is happening, and that's what I wish for you. When the mind is still, the body is still.

I took the following from a newsletter/website that I mention a couple times in this book. It is called, *Marc and Angel Hack Life - Practical Tips for Productive Living* (www.marcandangel.com). Marc and Angel Chernoff are a husband and wife coaching team that helps people with personal development. This excerpt from their newsletter on September 24, 2020 is all about control.

Most of the things we desperately try to hold on to, as if they're real, solid, everlasting fixtures in our lives, aren't really there. Or if they are there in some form, they're changing, fluid, impermanent, or simply imagined in our minds. Life gets a lot easier to deal with when we understand this.

Imagine you're blindfolded and treading water in the center of a large swimming pool, and you're struggling desperately to grab the edge of the pool that you think is nearby, but really it's not—it's far away. Trying to grab that imaginary edge is stressing you out, and tiring you out, as you splash around aimlessly trying to hold on to something that isn't there.

Now imagine you pause, take a deep breath, and realize that there's nothing nearby to hold on to. Just water around you. You can continue to struggle with grabbing at something that doesn't exist... or you can accept that there's only water around you, and relax, and float.

Truth be told, inner peace begins the moment you take a new breath and choose not to allow an uncontrollable event to dominate you in the present. You are not what happened to you. You are what you choose to become in this moment. Let go, breathe, and begin...

An easy exercise we can do to focus on what we can change is to take out a sheet of paper and put a line down the middle. On one side write down the things you cannot control right now, and on the other side write what you can control. Then form a plan of action that allows you to embrace the things you can control and let go of the things out of your control.

The health impact of our internal and external dialogue
In the early years of my dystonia, there was no peace or stillness in my life. Part of me at that time felt like my life was completely over so I gave up, isolated myself, and fell into depression. The other part of me was filled with rage over what dystonia and pain had taken from me. Looking back, I feel I had to go through all of it to learn more about myself, but it was a miserable existence that I probably didn't need to emotionally endure for as long as I did. The physical symptoms were a different story and my emotions fueled them to be worse.

Much of the reason for my initial emotional challenges was my ego thinking I was better than this health condition and how dare it happen to me. After this initial emotional shock, an identity crisis set in and I struggled greatly with my emotions and how I characterized my health problem. In other words, the words I used to describe my lot in life. My internal and external dialogue fed an angry beast inside me as my health continued to decline.

I had a revelation one day, after some other health scares, where I felt it was necessary to change my mindset and outlook if I wanted to get greater peace of mind to really understand what was going on with me and what options were available to try and get better the best I could. As silly as it might sound to some, I began by changing my words and how I was describing my life and my health challenges. I did a lot of physical treatments as well, but I had to change my mindset to motivate me to pursue them.

Regarding my language, I first began by replacing the words "should" with "could" and "need" with "want." As trite as it may sound, there are powerful distinctions. Should is nothing more than self-shaming and self-judging. Think of how it feels when someone else says, "you should do this or that." It is very minimizing, and we must understand that it is also minimizing when we say it to ourselves. The word "could" is open-ended and proactive, and creates options.

Replacing the word "need" with "want" creates a lightness in me rather than some daunting task. For example, "I need to lose 20 pounds" or "I want to lose 20 pounds" (in my case, I had gained 150 pounds, so I had a lot more than 20 pounds I wanted to lose – see Chapter 15 to read how I lost the weight). The second sentence, the one that begins with "I want to," is far more motivating and fun sounding to me. "I need to" is punitive and "I want to" is energy producing because it promotes initiative.

Before continuing, the reason this is so important is because when we label something with negative words (especially a negative adjective) it creates a negative feeling and stores a negative emotion and memory in the body. This creates stressful biochemistry that prevents peace and healing, and promotes avoidance of uncomfortable feelings and situations. When we give loving adjectives to events and experiences, we create biochemistry that promotes healing. So, this is not just silly semantics. It's biochemical and we need to acknowledge this fact.

Other words I changed were those that brought up feelings of anger, guilt, resentment, and loss. It was a matter of changing the adjectives. For example, I used to say things like, "this stupid dystonia," "my useless life," or "my horrible pain ruined everything." I said those things all the time, among others, and it made me feel even more miserable.

Our words create habits of thinking that create our emotions. We can use words that create a low energy, painful sensation in the body, or words that create a high-energy, joyous feeling in the body, or one that is neutral; the second two being the goal.

For me, this is the nuts and bolts… when we judge anything (good or bad) we define it ("this horrible pain," "that damn surgery," "I hate that I can't run anymore! Stupid neck and back!" "my rotten doctor," etc.). When we define something, we give it life because of the emotion attached to the word before the "thing." That thing then begins to define us, which can either lift us up or tear us down because of the words and emotions we attach to it. Take pain, for example. There is nothing stupid about it. It's just pain, but if I give it the "stupid" label, it gives the pain more life, and for me, more pain, both physical and emotional.

Please choose your words carefully because they do have a powerful impact. I am not at all saying, "just be positive" and everything will be fine. What I am saying is that the words we use to describe anything in life create emotions that negatively or positively impact our relationship to our experiences, which in turn, impacts our health.

There are a lot of things we can't control in this world. What we can control are emotions, judgments, attitudes, and perspectives. If we exert control in these areas, we can make any life experience a positive or neutral one, which will reduce the stress impact on our mind and body.

The challenge of change
My life before and after chronic pain from dystonia are as different as night and day. I went from a very active lifestyle to one that was extremely sedentary. For most of my life, I played organized and recreational sports all year round. My two main sports were golf and baseball. I could easily walk 18 holes several times a week and some days I played 27 or 36 holes. I played baseball from a young age all the way through college, practicing or playing games every day of the week. I loved it!

I also never passed up the opportunity to swim, bike, play tennis, racquetball, basketball, soccer, or ultimate Frisbee, to name just a few of my favorite activities. In the mid 1990's, I trained to be a placekicker in the NFL. Along with working full time, I was training twice a day until a hip injury ended that dream. I then studied karate for several years and earned the level of brown belt. Long story short, I never sat idle for long. When dystonia prevented me from living my active life, it was a major shock to my psyche.

For the first five years I was miserable. I had a lot of negative self-talk about how I could no longer do the things I loved so much. I characterized dystonia and pain as the things that "ruined my life." I was deeply frustrated, which caused a lot of anger and bitterness, as well as jealousy for people who could do all those things. This made my dystonia and pain worse because negative emotions cause increased stress and muscle tension. I had to shift my thinking if I wanted to live a happier and healthier life.

It was hard work, but I eventually came to understand that change is a natural part of life over which we have little to no control. Just ask any aging person about their former abilities compared to their current abilities.

Healthy aging requires accepting change just as healthy coping with any other health condition or other life challenge requires accepting change.

I came to understand that certain things do not last a lifetime, so I thought of all the good times I had playing baseball and golf (and other sports), said thank you for all those times, and let them go. I had to say goodbye. I had to release the past so I could live in the present and focus my energy on the direction my life was heading. Turning to gratitude completely changed my life. I was free of the grief I was experiencing about things I was trying to hold onto that were no longer a part of who I was. This opened the door for new, equally fun and rewarding things to come into my life.

Patience when things change

Just as it is for me, change is not easy for most people. If we have been a certain way for many years and something alters the course of things, it can be a challenge to adapt. Human beings are creatures of habit. We not only develop habits of thinking and behaving, we create routines in our lives. Even if you feel like a scattered person, scattered is your routine. When anyone's routine is dismantled, for any reason, learning to adapt to the change can take time. When this happens, be patient with yourself.

Change is often a slow process. Not always, but it often takes baby steps to get to a place where we want to be or become the person we want to be. Too often we rush the process and don't reach our destination. We may not even know what the destination is when we are in the midst of change. This is why we must trust the process and trust that everything will work out just as it was meant to be.

> *The only way to make sense out of change is to plunge*
> *into it, move with it, and join the dance.*
> - Alan Wilson Watts -

Everyone and everything grows and changes at its own pace. If you look at nature, which I believe to be one of our best teachers, animals, plants, trees, grass, etc., all grow at a different rate. As someone who loves plants, and I have dozens around my home and office, I am fascinated by the way they change and grow. Some grow like weeds and some barely change at all. Watching the process unfold in all of them is a great lesson in patience and allowing. In other words, they teach us how to let go and trust the flow of life, rather than the futile attempt to try and control the flow of life.

Regardless of the speed of growth and change, plants and all of nature do not try to speed it up. Nature simply is. It also doesn't force change or growth. It simply allows. Plants don't put pressure on themselves or do anything other than naturally allow themselves to grow at the pace they are meant to grow. We can learn a lot from this and practice doing the very same thing. We are no different if we make that choice.

When you are experiencing adversity and change in your life, big or small, try not to put too much pressure on yourself to get through it at a certain pace. Let the pace set itself. Take baby steps, which in retrospect you will see are giant leaps toward the person you want to become. There is no timetable. Let the results of your progress determine the timetable and allow yourself to flow with the natural process of things, rather than forcing them to happen. To modify the line from the movie Caddyshack, rather than "be the ball," "be the plant."

The following is a prayer by Michael Leunig about how to go with and grow from change. The most powerful part of this for me is the line: "To undertake the journey without understanding the destination." This is so true, as change requires trust and faith that everything will work out, and that it is important to immerse ourselves in the flow of the unknowns of life without resistance or interference. Change is inevitable and when we resist change, we increase personal pain and suffering.

> God help us to change.
> To change ourselves and to change our world.
> To know the need for it. To deal with the pain of it. To feel the joy of it.
> To undertake the journey without understanding the destination.
> The art of gentle revolution.
> Amen
> Source: http://www.leunig.com.au/works/prayers#

Below are two great quotes about patience:

> When you encounter various trials, big or small, be full of joy.
> They're opportunities to learn patience.
> - Scott Curran -

> Patience is the calm acceptance that things can happen in
> a different order than the one you have in your mind.
> - David G. Allen –

Chapter 5
Don't just "be positive" – Be honest

When people are struggling with anything in life, be it a health condition or something else, I often hear them say the following: "I am trying to be positive, but it is so hard!" Other people see us suffering and sometimes tell us to "just be positive," as if that is going to solve our problems.

Having lived a very painful 20 ongoing years with dystonia, I know how hard it is to be positive and how it feels to be told that all we need to do is be more positive, which is basically a disregard for how hard the struggle is. I do not in any way discount the power of a positive attitude, but people sometimes think that attitude alone is the problem or solution. Attitude is very important, but usually only consistently helpful if it is attached to an action towards alleviating or solving problems. In other words, attitude is the necessary precursor for action/change.

For the many years I lived with more brutal pain from dystonia than I do now, along with severe, involuntary, persistent muscle contractions 24/7, anxiety, and deep depression, "being positive" was not even in my vocabulary. I wanted to die and everything in life, and I mean everything, sucked! That was my reality and if you read my story in Chapter 1, you know just how profound my depths of helplessness and hopelessness were, and I still suffer with all the same challenges to varying degrees. The difference now is my attitude about my challenges, which has been a huge motivation for change.

My attitude is based on a level of acceptance I have reached, as well as a level of improvement with my health that I have achieved and sustained. It is also based on my belief that everything has a solution. My accomplishments in life are not from being positive without taking action to create change. I have to put in the work every single day and not just talk the talk without walking the walk.

When our health or something else limits our activities, we lose parts, if not all, of the life we once had, making it difficult to not be sad, angry, and scared, to name just a few emotions. This is why "being positive" is so hard. Although, I think these emotions are a necessary part of processing trauma and pain, which makes them positive. That comment aside, what exactly does one mean when they say, "be positive" or "I am trying to be positive?" It is a different answer for everyone I'm sure.

I think more than anything, it means being optimistic, but as I discuss below, we have to be optimistic about something tangible and realistic based on positive experiences and outcomes, such as a treatment that helps or when we can relate to another person who has been in our shoes and triumphed (two of many examples). Any ounce of evidence that hope exists provides true optimism, fostering a "be positive" attitude; and when you find things that help, hold onto them for dear life. Every "little" thing that helps adds up. When people ask what helps me most, I list a dozen or more things because I do so many things, even if they help just a little. I consider everything to be a piece of my health management puzzle.

It is when we get consistently reliable results or consistent change in the direction we want to head that we have real reason to be optimistically and confidently positive, versus trying to force positivity because we are told to "think positively." HOWEVER, I truly do believe that fending off negative, low energy thoughts and changing or reframing them to positive, affirming thoughts, to be a useful exercise. It is just far more powerful when attached to something tangible.

To me, being positive is a mindset of non-avoidance. In other words, being positive is when we actively acknowledge our struggle and focus on solutions rather than problems; looking at obstacles as challenges to overcome rather than setbacks. It does not mean denying the existence of mental and physical pain that everyone experiences to varying degrees. If we deny it or ignore it or try and "be positive" when all hell is breaking loose, there is no way through whatever challenge we are facing. There must be more than just saying the words. There must be meaning and purpose to our lives beyond suffering that we strive to achieve, and it must be practical and attainable to feel hopeful.

Being positive also means taking good care of ourselves, which can be hard because many of us want to do more for others than ourselves and perhaps live with guilt for putting ourselves first, so maybe do so with this thought...treat yourself like someone else you are responsible for taking care of.

For those who have read my other book, *Diagnosis Dystonia: Navigating the Journey*, and/or my articles and blogs, you could make the claim that I am all about positivity. This is true to a degree so let me clarify; my message is not, "just say and think positive thoughts and everything will be fine." Not even remotely close, but that is how my message is sometimes perceived and how some people mean it when they talk about "being positive." As many of you have probably experienced, it doesn't work long term because that thought alone is essentially meaningless. Other thoughts and a proactive plan that produce favorable results must accompany it. Having an upbeat attitude accompanied by action that creates positive momentum towards change is my message.

Without a plan (setting attainable goals and steps to achieve them) attached to "being positive," for a lot of people it ends up turning into more suffering. They think they have a handle on their situation by only saying the words, "be positive," because this is what our culture jams down our throat. When the you know what hits the fan, these people fall even harder and hurt more because they feign positivity and avoid confronting their suffering. It can be a dangerous game. Except in certain situations and around certain people, there is no reason to pretend that life is nothing but a bowl of cherries if it isn't, so don't deny it. Let it be what it is and express your emotions.

Those of us who suffer with anything in life (which basically means everyone if you are alive) need to grieve short and long term life challenges, and with that comes a lot of emotions that may be viewed as negative... but they are all okay to have and healthy to express. Indeed, I think it is a very helpful thing to purge our emotions because expression of true feelings means we are facing our problems honestly. It is more stressful living in a fake world of positivity or a chronic world of negativity, especially when neither is reality.

Rather than try and "be positive," I think it's more important that we try and maintain an upbeat attitude which creates an energy of hope more so than suffering. So instead of "being positive," be honest, realistic, and proactive by looking for options versus obstacles. Work hard to accept that things are tough, roll with them, be in a solution-oriented mindset rather than a reactionary one, and if you have moments where you need to scream and yell and cry, by all means do so, but if you live in this place all the time, it will make suffering worse because it becomes habitual and create stress chemistry in the brain that can prevent healing.

Every thought releases some type of chemical. When positive thoughts are generated, when you're feeling truly happy or optimistic, cortisol (stress hormone) decreases and the brain produces serotonin, creating a feeling of well-being. When serotonin levels are normal, one feels happy, calmer, less anxious, more focused, and more emotionally stable. Dopamine is also a neurotransmitter that helps control the brain's reward system and pleasure center. This is discussed in further detail in Chapter 3.

When we are anxious, fearful, under stress, or angry, the brain draws precious metabolic energy away from the prefrontal cortex and it's difficult to take in and process new material or think creatively.

As I mention several times throughout the book, I like to say, "how do I/we make the best of a difficult situation." This is a non-reactionary, non-emotional, rational way of recognizing that a tough situation exists and there are ways to make it better if we are open to options, rather than shutting down and giving up and being angry. This approach reduces the stress chemistry I discussed above.

No amount of anger will take your pain or other problems away. Anger only stirs up stress chemicals which make our physical and emotional pain worse. As much as you may resist this next thought, we MUST find a way to cohabitate with our pain/problems, no different than anything we don't like such as the shape of our nose, gray hair, wrinkles, excess weight, or anything else we would prefer not have.

Also critical is to not get too high or too low emotionally, so the way we characterize life events is very important. Be as even keeled as possible. An aroused nervous system cannot heal, which is why we must calm our minds (see Chapter 16 for mind calming techniques). View your obstacle as a challenge to overcome, which will change your mindset and reduce the negative toll your reactions to life events have on your health.

Life events in and of themselves are not the main problem. It is how we react/respond to them that determines the short-term and long-term health of our mind and body. If we can control our emotional reaction to pain or other physical ailments, or any other life experience, we can reduce the trauma it has on us. This is how we win the "fight" and when we can say, "I am being positive," and actually mean it and reap the benefits of living in this mindset.

Chapter 6
Mindset towards challenges

In her book, *After the Diagnosis*,[1] Dr. JoAnn LeMaistre describes two approaches to the experience of serious illness, but this can be applied to anything in life: (1) a Pollyanna approach that denies altogether that there has been a real trauma, and 2) a gloomy perspective of resignation, self-denial, and helplessness. Both perspectives distort the reality of illness and/or adversity. The Pollyanna viewpoint holds little reality and the resignation viewpoint holds little hope.

The Pollyanna approach is typified by personal stories or testimonials of complete recovery from extreme illness or disabling conditions and situations. These stories tug at the heartstrings and really catch people's attention. I know people who do this. They have short lived improvement in symptoms or life circumstances, and they shout to the world how wonderful they feel or how amazing something has worked for them, and not long after, they resort back to their suffering, sometimes worse than before.

Never having given the improvement/change enough time to know if it was temporary or permanent, the emotional high and glorious message to the world is based on little evidence. Besides creating false hope to others by overplaying the likelihood of miraculous change, these stories underplay the sadness and feelings of hopelessness that are part of physical and emotional trauma for many.

Many people deny the existence of their suffering and pretend that everything is better than fine, when it is far from fine. This distortion of reality intensifies their suffering (usually behind the scenes) and it gives unrealistic expectations which creates a rush of hope and then a crash of disappointment when people do not see the same improvement others claim to get. The Pollyanna approach can set people up for a crash and burn.

I am all for being optimistic and even having a general overall Pollyanna outlook because it helps us see the silver linings in life's challenges, but it is based on reality and not false hope, or merely the words, "just be positive," as discussed in the previous chapter. As I mentioned, having a positive attitude must be attached to a positive experience for one to have hope. It can also be based on life stories from others who have truly found measurable change that is sustained. This offers real hope to others that they too can get better from whatever ails them.

The second perspective LeMaistre describes in her book views a person as a failure. This is the person who does not respond to modern medicine and the lack of recovery is perceived as the patient's fault. I know countless people who have been told by others that their health problem is their fault. The same holds true for divorce, weight issues, work issues, financial burdens, child rearing, etc. People love to play the blame game and judge others for their perceived faults without considering all extenuating circumstances.

This attitude of blame accounts for some of the worst psychological abuses by healthcare practitioners, family, friends, and caregivers, often typified by statements such as, "stop complaining. It can't be that bad" and "just get over it." The result is often shame and isolation. I have heard things like this from many people from all walks of life, from doctors to family to friends to mere acquaintances. It caused a lot of anger and resentment. I have since learned to not care because I know the truth about me and my life. Plus, judgments from others are a reflection of who they are and not who I am. They are based on their perspectives, wounds, and life experiences. It is about them and how they view the world.

As difficult as it can be, we have to take power back. There is an incredible amount of internal peace and freedom when we detach from other peoples' judgements and behaviors. The way people treat us is their problem. How we react is ours. We can't blame others for making us feel a certain way because no one makes us feel anything unless we let them. How we feel is 100% our choice. Opinions from people are going to be there no matter what we do in life. More often than not, this is about the other person not knowing what to say or do, or because they are wrapped up in their own issues, making it too difficult to be there for us the way we need. Even the most compassionate person may not know what to say or do.

We all desire to be understood by others, and maybe this starts with our understanding that no one can ever be fully understood. This might be a better mindset, rather than getting angry when people do not acknowledge us and our challenges. As much as others may fall short of what we want and maybe expect, being there for ourselves is first and foremost.

Maybe we are not meant to understand certain things. Maybe these things happen to help teach us to accept that some things in life simply are the way they are, no matter what we think about or do about them, that we can't control everything, and that we have to learn to be okay with what we can't always comprehend. Sometimes we needlessly suffer trying to figure out why things are the way they are, without ever finding out. At some point, we must accept things for what they are and let them go, and then practice gratitude for all the blessings we do have, which leads me to the next section.

> *Your peace is more important than driving yourself crazy trying to understand why something happened the way it did. Let it go.*

Living in gratitude

In recent years, I have really learned how gratitude for everything in my life is so powerful that I am frequently saying thank you for things I never would have thought I would be saying thank you for in my life. Anytime something goes right for me, I say thank you. Anytime something goes in a direction I don't like, I also say thank you. This is because I truly believe that everything happens for a reason and even what I perceive as a bad thing is for my own good. If I give in and trust this belief, everything always works out. That is why this book is called, *Beyond Pain and Suffering* and not *How to live a life of pain and suffering*.

I believe there are lessons we are meant to learn from everything. It could be anything such as patience, forgiveness, learning to slow down, or working on overcoming anger, bitterness, and other personality traits that are not very desirable. Or simply an awareness of something to help change our perception to one that serves our higher good. For example, we need to be careful how we bookend our days. If we wake up saying we didn't get enough sleep and/or go to bed at night saying we didn't get enough done, we are judging and shaming ourselves, and creating a mindset of scarcity. Instead, be grateful for the number of hours you did sleep and acknowledge all the things you did accomplish that day. Gratitude for everything creates new perspectives and a new outlook on life.

In situations where you might react with anger or other impulsive behavior, step back and use it as an opportunity to be patient, kind, and compassionate. I can point to certain things in my life that have happened (even years ago) that rear their ugly head from time to time and still bring out the exact same emotions as if the event had just occurred. After going through a short bout of whatever emotion is brought out, I often find myself laughing and saying "thank you" for it appearing in my life again because I clearly have not properly dealt with it and need to learn to LET IT GO, something I am not very skilled at doing. Therefore, the fact that I am bad at letting things go means that every time it happens, I have the opportunity to improve that part of myself. What a gift!! Let me share a couple of examples to make this more tangible.

A number of years ago, I was involved with someone on a new business project. Things were going quite well and then took a turn for the worse when we brought a new person on board. Long story short, the project did not work out and I was blamed for a lot of it, much of which I was not responsible. In all honesty, at least from my perspective, it was quite unfair and unreasonable. The other person was without most of the facts of what happened, yet still concludes that I was to blame. They took little responsibility and to this day, still bring up how it was mostly my fault. Every time they do, which is only once in a while, I am filled with anger and a strong feeling of misunderstanding and unfairness.

To avoid an argument that would go nowhere with this person because of their stubbornness and lack of perspective back then because of intense stress they were under in other areas of their life, I let them speak their piece and then get on with my day. However, as I mentioned, I am unable to move on with peace of mind until I process my frustration.

I run through my head the events that took place and will sometimes, out loud, talk it out as if I am conversing with this person. Since the other person refuses to see their involvement, I have to work through it myself. It's really quite comical the way I talk to myself, but no one sees it because I am always alone when I vent. But this is my current process to get it through my system so I can get it off my mind.

There is an important point I want to make about how we process things - if we judge how we process things on top of how we process things, it prolongs the struggle and makes it more painful. I accept that this is my process, without judgment, which makes the emotional pain far less intense and long lasting.

Every single time I am impacted by this person and/or situation, it reminds me that there are some things in life I simply can't change. Some people will be so stubborn that there is no way to change their opinions, as in this case. However, I can also be like this when it comes to certain things, so I have to take responsibility for my own life and be mindful of how I treat others. This is where gratitude comes in. I am being shown how it feels to be treated this way, so I hopefully never do it to anyone else. With this knowledge, every time this happens with this person or someone else (which is not that often), I say thank you.

As I am writing this, I am thinking of all the details of the incident. While I was in the right about many things and feel the issue has still not been fully resolved, I have no emotion about it. This tells me that I am growing because there was a time when I couldn't share this story without getting stressed out. However, I am sure if this person mentions it again, I will feel some emotions. But, because I am working through it each time it happens, the emotions have weakened and the stress impact on my body is less. This tells me I am making progress, which is the best we can ever ask of ourselves, so be sure to acknowledge yourself for any growth you make, no matter the size.

> *Progress is not linear. It zigs and zags. It reverses. It faces setbacks.*
> *Sure, we can hope it bends towards truth, but we*
> *cannot expect it to march in a straight line.*
> - The Daily Stoic Newsletter -
> 7/6/2020

A "pain"ful lesson for which I am grateful

I want to share another experience where the power of gratitude helped me. About a year ago, I had an incident that brought back many bad memories of my worst years of pain. I was racing around trying to get a lot done and I moved in a strange way when suddenly, my body was frozen in screaming pain. The pain was in a different part of my body than where I usually have pain, but the shocking pain itself was similar. I had thrown out my hip and low back to where I was barely able to sit, stand, or walk. No position was comfortable. The pain kept hitting me like a nail gun.

At first, I was very distraught because it stopped me in my tracks and I had things I needed to do. A stressful, worried reaction is also typical in these situations. After assessing the damage, I came to terms with what happened and spent the next 48 hours laying on the floor on ice and heat, as well as using topical pain lotions, a TENS unit, the Oska Pulse (PEMF therapy device for pain), and a magnetic back/waist wrap. I also used massage machines and trigger point tools, and I saw my chiropractor for a low back/hip treatment. I also increased my intake of anti-inflammatory herbs like ginger and turmeric. Dealing with dystonia is hard enough, let alone anything additional, so I didn't give myself a choice other than do nothing but take care of myself.

After doing everything I could think of to try and alleviate the pain, within 4 days the pain was at least 80% gone and I was able to move around like I was prior to the incident. I know this is totally different from long-term, chronic pain like I have with dystonia and other people have with different ailments. I just wanted to share this particular incident as an introduction so I can describe how pain has completely changed who I am and my outlook on life.

During this short period of time I was injured, I was reminded once again how much I take my health for granted, even health that is already compromised by a neurological movement disorder, which has been an even greater teacher for me, long-term, about really appreciating life and not taking even the seemingly most mundane things for granted. I was even grateful this injury happened.

Yes, as crazy as it sounds, a part of me was happy I hurt myself. I had been feeling so good that I was overdoing it. My body finally said, "no more!" and I was forced to rest, which I should have been wise enough to do on my own, especially someone like me who always emphasizes self-care and life balance. Well, I sure got my fill of self-care those few days. Slowing down helped me realize that a lot of the running around I was doing was counterproductive.

When severe pain strikes, whether it lasts hours, days or years, it is an amazing teacher in so many ways. Pain forces us to slow down and look within, and perhaps to a higher power to put our faith to the test. It teaches us to not take anything for granted and appreciate absolutely everything, whether it be a pretty flower we see or something more profound such as the love and support of a family member or friend; or the roof over our head, food on the table, the cars we drive, and the ridiculously expensive phones most of us carry in our pockets where the world is at our fingertips in mere seconds. I could list a thousand things that we all take for granted far too often. It is during times of great pain and suffering, whether it be physical or emotional, that helps put life into better perspective and see what is most important.

Pain teaches us to not take what we have in our life NOW for granted, because it makes us aware of just how much we took things for granted before. It makes us more mindful of the good that remains in life, which most of us probably neglected too much previously.

Many of us grieve the loss of our former selves when we have limiting pain and other health conditions (or just changes from natural aging) and realize just how much we may have taken that former person/life for granted... which I hope teaches the person we are today to better appreciate everything from this day forward.

After my recovery from this short setback, every time I felt a twinge of additional pain in my hip and low back or somewhere else, as opposed to getting angry, I said "thank you." I literally said it out loud. I also say "thank you" when I feel well, of course.

This is because every time I feel additional pain it reminds me how good my life really is with so many blessings. In order to have a joyful life, I have to maintain this attitude of gratitude for all that I can do, versus focusing on all of the things that are difficult or that I can no longer do. I choose to be grateful for the pain and falls in life. They alert me to what I have so I cherish them more. Gratitude for everything is the main ingredient in the recipe for joy.

> *With gratitude, optimism is sustainable.*
> - Michael J Fox -

A tool for practicing gratitude
In my coaching practice, I often ask clients to make a list of things for which they are grateful. Most people make a list that mainly includes the big things in their lives, such as family, friends, work, home, food, car, etc. These are all very important, but to practice gratitude on a deeper level, it helps to really break down those big things into smaller things. In other words, take those big items and list the reasons you are grateful for them.

We can do the same for things we never think about too often, if at all. Like a pen, for example. It may sound silly, but think about how much a pen helps us, such as the ability to write a grocery list or a reminder note or a letter to a friend, the varied colors available to us for a creative project, a click, twist, or cap option, etc.

How about electricity, indoor plumbing, lightbulbs, refrigeration, a garbage disposal, WIFI, the moment we approach a light on the road and it turns green, the parking spot right next to the store, a grocery store with everything (and more) that we could ever want and need, etc.? When is the last time you found yourself being thankful, and literally saying "thank you" for things like this? There is so much we take for granted.

I recently cut my index finger on my non-dominant hand and had to put tape over the band-aid to keep it from sliding off. For the next few days, it got in the way a lot, making me realize just how important this finger is for SO many things. I have cut my finger many times in the past, but this time I really paid attention to how much it got in the way and how much I take my body and its amazing abilities for granted.

Our body is incredible beyond words and we often don't think just how remarkable it is and how well it works for us, especially if we have a health issue. When we have a health issue, the problem with our body is often the only focus, but there are SO many other things going well with our bodies that are easily forgotten.

That being said, take some tape and wrap it around the tip of one of your index fingers for one day (see the image below for the section to apply it). Tape it so your first knuckle on your finger is covered so you can't fully bend the top portion. See how it feels to do different activities that day. I bet you find that it gets in the way of many things. If we take this one inch of one of our 10 fingers for granted, imagine how many other things about our body, and the rest of our lives, we also take for granted.

The power of forgiveness

Forgiveness is equally powerful as gratitude, and the two go hand in hand. After many years of pain from this person I mentioned above (that I allowed to inflict upon me – we can never forget that no one but us is responsible for how we feel), being in a mindset of forgiveness has been very helpful. As I stated, I am still bothered by it so I have not completely risen above it, but I am getting there. Along with forgiving others, we must forgive ourselves for the personal torment and torture we put ourselves through.

I am going to share a story where I practiced forgiveness and the result I was going for was immediate. Someone contacted me about modifying a program I created to use as a presentation for something that it was not originally intended. I spent nearly a year creating the program, so it was a labor of love, just like this and my first book. I had no problem with him using the program. I was happy he was. The only thing I requested was that he put my name and website at the end so I received credit. This was done, but not the way that we had discussed and agreed.

After asking for the change to be made when it was sent to me for final approval, he refused. After asking again and explaining why I wanted him to modify that one piece (which I shouldn't have had to ask in the first place since it was my program and what was agreed upon), all I received from this person was an arrogant, passive aggressive response, and the edit was never made. He even ignored my follow up emails, after being so responsive while he was in the process of getting what he wanted.

For about a week I was furious. I couldn't understand why he was being so unreasonable. It wasn't even about me getting credit the way we discussed. It was that I couldn't wrap my head around how arrogant and unprincipled this person behaved. I like to understand things and I couldn't figure out his actions and aloof attitude. Up to that point, he had been very professional and ethical, so his behavior didn't make sense and nothing I could think of made it clear to me as to why. I reached a point where I had to stop torturing myself.

The next time I was thinking about him and trying to understand why he acted this way, I realized that this is how he is and there was nothing I could do to change what happened no matter how I felt about him. I could only change how I felt. So, I literally said out loud, "I forgive you" (saying his name). I even apologized for him having to live a life like this where he feels he can treat people so poorly and what it was in his life that drove him to be this way. To be that insensitive and self-righteous must be an awful way to live.

Rather than feel anger, I shifted to feeling bad for him that he lives in such a way where he feels that this kind of behavior is okay. From that moment on, I have never felt a single emotion at all about this person or this incident. I don't even care anymore that he did not honor my request; nor am I bothered by not understanding his behavior. By saying, "I forgive you," I set myself free of the entire situation. And I did this while I was alone. I didn't need for this other person to be present because it was about me, not him. I said it to free myself from the pain I allowed myself to feel.

It sounds so simple, and quite frankly it is, that it is almost hard to believe that this freedom can happen in an instant. By practicing this on a regular basis, we can dramatically reduce stress in our lives and reduce the out of control emotions many of us experience. Learning to "let go," in my opinion, is probably one of the most important things to our mental and physical well-being.

How forgiveness sets us free

As shared in the examples above, forgiveness is a very mindful, intentional, and voluntary process by which people undergo a change in feelings and attitudes regarding an offense and let go of negative emotions such as anger, resentment, and revenge.

Whomever or whatever hurt or offended us might remain a part of our lives, but forgiveness can lessen its grip on us and help us focus on positive parts of our lives. Forgiveness helps us move away from the role of a victim by releasing the control and power the offending person or situation has on us. As we let go of grudges, we no longer define our life by how we have been hurt. Forgiveness can even lead to feelings of understanding, empathy, and compassion for whom or what hurt us. Forgiveness is also a way of being more compassionate towards ourselves.

Forgiveness does not mean that we condone, excuse, or forget what happened, or deny the responsibility for whom or what hurt us, and it does not minimize or justify it. We can forgive without excusing the act or the situation. We forgive so we can detach ourselves, bringing a sense of peace that helps us get on with life and live in the present.

In many instances, we come to realize that the situation(s) we felt hurt us the most actually made us a better and stronger person. In its finality, we can learn to appreciate the "harm" that was done without spite or negativity.

When we look at the word forgiveness it is comprised of the words "for" and "give," It is an act of grace. It is more than just a positive attitude. It helps us see everything in a different way without our ego interfering.

As Mark Twain said, "forgiveness is the fragrance that the violet sheds on the heel that crushed it." It is better to look at "wrongs" that are perpetrated as lessons for us to learn from to help us in the future.

Forgiveness can set us free from emotional baggage. The less baggage we store in our mind and body the better. If we are unforgiving, we might bring anger and bitterness into new relationships and experiences. Our life might become so wrapped up in the "wrongs" we experience that we can't enjoy anything else. We might become depressed or anxious. We might feel that life lacks meaning or purpose and lose valuable and enriching connections with others.

Work on forgiving those who may have wronged you. Forgive whatever adversity you have in life as well. If we allow it to have a firm hold on our life, it not only hurts us; it can change how we relate to other people because we bring some degree of anger, bitterness, and impatience to every interaction.

Also, forgive yourself for mistakes you have made. This is a big one that we often neglect. For an interesting and powerful way to resolve issues with ourselves and others, please check out Ho'oponopono, a Hawaiian practice of reconciliation and forgiveness.

Moving away from emotional pain
Forgiveness sets us free to move forward and leave pain behind. However, there are things we can all grieve if we sit and really allow ourselves to go to that head space. I can easily look back at times in my life that are different from now and get depressed. Instead, I prefer to live in gratitude for those things, let them go, and focus on the here and now.

While I am not doing things with my life I thought I would because of my health condition, I am doing other positive things with my life because of it.

I am grateful for all I have experienced because it offers me the opportunity to grow in ways I never imagined. It also gives me the opportunity to help others with their life challenges.

We become better because of what we went through, better than
if we had resisted and never been broken in the first place.
- Nassim Taleb -

What a gift to be given life lessons that help us and others find hope and meaning in our lives. It is certainly a challenge to be in this mindset, and I am not all the time, but I know that we have to be like this if we want to find meaning in our struggle and joy in our lives. I learn every day how important it is to be grateful for EVERYTHING in life. Being grateful for literally everything in our lives is one of many ways to help us see things from a different, and often healthier, perspective.

To offer an example of an opposite mindset, I once worked with a client who had mild chronic pain symptoms; mild compared to many others I know, but to her it was severe. She was in her late 20's and studying to be a doctor. She complained incessantly about how her life had been ruined.

She was stuck in the depressed "why me?" mode of thinking, even though she found some symptom management techniques that were significantly helpful. She just simply resented the fact that she had dystonia, regardless of how much or how little it affected her life. She felt like she was above it.

I tried to impress upon her how fortunate she was to have this experience. I told her that when it came time for her to be a doctor, she would be much better able to empathize with her patients thanks to having dystonia. Her patients would be so lucky to have a doctor who had the capacity to put herself in their shoes, much like the movie *The Doctor* with William Hurt (a great movie to see if you haven't already, or to watch again).

She had a choice to continue grumbling about her health challenge or see the blessing in it because of the many fortunate patients with whom she would come in contact throughout her career. It was all about perspective and choosing to view her life in a different way. She is now helping many people, largely in part because of her personal health challenges. In my mind, everything she went through was meant to be and she will be a better doctor because of it.

Is there is a reason for everything?
Like the story I just shared, I believe everything in life happens for a reason. Sometimes we can figure out the reason and other times not, but I live my life with the belief that nothing is happening TO me. Everything is happening FOR me and I am exactly where I am supposed to be at every given moment. I may not always like the circumstances, but I am here for a reason and there is something to learn. Not everyone may agree, but this is my belief.

If we keep our focus on gratitude instead of bitterness and anger, life is less stressful and more fulfilling. It isn't easy to live in this state all the time, so I have to frequently remind myself, similar to most people.

You may have heard the following quote: "The most beautiful stones have been tossed by the wind and washed by the waters and polished to brilliance by life's strongest storms." We will have many storms throughout our lives and they all help us grow. Instead of running from the storm, it is best to find a way to dance in the rain and play in the puddles.

Most of us can think of a previous challenge in our lives and list things we learned from it. In most cases, we learned why we had to go through it after it happened. My suggestion is that we find the meaning as we are going through it if we can. One way of doing this is by "going into" the pain of the challenge and really feel it. Talk to it. Ask it what it wants you to learn. Sit with it and be still with it.

Instead of fighting, it is better to embrace the storm so we don't prolong the pain. If we are open to learning lessons we are being taught, the storm will not last as long. Storms in our lives help us if we let them. We can be angry and resentful, or we can be a student. The choice is ours. Remember that any setback in life is a setup for a comeback and we have the choice to become either a victim or a victor.

Victim or victor mindset
When we don't use the power of the mind to be at peace with the trials and tribulations of life, specifically gratitude and forgiveness, we can feel like a victim when faced with tough times. I had a victim mentality for years after developing chronic pain from dystonia.

The term "victim mentality" refers to people who blame someone or something else for the unpleasant things in their life. It is very common to do because projecting is instinctual and less painful than looking inward. In other words, life is easier when we play the blame game. It helps us rationalize why we are not growing and moving forward. "Victim mentality" also applies to people who believe that undesirable life circumstances only yield negative outcomes.

Feeling like a victim is normal when confronted with a life changing event, health condition, or other similar circumstance, but it can be destructive if we remain in this state of mind. We become isolated, depressed, bitter, angry, and resentful. It not only impacts us, but others around us as well.

Victims are only focused on themselves and upset with all the things they do not have or cannot do, whether it is because of financial constraints, health limitations, a combination of both, or something else entirely. The victim will always find something wrong and live a life of excuses. You probably know some of these people. You may even be one of them.

Many people make themselves unhappy simply by finding it impossible to accept life just as it is presenting itself right now. You don't have to be one of them. Victims will ask "why me?" in a sulking and moaning ("poor me") manner when something happens that they don't like, similar to the girl I mentioned a couple pages back. Asking "why me?" in an inquisitive manner is more proactive and might yield more answers because it puts us in the role of an unattached observer where we can be more objective.

For the first few years with dystonia, because of how my life literally took a complete 180 turn from the ridiculous pain and unrelenting muscle contractions in my neck and back, I was stuck in the "why me, poor me?" frame of mind. It got me nowhere but depressed. I had to change this question if I wanted freedom from my mental anguish, which was feeding the physical pain. Instead of asking, "why me?" I began asking, "why not me?" - "how can I learn to live with pain?" - "how can pain help me learn and grow?" - and "how can I help others who are also suffering?"

I was no better or worse than anyone else so if it happened to me, so be it. There was nothing I could do to reverse things so I needed to learn to accept it and find the good in it, even when I was in crazy pain and could barely function. I also had to find a way to help others. One of the best ways to get out of our own way is to be of service to others, which I began to do in the form of writing, volunteering, consulting, and life coaching.

When we dwell on our problems it puts us in a hole that is difficult to get out of. We may even find comfort in the depressed world we mentally create and are unmotivated to find solutions. I did it and I see others doing it all the time. People complain about everything: the weather, their job, car, family, spouse, bills, yard work, etc. What's the point? There is nothing inherently wrong with any of these things. The only thing wrong is our perception. There is great quote by Abraham Lincoln about perception:

We can complain because rose bushes have thorns
or rejoice because thorn bushes have roses.
~ Abraham Lincoln ~

A big part of the victim mentality is due to being stuck in the past; how life was before "the problem." I put "the problem" in quotes because any word(s) can go here, so I do not want to make it about anything specific. Find a way to release the past. It is not who you are. You can be whomever you want right now. You just need to make the choice, set the intention, and act it out. This is YOUR life.

Victim status embodies all that I reject about the struggles of life. The challenge is to live and function well under all circumstances, including those never anticipated.
- Richard M. Cohen –

By no means is it as easy as I am making it sound. I completely understand that it is a process that unfolds one day at a time. We just need to allow ourselves to let it unfold so we are free to live our lives. Become part of the process rather than trying to force the process.

The pessimist complains about the wind.
The optimist expects it to change.
The realist adjusts the sails.
~ William A. Ward ~

When I get stuck thinking about my life before dystonia and pain it can get me down. I could be on top of the world and all of a sudden I try to do something my body won't allow me to anymore and I am reminded of how life once was. Feeling sad about it is momentary though because I don't allow myself to dwell. Instead, I think new thoughts and involve myself in other activities. We must understand that the happiness of our life greatly depends on the quality of our thoughts.

A popular quote most of us have probably heard is, "The past is history. The future is a mystery. Today is a gift. That's why it's called the present." Do your best to enjoy the gift of this moment. An affirmation I like to use to help me when I am stuck in days gone by is, "I release the past. I am free to move forward with love in my heart." I say this over and over until I feel it resonate within me.

Also, whenever I go through painful emotions, whether it be anxiety, sadness/depression, misunderstanding, feeling judged, etc., my mind races like a broken record, playing over everything that contributed to all of the things that created those feelings. Eventually, I reach a point in my processing where I take responsibility for everything that I'm feeling, and it is then and only then when I can put my mind at ease by forgiving myself for allowing something outside of me make me feel a certain way. No one or no thing has permission to make us feel anything unless we give them/it permission. If we do, then we must assume responsibility for our feelings and the consequences of our choices.

I highly recommend the book, *You Can Heal Your Life*, by Louise Hay. Her belief is that we create every emotional and physical problem in our body. The following quote comes from one of my favorite chapters called The Body: "The body, like everything else in life, is a mirror of our inner thoughts and beliefs. The body is always talking to us, if we would only take the time to listen. Every cell within your body responds to every single thought you think and every word you speak. Continuous modes of thinking and speaking produce body behaviors and postures, and 'eases' or 'dis'-eases. The person who has a permanently scowling face did not produce that by having joyous, loving thoughts."[2]

Her book helps me look more closely at the mind-body connection, especially when my dystonia was severe and when I was going through some difficult challenges outside my battle with dystonia. I now see how my response to everything has a direct impact on my physical health.

I find the appendix of her book to be particularly interesting. It discusses how specific problems in certain body parts are connected to thought patterns. Take the neck for example. Louise says, "The neck and throat are fascinating because so much 'stuff' is going on there. The neck represents the ability to be flexible in our thinking, to see the other side of a question, and to see another person's viewpoint. When there are problems in the neck, it usually means we are being stubborn about our own concept of the situation."[2]

As it does me, this may describe many of you. I have always been a stubborn person. Throughout my life, whenever I felt I wasn't being heard or if I disagreed with something, I would tense up in the shoulder and neck area. I would also clench my teeth. I still do now, but to a much lesser extent thanks in part to the information in her book and a lot of years of practice with meditation, relaxation breathing, visualization, being more open to the opinion of others, and pretty much learning to not care so much about trivial things. However, stubbornness can be a great trait when applied in ways that help us, so it isn't always about the personality trait. It is how we use that trait. For example, when I apply my stubbornness to my self-care activities, I am benefitting.

I am not claiming that health conditions are created by our behavior or thought patterns, but I am also not discounting that they have an impact. Perhaps more than we realize.

Inner dialogue

What is your inner dialogue - the narrative you are telling yourself about yourself every day? This is your mental movie, so to speak. It is the feature film that plays over and over in your mind. The movie is about who you are: I am fat, my hair is too grey, I have too many wrinkles, I am not smart or funny, I am not lovable, I am not good enough, etc.

Would you be friends with this inner voice? If it were sitting next to you on a bus, you would probably change your seat. Pay attention when your movie is playing and realize that this movie is a train of thought that can be changed. Rewrite your script and intentionally, consciously design it the way you want to live and be, and then take steps to become it.

References
1) LeMaistre, J. *After the Diagnosis: From Crisis to Personal Renewal for Patients With Chronic Illness.* (1995). Ulysses Press.
2) Hay, L. *You can heal your life.* (1984). Hay House Publishing

Chapter 7
Understanding stress and changing how we fight it

Many of us talk about fighting or waging war against problems in our personal lives and in society. For example, "the war on drugs," "the war on poverty," "the war on terrorism," etc. For people with a health condition, especially one that is chronic, the war cry is "beat the disease" or "fight the disease." I think this can be problematic for some because when we say we are going to fight something, our body rears up and produces more stress hormones which makes it physiologically near impossible to heal or be as healthy as we could be. My perspective on "fighting" is based on what I share in upcoming sections in this chapter about the stress response, particularly something called the "freeze response."

"Fighting" needs to be put into proper context because when we wage war on something, it usually gets worse. Therefore, we need the proper emotional arsenal to be equipped with the necessary tools to effectively fight to become as healthy as possible. This is all very important because stress, especially prolonged stress, is dangerous for the body so we must learn to be at peace as often as we can for the processes in our body to function at their optimal level.

Please don't mistake any of this as me being a pacifist and that we shouldn't fight legitimate battles. There are battles that most certainly need to be waged, but there are many we wage for no reason at all or for the wrong reasons, or the wrong way, which makes us unhealthier.

I can't emphasize enough just how important it is to understand that the more we fight against anything, especially personal problems (physical or emotional) the more strength and control we give it, the more power it has over us, and the more it defines us. Instead of fighting against it, embrace it as a part of who you are and then FIGHT THE DESIRE TO GIVE UP ON YOURSELF during tough times. To me, this is the real "fight" and a far more productive battle. It also releases us from being so angry. Anger stirs up stress chemicals which make us feel unhealthy. So, by fighting against anything, the problem will always win.

As counterintuitive as it may sound, if we can learn to let go and find peace of mind with whatever is "wrong" with us, we give our body a better chance to heal. This is when we win the "fight" because we decrease the stress load on the body. I put the word "wrong" in quotes because "right" and "wrong" are nothing more than subjective perspectives. Nothing is inherently right or wrong unless we decide it is.

As we all know, stress can have a negative impact on our physical, emotional, and social health, such as increased pain, anxiety, headaches, physical weakness, increased tension, sleep interference, relationship problems, work challenges, family upheaval, etc. If your life is already filled with stress during normal circumstances, your response to additional stress is potentially catastrophic. Stress can affect us to such an extent that our nervous system is always aroused, keeping us trapped in chronic fight or flight mode because our body is conditioned, particularly if we are in pain, to always be on guard.

What is stress?
Stress is our body's reaction to an internal or external stimulus that disturbs its physical or mental equilibrium. When we are stressed, our body responds as though we are in danger. Our sympathetic nervous system is activated which increases hormones such as adrenaline and cortisol that surge through our body, initiating the fight or flight stress response. The fight or flight response becomes activated when we believe there is a chance we can outfight or outrun a perceived threat or stressful situation.[1]

There is also a response called "fawning." Fawning is where a person develops people-pleasing behaviors to avoid conflict and to establish a sense of safety. In other words, the fawn trauma response is a type of coping mechanism that survivors of complex trauma adopt to "appease" their abusers.

Stress experts around the world are now adding the word "freeze" to the fight or flight response with respect to the fact that instead of fighting or fleeing, we might sometimes freeze (like a deer in headlights) in painful or traumatic situations. This fascinating response to stress is discussed in the next section.

A little stress, known as acute stress, can be of great benefit to us. It keeps us active and alert, raising levels of performance during critical events, such as a sports activity, an important meeting, or a dangerous situation or crisis. However, long term, or chronic stress, can have detrimental effects on our health and can diminish our quality of life.

As mentioned above, stress can play a part in problems such as headaches, high blood pressure, heart problems, asthma, arthritis, depression, anxiety, pain, and muscle tension. Emotions such as anger, frustration, bitterness, and fear can exacerbate muscle tension. We also increase tension by closely monitoring our symptoms and having an over awareness of just how tight or sore we are,[2] or how uncomfortable we feel emotionally.

If stress is prolonged, adrenaline and cortisol maintain tension in the body. Over time, muscle tension can become habitual which pulls the body further away from relaxation. You may reach a point where you are no longer aware how constricted your muscles have become and relaxing them can be very difficult. In fact, if you try to relax, your muscles might tighten even more because they have forgotten what letting go and relaxed/tension-free feels like.

Keeping muscles tense drains much more energy than keeping muscles relaxed. This should alert us to the importance of practicing relaxation techniques because it is only when the body finds relaxation that it can reverse the damaging effects of stress.[3]

If you are someone who is living a high stressed life, you more than likely have an overactive nervous system, even at rest. It then takes only minimal stimuli for your system to become overloaded, causing an increase in the symptoms mentioned above. It is like a full glass of water where it takes only a few drops before it spills over.

The nature of life is such that we do not often know where or when something will trigger stress. Thus, it is important to learn how to manage our nervous system so we can handle stressors we can't avoid. We can do this by regularly practicing things such as mindfulness meditation, breathing exercises, visualization, and other mind calming activities. The more we practice and learn to accept the things that cause us trouble, the easier it is to deal with them.

Since stress and pain deplete our energy which reduces our ability to cope, identify your stress triggers and do your best to limit them or find new ways to respond to the trigger. Avoiding stress entirely is difficult so the best thing we can do is learn how to better deal with what we view as stressful. We may not be able to eliminate the stressors in our world, but we can change our reaction to them so we are not so dramatically affected.

Fight, flight, and freeze response

As mentioned earlier, the fight or flight stress response becomes activated when we believe there is a chance we can outfight or outrun our attackers (or any perceived danger and stressful situation). The freeze response differs in that it gets activated due to a perceived or real inability to take action. In essence, one feels helpless to fight or flee the threatening, painful, or stressful experience.

The sympathetic branch of the nervous system activates the fight or flight response. It tells the heart to beat faster, the muscles to tense, the eyes to dilate and the mucous membranes to dry up; all so we can fight harder, run faster, see better and breathe easier than we would without this response.

This response kicks in for real and imagined threats in as little as 1/20th of a second. The parasympathetic branch calms us down to rest, telling the body that the danger has passed and it can relax. The parasympathetic branch also coordinates the freeze response.

During the freeze response, the body becomes both tense and paralyzed at the same time. The thoughts, sensations, and emotions of the stressful experience become suppressed or internalized, not only in the mind but in the tissues of the body. This is called somatic memory (body/cellular memory) and can have damaging effects if the event or trauma experienced is not processed in a healthy way.

Somatic memory is often used by trauma therapists to describe symptoms that don't always have a physical cause, but can be related to past trauma, perhaps in childhood for example, and then forgotten by the mind but not by the body.

Trauma may result from a wide variety of stressors such as a health condition, accidents, invasive medical procedures, sexual or physical assault, emotional abuse, neglect, war, natural disasters, loss, birth trauma, or the corrosive stressors of ongoing fear and conflict. Experts believe that trauma is not caused by the event itself, but rather develops through the failure of the body, psyche, and nervous system to process adverse events.[4]

As described by Jonathan Tripodi, author of *Freedom from Body Memory* and Founder of the Body Memory Recall Approach (BMR), consider the interplay of a cat and mouse. When a mouse is approached by a cat it will run away. If cornered, the mouse might try to fight back. Once the mouse realizes that it can't win by attack and can't run away, it becomes paralyzed with fear (freeze response). The cat might swat at it with its paws and may even bite it, but the mouse remains frozen with tension. The cat will eventually interpret the mouse's frozen state as a sign that it is dead and will leave it in search of more stimulating prey.

Once the threat is over and if the mouse lives, it will come out of the freeze response by spontaneously discharging excess energy through involuntary movements including shaking, trembling, and deep spontaneous breaths. This discharge process resets the autonomic nervous system, restoring equilibrium. Body memory (or somatic/cellular memory) from the attack is released and the mouse walks away as if nothing ever happened.

The mouse has effectively survived and released the traumatic experience. It does not carry any tension from the attack and its body is again at ease. This is similar to a deer that freezes at the sight of headlights. When the threat has passed, it trembles violently which "shakes off" the event and then goes about its business without lasting impairment. This shaking is called neurogenic tremor.[5]

Neurogenic tremor is the natural response of a shocked or disrupted nervous system attempting to restore the neuro-physiologic homeostasis of the body. The tremor (vibrations) restores a relaxed muscle state to prevent the development of health problems. The tremors/vibrations signal the brain to release tension to return to a resting state. This helps us better adapt to our environment and this process of adaptation makes us stronger and more prepared to deal with difficult future experiences.[5-7]

Think of this in terms of the rhythm of breathing. We breathe in and we breathe out. Imagine what it would be like to inhale and then hold it. To a certain extent, this is what is happening while in the freeze response.

I think many of us can recall a time when we experienced our body shaking from a painful event or situation (a car accident or near accident, public speaking or doing something embarrassing in front of others, receiving bad news, a confrontation, a health scare, etc.) The shaking is a way of re-calibrating our nervous system. It is the body's way of naturally processing and releasing the event. If we resist the shaking, we prevent ourselves from healing from the event. This repression of trauma causes it to be stored in our muscles, which is what may cause some health problems. This being the case, while it might be uncomfortable to go through the shaking, the short-term discomfort of shaking is better than potential long-term damage. In short, let yourself shake. Don't resist. It is the body's way of healing.

The primary difference between animals and humans is that humans do not tend to go through the instinctual discharge of the freeze response, leaving us vulnerable to constriction and pain. Through rationalizations, judgments, shame, and fear of our bodily sensations, we may disrupt our innate capacity to self-regulate, functionally "recycling" disabling terror and helplessness. Living in this state can sometimes be the reason for physical and emotional/psychological health issues from developing or persisting, because when we hold onto an experience, we live it over and over when we are triggered by a memory of it.

When the nervous system does not reset after an overwhelming experience, sleep, cardiac, digestion, respiration, and immune system function can be seriously disturbed. Unresolved physiological distress can also lead to an array of other physical, cognitive, emotional, and behavioral symptoms. Trauma experts believe that the interruption of the freeze response (which animals rarely experience) contributes to what is called "kindling" in humans.[5]

Most people think of kindling as small, flammable pieces of wood that help larger pieces of wood catch on fire. As the name kindling suggests, a small spark applied to tinder will ignite a flame that eventually can grow into a roaring bonfire. Used in medicine, kindling is a term to describe a process of over-firing chemicals in the nervous system that triggers symptoms of post traumatic stress disorder, chronic pain, epilepsy, bipolar disorder, and other health problems. Kindling has been compared to spontaneous combustion, a chemical reaction that occurs when objects reach a certain temperature.

In neurology, kindling is a term used to explain how over-firing or neural excitability in the nervous system becomes self-perpetuating without much, or any, need for additional external triggering. We can use anxiety as an example. Picture anxiety as the log that is burning. When we feed the burning log (anxiety) with fear, worry, judgment, shame, etc., about the anxiety, this is the kindling that makes the anxiety (fire) grow.

As neuroscientist Joe Dispenza talks about in his many lectures and videos, unlike other animals, human beings can turn on the stress response by just thought alone. We can think of the past or something that is going to happen in the future, and we can turn on the same stress chemicals as if we are experiencing the actual event. If we keep these thoughts turned on, we are headed for health problems because no organism can live in emergency mode for very long.

Somatic experiencing (discussed below) contends that negative symptoms of trauma, such as anxiety, hypervigilance, aggression, and shame, result from denying the body the opportunity to fully process the traumatic event. Ideally, human beings should respond to trauma the same as the mouse and deer that I mentioned earlier. However, the release of the freeze response and the associated tensions and fear from the overwhelming event may instead occur gradually over time or not at all. With repeated unresolved trauma, syndromes can develop or existing syndromes can persist.

Perhaps kindling is why some of us developed health problems and/or why symptoms persist. Perhaps kindling is also why some people are so dramatically affected by seemingly innocuous stimuli. In other words, they have an over-stimulated nervous system and it takes very little additional stress to feel overwhelmed.

Living in protection mode
Think about your response to stress. Out of fear and not feeling in control, many of us live in protection/survival mode where we consciously restrict our movements (to the best of our ability) to try and decrease pain and other physical or emotional discomfort. For many, it is an automatic response.

Notice small warning signs in your body that your danger system has taken over, like sudden muscle tension or an elevated heart rate. When you notice this happening, take a deep breath and remind yourself that there is no real danger in the present moment.

Also, what would happen if we just allowed our pain or discomfort to be what they are without mentally or physically trying to fight them? Easier said than done of course, but think about the possibility of just letting go and embracing what we find unpleasant. Perhaps some of the tension in our body and damage from that long-term tension is from our intellectual brains keeping the symptoms of stress and trauma stored in memory. For real healing to take place, our body needs to learn that the danger has passed and that it is possible to live in the safety of the present. Our problem is that we resist feelings that are uncomfortable, making it difficult to move from this discomfort to feelings of peace and calmness, and safely trust our body's ability to balance and heal itself.

Imagine all things in nature (animals, flowers, water, trees swaying in the wind, etc.), and you will observe that there is non-resistance. Trees don't try to avoid swaying in the wind. They move at the speed of the wind without fighting. When moving water reaches a rock, tree, or other impediment, it finds a way under, over, around or through the obstruction. The flow of water doesn't increase to get beyond the impediment. Sometimes it takes years of constant movement to erode what is in its path. Just like water, it would be helpful to flow with the natural rhythm of life, rather than trying to control everything. Examples of words I like to use to help me visualize letting go include "melting," "swaying," and "flowing."

Since relaxation and self-healing are prevented when the freeze response remains active, if we get our mind out of the way, we might be physically and emotionally more at ease. It certainly merits consideration because the body is better able to remain balanced, vital, and adaptable to new experiences when we don't fight what is "wrong" with us so much.

I remember the day my Mom received a call from her doctor telling her she had breast cancer. She got the call while we were driving home from one of my doctor appointments. When she got the news, I was amazed at how calm she was. It was probably because we were still in the car and she had to focus on driving, the news didn't hit her yet, or she went into the freeze response to some extent.

When we got home, which was only about five minutes from the time she received the news, she stood in the kitchen completely numb with tears in her eyes, unable to speak. She then began to shake uncontrollably for a couple minutes. When the shaking stopped, she was able to clearly articulate the diagnosis, treatment, and prognosis. If I understand the freeze response correctly, this is what she went into and came out of successfully.

That was over ten years ago and I am happy to report that she remains cancer free. I often wonder if she would have gone through surgery and radiation treatment as well as she did had she not experienced neurogenic tremors and instead, held onto the shocking news that caused her such fear. Perhaps if she held onto the news instead of "shaking it off," her recovery would not have gone so smoothly.

When I speak with her about it now, she views her cancer as something she had, was treated for, and it is over. She doesn't hold onto any of it. It was taken care of and she has moved on with her life. She has no attachment to it, similar to a frightened mouse that "shakes off" an attack from a cat.

The more I think about how she handled the entire experience, the more I am convinced that the way we process bad news, a challenging circumstance, an acute or chronic health condition, or a frightening situation, affects our physical and emotional well-being.

Unlocking the freeze response

A method used to unlock the freezing and hypersensitive responses of the nervous system is called pendulation. Pendulation is the movement between dysregulation (trauma) and regulation (healing) within the body. It is the natural rhythm of movement between constriction and release inherent to all physical systems. It helps activate basic regulatory rhythms and stops nervous system rigidity and random responses, interrupting all kinds of traumatizing pain.

Pendulation is an aspect of a therapy called Somatic Experiencing, which was introduced by Dr. Peter Levine in 1997. Somatic Experiencing is a form of therapy aimed at relieving and resolving the symptoms of post traumatic stress disorder (PTSD), rape, auto accidents, post-surgical trauma, chronic health conditions, etc., by focusing on the client's perceived body sensations (or somatic experiences). It is a body-awareness approach that restores self-regulation and returns a sense of aliveness, relaxation, and wholeness to traumatized individuals. It is based upon the realization that human beings have an innate ability to overcome the effects of trauma.

Pendulations are done with the help of a Somatic Experiencing Practitioner. They help clients move to a state where he or she is believed to be somewhat dysregulated (aroused or frozen from present or past trauma) and then helped to return to a state of regulation (loosely defined as not aroused or unfrozen). This process is done in small doses called titrations, with progressively more levels of dysregulation as the client successfully progresses through pendulations.[5,8] Another technique is called Tension and Trauma Releasing Exercises (TRE), which is discussed in the next chapter.

References
1) Psychology Today, http://www.psychologytoday.com/basics/stress

2) WebMD, http://www.webmd.com/mental-health/effects-of-stress-on-your-body

3) Phillips, M. (2007) *Reversing Chronic Pain*. North Atlantic Books: Berkeley, CA

4) www.painsupport.co.uk. Retrieved on June 27, 2020

5) www.traumahealing.com, Retrieved March 29, 2014 from:
http://www.traumahealing.com/somatic-experiencing/

6) http://www.bodymemory.com, Retrieved June 27, 2020

7) Feldman, S., (2004). Biomechanical Stimulation Web by Spencer Feldman.

8) Phillips, M. (2007) *Reversing Chronic Pain*. Berkeley, CA: North Atlantic Books: 59-60

Chapter 8
Managing stress

When Dr. Peter Levine, author of the book, *Waking the Tiger*, gives lectures on surviving trauma, he shows a video of a lion chasing a baby gazelle to demonstrate how the freeze response works, which was discussed in the previous chapter. He explains that the video is short because the average time for a lion attack from start to finish is about 45 seconds. He makes the additional point that this is how long the victim's stress response (and our stress response) was designed to be activated; not hours, days, weeks, or years.

Unfortunately, those with chronic stress, pain, or illness often live in a body with a heightened nervous system that does not know how to turn off the stress response, even under normal conditions. This can have harmful effects and keep us in a chronic unwell state.

There is good news, however; we can learn stress reduction techniques and make lifestyle changes to better cope with stress and recover from the fight, flight, and freeze response. This is very important, as the constant release of stress hormones can slow down or prevent relief and recovery from the symptoms associated with physical and emotional health conditions.[1]

General health and stress maintenance can be enhanced by regular exercise, an anti-inflammatory diet (see www.deflame.com), and by avoiding excessive alcohol, caffeine, and tobacco. Instead of relieving stress and returning the body to a relaxed state, these substances tend to keep the body aroused.

Physical activity, such as aerobics, walking, swimming, biking, yoga, Pilates, tai chi, stretching, and weight/resistance training are all helpful for reducing stress. Scientists believe exercise increases blood circulation to the brain, especially areas like the amygdala and hippocampus — which both have roles in controlling motivation, moods, and response to stress.

These activities also serve as effective distractions from stressful events. Physical activity may also blunt the harmful effects of stress on blood pressure and the heart. Exercise is an extremely anti-inflammatory activity, so long as you exercise within your individual tolerance zone. Too little exercise is not enough for reducing inflammation and too much can be pro-inflammatory.

Working with a counselor who uses cognitive behavioral therapy (CBT) can also be an effective way to reduce stress. A typical CBT approach includes identifying sources of stress, restructuring priorities, changing one's response to stress, and finding methods for managing and reducing stress. As a life coach in the area of health and wellness, some of the main challenges my clients bring to our sessions include how to manage stress and stress triggers, and cope with unwanted and/or undesirable stressful life circumstances.

The benefits of talking to a therapist or coach is that the act of verbalizing our feelings helps us release tension, sort through problems, and gain new perspective. Feelings such as anger and frustration that are not expressed in an acceptable way may lead to hostility, a sense of helplessness, isolation, and depression. These often turn up as major themes in my coaching sessions.

Expressing feelings does not mean venting frustration on others, loading down friends with emotional baggage, or wallowing in self-pity. The primary goal is to explain and assert your needs to a trusted individual in a positive way where we don't necessarily change the past so much as we identify current habits of thinking and behaving, and then change these patterns moving forward.

Stress can also be managed by writing in a journal, writing a poem, or composing a letter that may never even be sent. Along with expressing our feelings, learning to listen, empathize, and respond to others with understanding is just as important for maintaining strong relationships necessary for emotional fulfillment and reduced stress. Music is also an effective stress reducer. It can reduce heart rate, blood pressure, and feelings of anxiety.

Removing ourselves from a stressful environment and listening to guided relaxation/meditation programs can also be helpful. Spend time focusing on your breathing while you visualize peaceful settings, such as floating on a raft on a lake in the mountains or lying on a private, white sandy beach. If you are able, take a slow walk and pay attention to the sounds of nature around you. Try to zone everything out except for the sights and sounds.

Limit the amount of time you spend on the phone, computer, and other forms of technology when possible. People may not be aware how significantly stressful they can be. If you are not sure how much technology is affecting you, turn everything off for a few hours and/or just leave your phone at home for the day.

I bet just the thought of doing this with your phone causes discomfort for many of you. If it does, you are probably overusing your gadgets. Allow your mind time to rest. The instant message world we live in promotes anxiety, so it is important to balance our usage. To read more about this, please see Chapter 11.

By following the above ideas, over the years I have learned to better deal with stress and anxiety. One of my biggest keys to managing stress is allowing myself to acclimate to an environment, feeling, or situation that is uncomfortable. Rather than looking for a way to escape, I "melt into" the experience and let time pass, which lets my body and mind adjust and be more at ease.

I allow all the uncomfortable feelings, as well as noise, movements, lights, and other stimuli that challenge my sensitive nervous system, come into my mind/body without resistance. I also make myself very mindful to not react, as if they are something dangerous. I don't allow myself to view them as a threat or judge them as noxious stimuli.

The longer I allow myself to acclimate like this, reminding myself that I am safe, the more my stress and anxiety dissipate which prevents my discomfort from getting worse. When we stay in the alarmed state, almost every external stimuli is recognized as a threat and we are on edge and want to run. This is the habit we want to exercise out of our way of being, by "allowing" and "not resisting." I recall having dinner with a client with high stress and anxiety who was visibly startled by every noise in the restaurant. Her nervous system was trained to view everything as dangerous because for much of her life, she resisted allowing herself to feel and release anything uncomfortable.

Dr. Claire Weekes, author of *Hope and Help for Your Nerves*, talks about this in the context of first fear and second fear. Some people who experience a flash of fear and anxiety from stress that naturally comes with anything uncomfortable, may often fear those feelings (sweaty palms, nervousness, headache or other pain, rapid heartbeat, shakiness or weakness) which adds a second fear; in other words, fear on top of fear. This is what causes us to panic and keeps us in fight, flight, or freeze mode (also called sympathetic dominant, referring to the sympathetic nervous system).

If we instead practice complete acceptance and allow the first fear to happen without adding second fear to it, it is significantly much easier to handle uncomfortable situations. It takes practice, but the more we do it, the easier it becomes.

Stress reduction techniques[2]
- Slow and deep breathing. Stop what you are doing. Breathe gently but deeply from your abdomen. On the out breath say to yourself, "Be calm. Be peaceful."
- When you are rushed, say, "There is plenty of time. Stay calm."
- When things don't go your way, say, "Everything is happening perfectly. It will all work out for the best."
- If you're feeling angry, anxious, or depressed, it is best to acknowledge the feelings and say, "Okay, I recognize this. I feel bad at the moment, but it will pass just as it has before."
- Talk to your family, friends, therapist, or support group about the situations you find stressful.
- Replace/reframe negative thoughts and judgements with positive thoughts.
- Write down your feelings.
- Utilize visualization techniques.
- Spend time in prayer and meditation.
- Get outside and be among nature. It can be very grounding.

When you feel stress (or pain), don't numb it, avoid it, or ignore it. Focus on what you are feeling and bring it close to your awareness. Breathe and give what you are feeling your full, thoughtful attention. Notice the specific feeling(s) in your body. Where is the feeling located and how would you describe it? Notice if you have any tension (in your mind and body) and try to relax the area(s).

Allow your breath to assist you in finding peace. Close your eyes, breathe in, and feel it; then breathe out and release it, repeating the process again and again until you feel more relaxed. Rather than resist your feelings, accept the moment as it is and yourself as you are. The short-term pain of focusing on your feelings will be better than the long-term stress and damage of avoidance.

Using various relaxation techniques like this and changing our mindset about our life situation can reduce added tension that is created beyond what is part and parcel of life. Relaxation does not come naturally for a lot of people. Learning (or re-learning) how to release tension and relax is a practice.

When you become skilled at body/mind relaxation, you will better recognize when tension is building up and be able to shut it down. It is crucial that we learn to release tension because it is only when our body finds relaxation that we reverse the damage of stress, which can then reduce pain. Find what works best for you and put it to practice.

A steady track for managing stress and heightened emotions

When it comes to stress in your life, do you ride a roller coaster of emotions or are you pretty even keeled? When you are under stress do you feel a physical impact, especially if you already live with a health condition?

These questions are important to answer because stress and heightened emotions, both of which feed off each other, can have damaging effects on our health if not properly managed, as was previously mentioned. When I don't manage life events well, it results in stress which increases my symptoms of dystonia and chronic pain. It also causes headaches and abdominal discomfort. I know many people in all walks of life who have the same response to stress. It is very common, which tells us how much most people need to practice techniques for better responding to stress.

Stress means different things to different people and what causes stress in one person may have little impact on another. Some people are also better able to handle stress than others, and not all stress is bad. In small doses, stress can help us accomplish tasks and prevent us from getting hurt, like slamming on the brakes to avoid hitting the car in front of us...a very good thing! These short-term stress responses are very helpful in these dangerous situations, but harmful when we are in this state when no danger is present or if stress is prolonged.

Going back to the question in the opening paragraph in this section about riding a roller coaster of emotions. I want you to visualize an amusement park that is filled with roller coasters and other rides, people, lights, noises, and other stimuli. It's fun for a little while but imagine living most of your life in the amusement park. For most of us it would be system overload. The amusement park is the image I want you to visualize as stress.

Now I want you to visualize the peaceful overhead tram circling the pandemonium of the park below. Better yet, picture a slow moving, open air train that quietly circles many amusement parks. The slow moving, steady train is where we want to live emotionally for better health. Let's take this a step further and make it more applicable to real life.

A train typically goes around in an oval, similar to many racetracks and running tracks. The majority of the track is straight and on each end there is a curve. The place we want to emotionally live most of our lives is on the straightaways and then not become alarmed when we hit that curve and our balance is thrown off. In other words, the more emotionally even keeled we are during ALL life events, the less of an impact stress will have on us.

Examine your life to see how much your mind is bouncing around in the raucous amusement park and how much of it is relaxed on the peaceful, steady train. If you are riding the roller coaster of emotions of the amusement park, it is totally fine. It just means some work needs to be done. The reason why is because a body and mind that has frequent up and down emotions, and is easily triggered by stress, is a body that is less prone to good health.

Just like the train that hits a curve, the same happens in life. We all hit curves that throw us off course. The key is to get back on the straightaway and keep the curves to a minimum. Every time you hit a curve, lean into it and flow through it smoothly to get yourself back on the straightaway. Repeat those words I just mentioned…lean into, flow through, and smoothly. Close your eyes and let those words marinate for a little while. Allow your mind and body to experience how those words feel.

If we fret whenever we hit a curve, rather than flow with it, the stress response kicks in and keeps the body in a state of alarm (anxiety) even on the straightaways. It is no different than staying in the metaphoric amusement park where chronic stress exists. It can feel like your head is inside a pinball machine.

For those of you who live with a health problem, you know full well how your symptoms are impacted by stress and heightened emotions. Even if you don't have a health problem, you have more than likely felt the physical impact of stress on your body. Someone once told me that whenever she gets a text message from certain people in her life that cause her stress, it immediately triggers a headache. Just seeing their name appear causes a headache, before even reading their message.

More remarkable is how, when faced with certain topics, movements, external stimuli, or other conditions, I have witnessed some people with chronic health conditions go from a 1 on their pain or other symptom scale to a 10, and then back to a 1, all within as little as a half hour or less! This speaks to the power of the mind and how stress, unresolved trauma, and emotional issues can profoundly impact our health.

I want to challenge you to take on a perspective that may be new to you or even sound a bit outlandish, given how ingrained the word stress is and how much it is part of our dialogue. I want you to take on the belief that there is no stress in the world. Set up this thought structure in your mind because when you think about it, how we respond to life events is what really determines stress and the impact it has on us.

Nothing in and of itself is stressful. It is our beliefs and judgments about events and experiences that determine our reactions that cause, or not cause, a stress response. Therefore, if this new thought process becomes your reality, your body can remain calm, even when you hit the curves in life or find yourself bouncing around in the metaphoric amusement park, which we all do from time to time.

Even if this assumption about stress is false, at least we put ourselves in a position to resist the messages we see and hear all the time from television, news, and social media that most of life is stressful. The phrase "stressed out" has become so overused that we have accepted and embraced stress to our detriment.

Believe it or not, the first time I ever heard the term "stressed out" was during final exams my freshman year in college. I never knew what it meant and I didn't feel what "stressed out" was supposed to feel like. However, it was such a common thing to hear that I began using the phrase also, and then I became stressed out from believing I was under stress even when I wasn't. What very much concerns me is how often I hear young kids saying this, more than likely from copying the adults around them without knowing what it means, and this sets them up to be stressed about things that are not stressful, which breeds anxiety. We have enough anxiety as it is, so we truly must be extremely careful the way we characterize stress.

Hypervigilance

Hypervigilance is a state of heightened alertness accompanied by behavior that aims to prevent danger. More scientifically, hypervigilance is an enhanced state of sensory sensitivity accompanied by an exaggerated intensity of behaviors whose purpose is to detect activity. Hypervigilance may bring about a state of increased anxiety which can cause pain and exhaustion, without the calming ability to "let go" and relax the mind and/or body. Picture a squirrel and how its very wide-eyed face is always on alert looking for danger. This behavior is a good visual of hypervigilance.

Hypervigilance makes it either extremely easy to focus (usually for only short periods of time because a hypervigilant mind gets tired) or very hard to focus because our attention is highly (hyper) scattered. Or, a person can be so hyper-focused on one thing that they are unaware or indifferent or insensitive to things going on around them.

A few characteristics of hypervigilance include excessive fear and worry, finding it hard to relax, overanalyzing situations and believing them to be worse than they are, being overly sensitive to people's tone or expressions and taking them personally, having trouble getting to sleep or staying asleep, finding crowded or noisy environments to be overwhelming, being reactionary, easily startled and jump or scream at things we suddenly hear or see, checking surroundings for a threat, finding it hard to focus on conversations, and having frequent mood swings.

It is very much like being stuck in the fight or flight stress response. In a nutshell, hypervigilance for many people is caring too much above and beyond that which is necessary and healthy. The next section explains what I mean by this in more detail and how I have decreased my hypervigilance.

The art of not caring – Reducing stress to improve our health

Having lived with chronic pain from dystonia for 20 years, I spent most of that time focused on treating the physical symptoms. This has been very important and helpful, but for too long I neglected the impact of my emotional state, which was one of anger, sadness, grief, bitterness, and intense hatred for what my life had become. I lost my physical ability to do anything without blinding pain, so these are not unreasonable feelings. However, I let these feelings last way too long and take over my life. As a result, I was overly stressed which worsened my health.

When I began to resolve these emotions, which is still a daily (lifetime) practice, and by accepting (being okay with) that it is a daily/lifelong process, it helped me better come to terms with my pain and life began to change. I began to practice mind calming activities such as meditation, breathing exercises, and visualization, as well as decluttering my life, removing toxicity, setting boundaries, respecting myself and my time more, not caring so much about things I have no control over, and learning how to let go and stop resisting what I didn't like about life. This helped me learn to not care so much that I had dystonia and pain, which was probably the biggest thing that transformed my life and helped me create a new one.

Not caring so much about almost everything significantly increased my level of health and happiness. Some other things that help lower my stress and increase my happiness meter include not watching the news, avoiding politics and political conversations, not engaging in the lives of people who suck my energy, not caring what people think about the life I need to live to best manage my health, and letting go of guilt so I can engage in self-care activities that are so vital to my well-being.

It was amazing the changes that took place when I stopped caring and worrying so much about how I felt, what others thought, and not exposing myself to petty drama. Being focused on doing as well as I can with whatever challenge I may have on a particular day, whether it is related to my specific health issue or not, was one of the missing links for me to improve my physical and mental health. So, my newest affirmation is, "I don't care. I choose to be happy."

I do not in any way mean that I am an uncaring person or without compassion. I am very much the opposite. I am a deeply passionate, very caring person. The problem is that sometimes I care too much about other people and things to my own detriment. I overextend my emotional attachment, which can be utterly exhausting. I know many of you can relate because I have conversations with people about this all the time.

The reason I chose the specific words, "I don't care. I choose to be happy," is to trick my mind. In other words, I use it to help slow down my overly caring, hypervigilant mind to care at a more normal level where it doesn't burn me out and cause emotional pain, which of course leads to more physical pain. I still care too much about certain things that it impacts my well-being, but I am getting better at not giving energy to areas that suck the life out of me. This phrase also helps me not ruminate about things as much.

If you are suffering from depression, you might want to be careful about using this phrase. However, if part of your depression comes from being disappointed by others, perhaps from giving so much of yourself and not getting much in return (in other words, you might be an "over-carer" like I described earlier), this might be an excellent motto or slogan for you to follow.

In the last few years, especially when working with coaching clients who have various health issues, I have become much more aware about the power of emotions and how much the mind and body are connected. So much so that I don't think we can reap the greatest benefit from our treatments and self-care, or enter a healing phase, if we are filled with anger, fear, hatred, jealousy, resentment, or anxiety, to name just a few intense emotions. These emotions ramp up the chemical factory in the brain that creates stress hormones that prohibit healing. The source of these emotions often comes from caring too much about too many things that are often not that important or about things we cannot change, as well as overthinking and overanalyzing. They can also be from having expectations that are not met. For more about this, please see Chapter 9, *The impact emotions have on our health*.

Please investigate your life to see where you are "over-caring" and "over-worrying" (hypervigilance) and probably over-exhausted. Stop putting your cares in those places so you can devote energy to what truly matters. Life is short and time is precious, so use it wisely by caring about what is most important to you and be careful, for the sake of your health and well-being, that you don't exhaust your energy in places it doesn't belong.

If you want to be sad, no one in the world can make you happy.
But if you make up your mind to be happy, no one and
nothing on earth can take that happiness from you.
- Paramhansa Yogananda -

The waste in worrying

Do you worry a lot? Do you ever find yourself worrying about worrying? How many of the things that you worry about actually come true? More than likely, most things you worry about never happen and it ends up being time wasted. There is a misconception that worrying protects us, but no matter how much we worry, we cannot change the outcome of most things. Worry is like a rocking-chair; it keeps us busy and gets us nowhere. There is a saying by Mark Twain: "I am an old man and have known a great many troubles, but most of them never happened."

I am a worrier; much less of one now after doing lots of work to get over my anxiety that caused me to worry, but I still fall into the trap from time to time. I also feel a need to be in control, which got much worse after developing dystonia. When my body began doing things out of my control, it increased my need to find some way to control my surroundings in the hope it would reduce my symptoms. This led to obsessive compulsive disorder (OCD), which impacted my life to such an extent that I had to seek therapy. Thankfully, with a lot of hard work I have learned to manage it.

I used to often worry that my health would get worse. This is reasonable to think about from time to time so we can remain diligent in our symptom management efforts, but to constantly do health checks and worry about the unknown is damaging. It can exacerbate physical symptoms and exhaust our minds, making us worry more. Worrying prevents us from living and enjoying the moments. Worrying about something that might happen may also become a self-fulfilling prophecy.

When I let go and just live my life, the symptoms of my physical illness calm down. Doing things I enjoy and engaging in life versus worrying about how I feel or how bad I might feel during or afterwards, always decreases my anxiety. It often comes down to a conscious decision to either worry and live in fear or take a leap of faith and live life to the fullest in the moment, rolling with the punches. Once we realize that worrying is the problem, not the solution, we can regain control of our anxious mind.

Remember that in life we are only guaranteed moments; this very moment. Once this moment is over, we are only guaranteed the next moment until all our moments are used up and life is over as we know it. I suggest we enjoy our time here as much as we can. Worrying is wasteful and leads to unhappiness. Also, if our energy is not squandered on petty things, when serious problems come our way, we will have reserves to deal with them.

I once heard someone say that if we are in control of something then why worry about it? And, if we are not in control of something and can't be, and it is going to happen anyway, why worry? Easier said than done of course, but this pretty much negates all reason to worry. It is better to prepare for what may lie ahead with self-discipline in our thoughts and actions in the present moment.

Two elements must be rooted out once for all - the fear of future suffering and the recollection of past suffering; since the latter no longer concerns me and the former concerns me not yet.
- Seneca -

Yesterday is over and none of us is promised anything beyond this very moment. We don't have tomorrow until tomorrow arrives. All we have is right now, so this is where our focus must be. When we focus on right now and the abilities we have right now, acceptance follows, giving us greater peace of mind. This helps us better learn to be okay with what we may view as not okay, so we can stop running from or fighting against life all the time. As Ferris Bueller said in the movie, *Ferris Buellers Day Off*, "life moves pretty fast. If you don't stop and look around once in a while, you could miss it." It might do us well to get out of our own way and enjoy the life we have, no matter what might be "right" or "wrong" with us. "Right" and "wrong" are just words. How we perceive them is what matters most.

Many of us need to stop worrying, wondering, and doubting, and trust that things will work out. Maybe not how we planned, but just how it is meant to be for reasons we may not understand; and maybe we are not meant to understand everything. Perhaps not understanding everything is a lesson in trusting the process of life, rather than trying to control everything. To help reduce this tight grip on life that so often adds more stress, below are two techniques to try.

Tension and Trauma Releasing Exercises (TRE)
A technique called Tension and Trauma Releasing Exercises (TRE) is being used by people around the world as a tool for releasing chronic stress, fear, worry, physical tension, and emotional trauma. It is also a popular way to release the everyday stress and tension from the daily pressure of life.

The exercises used in TRE help release deep tension from the body by evoking neurogenic muscle tremors (self-controlled muscular shaking process in the body) that I mentioned in Chapter 7. These gentle tremors reverberate outwards along the spine, releasing tension from the sacrum to the cranium. The exercises are a simple form of stretching and are used to gently trigger these muscle tremors.

Once the technique is learned and mastered after several sessions, the warm-up exercises can be accelerated or replaced with your normal exercise activity like walking or yoga, and the technique then becomes a quick and effective method for consistent relaxation. Eventually, these tremors will evoke themselves naturally in a rest position to reduce stress or tension that accumulated over the course of the day.

Since this shaking mechanism in the muscles is part of our natural behavior as humans that we can cultivate more effectively with practice, you might benefit from TRE. This shaking of the muscles (neurogenic tremors) increases the resiliency of the body because it causes deep relaxation that naturally reduces stress levels. It can release emotions ranging from mild upset to severe anxiety whether it is caused by work stress, excessive worry, conflict in relationships, and physical stress or trauma from accidents and health problems. Additionally, TRE has been reported to reduce pain, increase mobility, and aid in healing past injuries.[3]

Emotional Freedom Technique (EFT)

Emotional Freedom Technique (EFT) is another tool you might find helpful for managing stress. Founded by Gary Craig, EFT is a form of acupressure based on the same energy meridians used in traditional acupuncture to treat physical and emotional ailments, but without the use of needles. Instead, simple tapping with the fingertips is used to input energy onto specific meridians on the body.

Tapping is done simultaneously while you think about a specific problem (a traumatic event, an addiction, chronic or acute pain, an illness) and say positive affirmations. This is thought by practitioners to treat a wide variety of physical and psychological disorders, and has the advantage of being a simple, self-administered form of therapy.

As described by doctors, this combination of tapping the energy meridians and voicing positive affirmations works to clear the emotional blocks from your body's bio-energy system, thus restoring your mind and body's balance, which is essential for optimal health.

All of our thoughts have an impact on our nervous system which creates a feeling within us (happiness, joy, fear, shame, anger, frustration, etc.). Tapping certain points in the body can reduce negative nervous system reactions that have become habitual. If we tap during moments of distress, it is believed that it can decrease the physical and emotional pain we are experiencing. In other words, it is possible to shift the energy in our body that can impact physical and emotional trauma and pain.

Put the glass down[4]
The following story is a great example of how stress can very quickly mount:

A clinician walked around a room while teaching stress management. As she raised a glass of water, everyone expected she would ask the "half empty or half full" question. Instead, with a smile on her face, she asked, "how heavy is this glass of water?" Answers ranged from 8 oz. to 20 oz.

She replied, "the absolute weight does not matter. It depends on how long I hold it. If I hold it for a minute, it's not a problem. If I hold it for an hour, I'll have an ache in my arm. If I hold it for a day, my arm will feel numb and paralyzed. In each case, the weight of the glass doesn't change, but the longer I hold it the heavier it becomes."

She continued, "the stresses and worries in life are like the glass of water. Think about them for a while and nothing happens. Think about them a bit longer and they begin to hurt. If you think about them all day, you will feel paralyzed, incapable of doing anything. Remember to put the glass down."

Focus on what matters - rocks, pebbles, sand
A philosophy professor stood before his class with an empty jar. He filled the jar to the top with large rocks and asked the students if the jar was full. The students said that yes, the jar was indeed full. He then added small pebbles to the jar and gave the jar a bit of a shake so the pebbles could disperse themselves among the larger rocks. Then he asked again, "Is the jar full now?" The students agreed that the jar was full. The professor then poured sand into the jar to fill up the remaining empty space. The students then agreed that the jar was completely full.

The professor went on to explain that the jar represents everything that is in one's life. The rocks are equivalent to the most important things, such as family, health, and relationships. The pebbles represent the things in life that matter, but that we could live without. Finally, the sand represents the remaining filler things in our life.

The metaphor is that if we start with putting sand into the jar, we will not have room for rocks or pebbles. This holds true with the things we let into our life. If we spend all our time on the small and insignificant things, we will run out of room for the things that are most important. Take care of the rocks first – the things that really matter and are critical to our long-term well-being and happiness. If we deal with the big issues first, the smaller issues can still fall into place.

References
1) http://www.stressstop.com, Retrieved August 27, 2013 from:
http://www.stressstop.com/stress-tips/articles/fight-flight-or-freeze-response-to-stress.php
2) www.painsupport.co.uk, Retrieved on August 19, 2013
3) http://traumaprevention.com/, Retrieved June 27, 2020
4) Lindsey Biel, OTR- Retrieved August 13, 2013 from: http://sensorysmarts.com/

Chapter 9
The impact emotions have on our health

When I developed dystonia in 2001, it totally turned my life upside down where I went from being fully functional and very active to almost 100% debilitated with pain where I literally rolled around on my floor all day trying to find relief. This is no exaggeration. Sitting or standing for just minutes caused unbearable pain, not to mention also having severe, involuntary muscle contractions in my neck that forcefully turned and locked my head towards my right shoulder.

Needless to say, I was filled with great anger, shame, fear, frustration, sadness, bitterness, resentment, etc., for years, grieving the life I lost and trying to come to terms with the new one; one that I wouldn't call much of a life. I was merely existing. Hearing criticism from people who didn't understand the nature of persistent pain or something chronic and questioned why I didn't "just get over it" further fueled these emotions and made it more difficult for me to cope.

My intense stress and negative emotions kept me in the fight/flight/freeze stress mode almost 24/7. This created an environment in my mind/body where any kind of healing was near impossible, a common problem for many people. It was only when I chose to learn how to come to terms with the reality of my new life and that I needed to reinvent myself, that I saw changes.

This shift in thinking helped calm my mind, and by reducing this mental tension, it gave my body some relief. The change in my health was minimal at first, but it gave me hope and improved my attitude, which began to open new doors where my life began having meaning again.

This did not happen overnight. It was a process that took time, each day built on the previous day. The less I mentally resisted the reality of my life, the better I felt, a practice I still work on every day because I still have health issues related to dystonia that need to be addressed, as well as other challenges that are part of any life.

Please don't take any of this as me saying, if you simply change your attitude and accept your condition, you will heal. It takes a lot more than that, but acceptance is an important piece of the puzzle. We all know this, but it is hard to get there. Maybe this will help. Instead of "acceptance," I prefer to say, "acknowledging" and "coming to terms with." I think they means the same thing as acceptance, but for me they are more practical sounding and attainable, as they are more of a working definition/description that we can apply daily that helps the process unfold naturally, which is how it should unfold. We shouldn't force it.

When I think of "coming to terms" with anything, I think of a discussion, then an agreement, and then conditions set forth for actions and behavior to create change. I think this is the rational way to approach any problem. It helps take the emotion out of it. With this in mind, as crazy as it sounds, I talk to my pain. I ask it what it needs and then I take the necessary steps to try to improve it (one day at a time) by changing my habits and behavior. I work with it. I don't fight it. When I fight it, my stress level increase and life goes to the pits in a heartbeat.

As mentioned earlier in this book, "how do I make the best of a difficult situation" is my working phrase when things get tough. This keeps emotions from running out of control which keeps symptoms from running out of control, or further out of control.

We may not be able to control the cause of our pain and suffering in the moment, but we can control the response to our immediate circumstances. If we react to it in an angry or fearful way, it makes the pain and suffering worse. Therefore, managing our emotions is critical for keeping our suffering at a lower level than it has to be.

When we are highly stressed, angry, bitter, etc., the mind pours out inflammatory chemicals to such a degree that healing of any kind is near impossible, as mentioned above. All of these emotions are fine to have and we need to vent, but it is important to keep it temporary. Chronic high stress, anger, bitterness, etc., is not healthy. It keeps us locked in fight, flight or freeze mode, often without even realizing it.

As mentioned in Chapter 7, I believe fighting against or avoiding a problem is the wrong approach. Avoidance prolongs the problem and fighting against any adverse condition increases its power over us by ramping up the stress factory in the body. Instead of fighting against problems, we must learn to work with and through them. This is a very important distinction because the emotions attached to each approach are different, impacting the body in different ways.

I fought against my health situation for nearly a decade, which only made me more miserable. Accepting, or acknowledging and coming to terms with the condition, and the new dynamics of our lives because of the condition, being proactive in finding answers/solutions, rather than reactive, and then fighting the desire to give up on ourselves during tough times, is the real fight and the one we will always win, because this is how we rationally and successfully work through problems. I know I already mentioned this several times in previous chapters, but it is so important that I feel it is necessary to mention again.

Too often we only look for how to treat the physical symptoms and neglect the power of the mind and the role our emotions play on our health. Both need to be addressed. If you are struggling with any challenge in life, be it health or something else, I encourage you to examine your relationship with this challenge and how you judge/perceive this challenge; and then notice how much your approach might be fueling your symptoms.

We should be asking ourselves, "what can I do on a daily basis that puts me in a position to make a difference about my situation?" To find peace, we must honestly deal with our reality. Everyone is flawed and those who can be vulnerable by looking deep within themselves, become strong, powerful, and inspirational.

I am not in any way saying that our life problems are in our heads, meaning that we make them up. Quite the contrary. What I am saying is that our emotional reaction to life events can have a positive or negative impact on our existing problem(s) and how we feel overall, physically and emotionally. In other words, how we think is a choice and what we think creates our perspective. Our perspective then determines our behavior which determines our feelings, ultimately determining the level of joy or sorrow we experience in life, regardless of the challenge at hand. When we learn to control our emotions, reactions, judgments, and stress brought on by any difficult experience, we are better able to manage that experience and the mental and/or physical pain it may bring.

Holding in emotions is like holding our breath
I want you to picture what it feels like to hold your breath with your mouth closed and your fingers holding your nose so you can't breathe any air. Few of us can go very long before we have to let go with a huge exhale followed by a deep breath. From the moment we hold our breath until we exhale, we can feel the build-up of tension, which for many people is unsettling

because the feeling of not breathing is horrible. Something similar happens to us when we hold onto our emotions.

When we hold onto emotions, we eventually reach a breaking point when they come flooding out, sometimes, maybe too often, in the form of verbally lashing out or a health issue. For some people it is in the form of panic attacks, and in more serious instances, a seizure, heart attack, or stroke. For those of us who live with chronic health conditions, like I do with dystonia where I have involuntary movements and pain, holding in emotions can increase these symptoms, which we certainly want to avoid. In short, an improper expression of feelings/emotions creates internal stress which has a physically damaging impact...no matter who you are.

In a single 24-hour day, we all go through many emotions; too many to count. They often change from moment to moment. Some are fun and some are not so fun; quite painful for many to be more accurate. The fun ones are easy to express via laughter and jovial conversation and other expressions. The painful ones are far more difficult to express for a variety of reasons.

First and foremost, it is not comfortable so we might deny or avoid them; we also may not want others around us to see how we are really feeling, as there can be shame and embarrassment, or a feeling of "less than" when we are having a tough time. As difficult as it can be for a lot of people, it is important that we purge ourselves of these feelings privately or to a trusted individual, which is no different than letting out a breath after holding it in for too long.

The problem that many of us run into is that we don't regularly express our feelings, so they build up. Another problem many of us run into is that we resist what we do not like or what does not feel good, so we do all we can to not express painful feelings/emotions. This is human nature and we all go through it. However, I think we would all agree that this is not the healthiest way to live.

Anytime we experience something in our lives that creates an emotion it leaves an imprint. If every time we think about it and allow ourselves to have an emotional response to it, it increases the imprint on our brain. Over time, this makes us react to anything related to that stressful event as if we were experiencing the event again in real time. This is why these things are called a "trigger." When this happens, it creates muscle tension and other physical ailments, which is why it is so important to process emotions and not keep reliving them. Embrace how you feel, no matter what it is, and then let it out. When we resist, it stays with us.

Allow yourself to feel the feeling. Sit with it. Don't label it or judge it. It simply is what it is. Let it just be that. For as long as you need to sit with it, do so, and then let it go just like a breath and let more calming feelings enter. The key thing is that you do not force positivity if you do not feel positive.

All of this is far more difficult than I am making it sound. It is HARD to deal with painful emotions when they hit is, but if we go through that pain in the moment rather than masking it, hiding it, pushing it away, doing replacement/avoidance behaviors, etc., we make it easier for ourselves in the long run because we will process it more quickly. It's like dirty laundry. If we have a load and do it until it's finished, it's over. If we let it pile up, it becomes so overwhelming we don't know where to begin. Then we don't want to do it because it seems like too much work.

In the same way, if we just breathe in and exhale the moment, it will pass faster. It is easier to be an exerciseaholic, a workaholic, a cleanaholic, etc., than it is to deal with stuff, all of which is re-enforced by society, but is it healthy? Of course we all know the answer to this question.

Going back to the very beginning, imagine your emotions being like your breath. We inhale and we exhale. The breath comes in, the breath leaves. When we hold it, we can't breathe and our nervous system and organs can't properly function. The same thing happens with emotions. If we don't allow ourselves to feel them and express them, it is like holding our breath, and we carry those emotions around with us, hidden below the surface. These feelings/emotions get stored in the cells/tissues of our body. It is called somatic memory, as discussed in Chapter 7. What this eventually does is create physical and emotional pain, and if we are already in pain, it creates more pain.

When we are able to express emotions in a healthy way and really put this to practice on a regular basis, it helps us flow better with everything, which will bring us closer to that healthy balance we are seeking. I strongly encourage you to read about the fight/flight/freeze response in Chapter 7 of this book. I also encourage you to research the work that trauma experts are doing regarding the stress response and the sympathetic nervous system.

Our goal is to engage the parasympathetic nervous system, which is the calming, restful side where we find peace. I also encourage you to look into the work being done by Dr. Joe Dispenza (www.drjoedispenza.com), who has devoted his life to these topics.

Finding relief in the midst of a serious pain episode
I want to give a real-life example of how our emotional response to life events can help us or hurt us. While attending a college basketball game with my father in 2019, I hurt my back and experienced severe pain unlike anything I have in a long time. The timing was interesting because the week before I wrote an article about the impact emotions have on our health. It was as if I were being tested to see if I would follow my own advice and if my contention about pain and emotions held any water.

About 15 minutes after we sat down, I turned to my right to say something to my Dad. All of a sudden, I had screaming pain shoot like a lightning bolt from the center of my spine radiating all over my back. It literally took my breath away. It has been years since I have had pain so intense and instantaneous in this part of my body, so I was very quickly alarmed.

Since I was blindsided, my initial reaction was panic (I am used to dealing with pain as a way of life, but this was different). Then I thought I might have just temporarily tweaked something and it would probably just go away (it felt like a cramp in my spine with pain shooting outwards like lightning bolts). Unfortunately, this was not the case and fear took over because this was the exact spot in my body that began to contract/spasm when I first developed my most severe symptoms of dystonia 20 years ago.

Although it hurt like crazy, I was able to stand, so I slowly got up and very gently tried to stretch a little. That did not help at all. It actually made it worse and taking a deep breath was extraordinarily painful. My heart began to race with fear and my breathing became rapid and shallow; a true fight or flight response.

My Dad asked if I wanted to leave, but my concern was moving and making it worse because we had quite a few stairs to go down and a long walk to the parking lot in cold weather. My body was in too much trauma. I needed to sit a bit longer to see if it would get a little better. I also needed to calm my worried mind the best I could for the walk to the car. I knew if I were in rushed panic mode, my muscles would contract more and make it worse.

Running to the car is what my reactionary fight/flight system was telling me to do, but my rational mind thankfully knew better.

So here I was in horrible pain with several thousand fans screaming and going crazy at what turned out to be a very close game which was won at the buzzer... by the opposing team, but exciting, nonetheless. Emotions were super high in the building. Talk about testing my ability to relax in a boisterous, highly stimulating environment in the midst of severe pain that came on in an instant!

In my mind I went over all the things I knew were important to do in that moment, panic being the last thing. I looked straight ahead watching the game, very passively, and mindfully focused on my breath. I said calming affirmations and prayers, and I visualized my body at rest and peace.

If I resisted the pain, my body would have seized up more than it was, so I had to let go and find the rhythm of my breath. I basically went stoic; totally within the pain to find peace. I literally zoned out the noise and activity as if it were a blur. As humans, we typically want to run from pain, but this usually makes the pain worse. I had to sit with it.

It helped about 10 to 15 percent in terms of pain reduction, but my mind calmed a lot more than that, which was the difference maker for me to get to the car when I felt ready to leave. My goal was to make it to the car without getting worse. That's why I decided to stay versus run home, which was my initial reaction out of fear. I knew that panicking and running would make things worse, so I took things in small steps.

I mentally prepared myself for the walk to the car doing all the things mentioned above. I then had my Dad wait until I got comfortable in the car before he began driving so I could prepare myself for the movement of the vehicle. When I got home, I took a moment before I got out of the car. I then waited until I was ready to walk to the house. I then did a few things to try and help: ice, heat, massage, and trigger point work, but mainly just lying down focusing on my breath. I also tried to get my mind lost watching a peaceful nature show.

I didn't sleep well and woke up the next morning with a lot of pain, but a little less than it was the night before. The next few days I did nothing but rest on ice and heat, lots of mindful relaxation breathing, I loaded up on anti-inflammatory supplements, used my trusty Oska machine (PEMF therapy device for pain) and just laid on my back. Basically, I pretty much zoned out spending most of the time lying flat as a pancake.

Although most of this was very boring, I made it a priority to strictly focus on self-care so I would be functional as soon as possible. I took care of myself without guilt, something that can be hard for me and others to do, but absolutely essential! About 4 days later, I was back to normal.

It was a scary experience, but I was kind of grateful to have the opportunity to see just how much I would be able to follow my own advice amid trauma to see what it would do to my pain and ensuing recovery. Having practiced all the things I mentioned above for years (meditation, relaxation breathing, visualization, mindfulness, etc.) it better prepared me for this moment.

Had I only practiced these things during times of stress and not made it part of my daily lifestyle, my body and mind would never learn to calm itself. This is something I stress (no pun intended) to my life coaching clients all the time. In order to be prepared when the worst happens and not make a situation worse, we have to practice mind calming activities when we are already calm, so our mind/body are receptive to learning or relearning how to be at ease.

We are not able to effectively learn and benefit from these relaxation tools if we only practice them on occasion and only when we are anxious and in trauma, which many people do. It won't help. Think of it in terms of sports. Athletes/teams practice thousands of hours for only a handful of games. Think of your "game" being these stressful and traumatic situations, and all the other time when you are not in as much distress as time to practice.

I hope this example, and other things mentioned in this book (like the similar story I shared in Chapter 6 about injuring my hip and low back), helps you truly take to heart just how much our emotional reaction to pain and any adverse condition we experience in life can either help or hurt us, and just how powerful it is to go within and not resist the pain. This is vital because anytime we have an emotional response to any stimuli, it increases adrenaline and cortisol and other stress hormones in the body, causing muscle tension, pain, shallow breathing, change in circulation, among many other things.

When we add fear and stress to fear and stress, it is a recipe for disaster, meaning it can hurt us more than we already are. This was exactly what I did not do, which I know prevented the situation from being much worse that it could have been.

Whenever you are in pain, especially above and beyond what is normal, please be mindful of how you react/respond to it. It will almost always determine how much worse it may get and how quickly or slowly you may recover from that particular event. I can't emphasize this enough. Lastly, whether or not you have a health condition, please don't ever take your health for granted. It can disappear in an instant.

References
1) Phillips, M. *Reversing Chronic Pain*. (2007). North Atlantic Books: Berkeley, CA

Chapter 10
The stages of grief and their importance

Learning to live with any adverse event or situation in life is a process. Like all processes, there are different stages with different characteristics. Each stage toward wellness usually involves loss, grief, and acknowledgment of internal pain, which leads to acceptance.

It may sometimes seem that you have no reason to live or that you are living only to experience hardship after hardship in life, just hanging by a thread. Even so, the reason for living and the incentive for becoming psychologically well is the potential for the future.

As with the death of a loved one, it is common for people with a health diagnosis, job loss, a relationship ending, and other life changing events to go through the stages of grief. When something alters one's life to an extent that there is a significant void and/or they are no longer able to do things they once could, it can cause a great sense of loss which initiates the grief cycle.

When my dystonia became severe in the early 2000's, I lost all sense of self. I didn't know where I fit into the world anymore. I was no longer a student, a businessman, an athlete, or a traveler. I also no longer felt like a friend, a brother, an uncle, a son, or an active member of society. I was a guy who lived on the floor in writhing pain who basically did nothing but eat and sleep. This may sound melodramatic, but that truly was my existence. I was overcome with deep sorrow. I felt a deep sense of personal loss and had an identity crisis.

It was important for me to understand grief to be better equipped to process the significant changes to my life and accept new challenges that dystonia added. Grief is an important process that many of us need to go through to be mentally healthy.

Grief is a personal journey. It is a process that takes time. As difficult as the process may seem, there is hope, and learning the stages of grief can be the beginning to understanding that grief is part of the journey, not the end of your journey. Take your time to grieve. Allow yourself to do it in your unique way and remember that help is available if you feel grief is significantly impacting your life.

Stages of grief

The information below is a compilation of the work done by Elisabeth Kubler-Ross, M.D. The late Kubler-Ross was a Swiss-born psychiatrist, a pioneer in near death studies, and author of the book, *On Death and Dying*, where she first discussed what is now known as the Kubler-Ross Model. In this work, she proposed the five stages of grief as a pattern of adjustment. People experience most of these stages, though in no defined sequence.[1] There are additional stages that have been added over the years, but the Kubler-Ross model is still widely accepted as the standard.

Kubler-Ross did not intend for this to be a rigid series of sequential or uniformly timed steps because people do not always experience all of the grief cycle stages. Some stages might also be revisited, and some stages might not be experienced at all. Rather than a steady progression, people tend to ebb and flow between stages. The five stages are also not linear or equal in their experience. Grief and other reactions to emotional trauma are as individual as a fingerprint.

The grief model is perhaps a way of explaining how and why "time heals," or how "life goes on." If you do not go through some or any of the stages, it does not mean that you are going through grief "incorrectly." We all experience grief in different ways.

While Kubler-Ross' focus was on death and bereavement, her grief cycle model is a useful perspective for understanding emotional reaction to personal trauma and change, irrespective of cause.

1. *Denial* – Denial is a conscious or unconscious refusal to accept facts, information, and realistically relating to the situation. It is a defense mechanism and perfectly natural. Some people can become locked in this stage when dealing with a traumatic change that cannot be ignored. A chronic health condition, especially when pain is involved, is certainly not something that can easily be avoided or ignored, so denial in the literal sense is probably not very common.

Rather, we know something is wrong, but we may ignore the extent to which it affects us, wishing it would go away. Some days you may be tempted to pretend you never received bad news. However, facing the reality of the situation head on is usually the best way to cope and move forward.

2. *Anger* – People dealing with emotional upset can be angry with themselves or with others, especially those close to them. Knowing this helps us keep detached and non-judgmental when experiencing the anger of someone who is very upset.

I have experienced anger plenty of times, all to varying degrees. It may spark from my symptoms, my frustration with doctors and ineffective treatments, indifference or lack of acknowledgement from others about my situation, or the frustration of not being able to do some things I enjoy. Sometimes anger feels like the only appropriate outlet. Personally, I have exercised anger out of most aspects of my life because there is so much to be grateful for that redirects my focus. Anger is also an energy wasting activity unless it is used as motivation for change.

3. *Bargaining* – The bargaining stage is characterized by attempting to negotiate with a higher power or someone or something you feel has some control over the situation. You might make promises in return for the painful situation not to occur or for things to go back to how they were before the loss or change.

You may find yourself intensely focused on what you or others could have done differently to prevent the loss or change. You may also think about how life could have been if not for this unpleasant situation. While these thoughts may help you begin to accept the loss or change, bargaining rarely provides a sustainable solution. "Only if" and "what if" thinking doesn't change the past, but it can prepare us for handling things differently in the future.

4. *Depression* – Although this stage means different things depending on who it involves, it is sort of an acceptance with emotional attachment. It is natural to feel sadness, regret, fear, and uncertainty. It shows that the person has begun to accept reality.

Although, this reality can often keep people stuck, especially those with chronic health issues. When we are constantly reminded of our pain and how life once was, it is challenging to break away from depression. If you live with depression, it would be wise to seek out a trusted friend or therapist. Please also see Chapter 11 on depression.

5. *Acceptance* – Acceptance is one of the greatest challenges for individuals and also one of the most important to achieve for progress to be made towards living a fulfilling life. This stage varies according to the person's situation, although broadly it is an indication that there is some emotional detachment and objectivity. People dying can enter this stage long before the people they leave behind, who must also pass through their own individual stages of grief.

Acceptance for many people I know is usually the stage we reach and retreat from most often. When we are having a good day, acceptance is easier, but on tough days, it can be a roller coaster ride where we may fluctuate through all stages.

What we resist persists, so accepting our current situation is essential for forward progress. Without acceptance, the fight with pain can end up in a battle with ourselves that we will continue to lose. Everything we fight weakens us and everything we embrace strengthens us. Please really think about this statement, as it may sound counterintuitive. Perhaps much of this book sounds counterintuitive, and that, in my opinion, is because we have been conditioned by poor habits of thinking that result in poor coping mechanisms and a struggle to process and ultimately detach from painful situations. This book strives to teach how to better process adversity, by thoughtfully facing it rather than avoiding or running from it.

It was very hard for me, but I had to learn to accept that there were things I was no longer going to do when my body was compromised from dystonia and pain; some by choice because of how they make me feel and some because my body does not allow me to do them. Several formerly important parts of my life are gone. I can't bring them back so there is no point fighting any of it.

As I continue to get better, perhaps I will be able to do some or all of those things again, but for now, I am very content with who I am. I passionately embrace what my life is now, so not doing activities I once loved does not faze me at all, and I love that liberated feeling. They are simply not a part of who I am anymore, and I don't fight to try to be something I am not.

One of the keys to acceptance is learning to accommodate our challenges. Too often we fight against them, rather than embracing them as a part of our lives (you may notice that this is a common theme in this book). We must find a way to make our challenge our friend. Yes, you read correctly.

Learn to treat your challenges as your friend so the inner battle and turmoil you are experiencing will end.

This may sound like an unusual concept to some of you, but it truly is the secret to living a meaningful life. If I heard this at a different time on my dystonia journey when I was filled with anger and grief, I would have been furious, so I understand if this causes you anger or other emotions. In recent years, I have come to better understand this concept of befriending challenges, and it has served me well.

Work on accepting any challenge as part of your life so you can move on, similar to the way practicing forgiveness sets us free from past events. Please see Chapter 6 for more about forgiveness.

If you can get up after getting kicked in the gut, regardless of how many times, you have more than a fighting chance at a quality life. Let the process of grief play itself out and do your best to roll with the stages. Your internal strength and perseverance increase every time you rise from falling.

References
1) Based on the Grief Cycle model first published in *On Death & Dying*, Elisabeth Kubler-Ross, 1969. Interpretation by Alan Chapman 2006-2009. Retrieved on April 21, 2013 from: http://www.ekrfoundation.org/five-stages-of-grief/

Chapter 11
Understanding and transcending depression

Living with anything painful in life (health problems, tough relationships, bad work situations, etc.) requires us to adjust to the demands of the unwanted conditions, and in some cases, an uncertain future. It may impact our independence and change the way we live, how we see ourselves and how others see us, and how we relate to others and how others relate to us.

Sudden and unexpected changes to plans, minor or major, can alter our lives in many ways. Feelings of shock, anger, grief, loss, and sadness are common. These feelings usually pass with time. However, if they cause ongoing stress, we are at risk of developing depression and anxiety, two of the most common problems people face today, to the point that it sometimes seems as if almost everyone is medicated for something.

For some perspective regarding medications for depression alone, according to Globe Newswire (Apr 21, 2020), the global antidepressants market is expected to grow from $14.3 billion in 2019 to about $28.6 billion in 2020. This does not account for those people who are mildly or occasionally depressed that are not taking medication.

Any kind of stress can cause despair or sadness, which is normal. However, if it persists, it can turn to depression. The challenge for you and your doctor is to decide whether symptoms of depression are just a normal reaction to stress or so intense and disabling that you require specific treatments for the depression itself.

Depression is quite common, so it is important to recognize and understand the symptoms. Be open and honest about your feelings and share them with your family and healthcare team. Depression is not a weakness. It is an obstacle to overcome and an opportunity for massive personal growth, as discussed in upcoming sections.

Common symptoms of depression
- Irritability and restlessness
- Apathy
- Feelings of guilt, worthlessness, and/or helplessness
- Feelings of hopelessness and/or pessimism
- Overeating or appetite loss; significant weight changes
- Insomnia, early-morning wakefulness, or excessive sleeping

- Difficulty concentrating, remembering details and making decisions
- Fatigue and decreased energy
- Thoughts of suicide; suicide attempts
- Loss of interest in activities or hobbies once pleasurable
- Cramps or digestive problems that do not ease, even with treatment
- Persistent sad, anxious, or empty feelings

We and our family members often overlook the symptoms of serious depression, assuming that feeling sadness is normal for someone struggling with life challenges. Symptoms of depression such as fatigue, pain, anxiety, and insomnia are also common features of an average person's hectic life today, adding to the difficulty of deciding whether it is clinical depression or the rigors of day to day living that eat at us.

Situational depression

Always be on your toes mentally because sometimes when things begin to look brighter, we are tempted to relax and might be caught off guard when a bout of depression recurs, which is totally normal for everyone. We all have highs and lows. The important thing is to not be alarmed when it happens. Life can be unpredictable, so be prepared that one day of feeling well may not transfer over to the next day. Also, the excitement associated with mastering new living skills can give way to new feelings of despair when we begin to recall how much simpler it once was to do routine things.

Nostalgia may bring on sadness and discouragement. If something reminds us of what life was like before the current problem we are facing, depression is possible. This is an ongoing mental battle for many of us… and it is totally normal and okay to feel this way. It is, as they say, part of the human condition.

On a personal note, while I am now in a better place mentally and physically with my health challenges, and proud of the things I am able to do again because of all my hard work, I am sometimes reminded of things I used to do and how easy they were compared to now. This can be frustrating, but I have to remind myself that I am doing the best I can. This is all I can ask of myself. If I don't reframe my accomplishments based on my abilities, then I am not living in reality. When I reframe how I feel about how far I have come, it puts me in a headspace of immense gratitude and love for my life.

The more I focus on the life I have created for myself now versus the one I used to have, the more upbeat I am. The more I involve myself in new ventures and new ways of living; fun events take the place of unhappy memories. Everyone must do this. Changing and adapting is universal to life.

Difficult life changes/Self harming thoughts
When we are faced with a difficult life challenge, experiencing fear, anger, depression, and anxiety is normal. We not only experience painful physical and emotional changes, and perhaps the loss of some of our competencies, we have many questions.

How will it affect my life? Will it get worse? Will it get better? How do I cope? Will the pain ever go away? Is it all in my head? How did it happen? Was it my fault? Will I still be able to work? Will I be able to take care of my family?

The questions are endless and not all of them can be easily answered or answered at all. This can lead to anxiety and panic which will make the problem worse, so please be careful. Seek answers one at a time so you are not overwhelmed trying to solve everything at once. Prioritize your concerns.

At my worst with my dystonia, anxiety, and depression, my energy was strictly on how I could end the ridiculous pain. Literally, nothing else mattered. It was a very scary and confusing time for me because I felt so lost and alone. I kept telling myself to be patient and that I would find my bearings, which I did.

Suicidal ideations
Problems cannot be wished away so a lot of us experience intense fear, anger, and sadness. Where anger and fear exist, anxiety, isolation, and depression often follow. Add physical pain and a sense of helplessness and life can lose all meaning. If these feelings persist, the most perverse thought one can have is suicide.

I thought about suicide. I no longer do, but when my pain was severe and my neck and back muscles would not stop contracting and twisting because of dystonia, it crossed my mind. I would say that I wanted to die, but I never talked about my actual suicidal thoughts with anyone. I was afraid. It seemed taboo.

I wish I did because I really needed some perspective about what I was feeling. There was no shame in feeling the way I did, but in the moment I was confused and afraid. I didn't know who to talk to or what to say. Looking back, I could have talked to family, friends, therapists, and others with dystonia. I now know that would have helped a lot.

Thoughts of self-harm passed when I learned more about my health problem, treatment options, coping tools, stress management techniques, and finding out that there were others who felt just like me. I wasn't alone!

It also helped when I began to focus on the things I could do versus all I had lost. It took great mental fortitude to find meaning in my life, but I did and it grew as more time passed. There is meaning to your life as well, no matter how much suffering you experience. Please have faith and be patient with yourself.

If you have any thoughts of suicide, please speak to someone. It is not uncommon to have these thoughts so please talk about it. You will be doing yourself a big favor, as well as others by opening the door for them to feel comfortable talking about it. If you are in the United States, you can also call the National Suicide Prevention Lifeline (1-800-273-8255).

None of us are immune to the challenges of life. At some time or another we all endure tough experiences. When adversity comes, how we respond to it determines what happens next. Life experiences become tragedies if we make the conscious decision to make tragedies out of them. We can either resist or we can accept challenges. If we choose to view all challenges as opportunities for personal growth, they can be a driving force for positive changes, a common theme in this book.

Thinking our way into depression

Having gone through long and short bouts of depression, I fully acknowledge its presence and the reasons for its occurrence. The way we process life conditions affect us emotionally. Our emotions then impact our thoughts which play a significant role in our state of mind. After developing dystonia, I fell into deep pits of despair, largely in part because I didn't have the tools I do now.

While I acknowledge the seriousness of depression, there are times when we falsely classify what we are feeling as depression, when in fact we are simply experiencing the challenges that are part of the process of living. This can lead to a self-fulfilling prophecy so be careful how much power you give to momentary depressing thoughts. Also be careful how much you are exposed to things that toy with your emotions. With social media (and media in general), and the instant message lifestyle in which we live, we are practically being set up to be anxious and depressed. We should all be mindful of this reality.

While it is normal to go through bouts of depression at times, we have the ability to ward off chronic depression; we even have the ability to avoid bouts of depression. If we can recognize the signs, we can shift our thinking to change our mood. That is basically what depression is; a temporary mood that engulfs us because of thoughts we are generating.

Depression begins like the head/source of a river, usually starting with a small trickle in a mountain that opens up to a massive waterway further downstream. This is maybe a good way to visualize how depression can begin with minor uneasiness to full on, crippling sadness that never dissipates. Like a river that empties into a gulf, sea, or ocean, our sadness can flow into every aspect of our lives and take us down some very scary, dark paths. Seeking help before it reaches this point is critical.

Depression, in my opinion, is a complicated mind trick. Since the mind can only think one thought at a time, we have only one attention. Since the pain of depression is so persistent, we give it our one attention. Since our feelings are located in a separate part of the brain from our cognitive area, we are temporarily disconnected from the totality of our experience. We feel lost, helpless, and powerless, but we are not helpless or powerless at all.

Since we can only think one thought at a time, we can think any thought we want. This principle is based on neuroscience and is also the basis for transcendental meditation and hypnosis. If this principle were not true, there could be no such thing as medical hypnosis for brain surgery or how we form a new habit.

We are not forced to feel painful feelings like depression. It is caused by a chemical imbalance in the brain that we have the ability to change by changing our thoughts, which changes habits and behavior.

Thoughts like "I am depressed." "I am fat," "I am in pain," "I can't get out of bed," "life is terrible," etc., power up the chemical factory in the brain causing it to churn out buckets of stress chemicals. This causes the brain to become more chemically imbalanced, plunging us deeper into depression. These thoughts may be true, but we are better off not replaying them over and over in our head, unless we use them as motivation to change those things about ourselves. If we do not change our thoughts, they become habitual, which makes it much harder to reverse.

We do not have to give attention to a thought merely because it pops into our brain. Nothing is actually forcing us to think them. We can choose to think neutral or positive thoughts long enough for the chemical brain factory to power down and balance out.

When we have positive thoughts, the pituitary gland disperses endorphins which are effective in releasing energy that eases healing and relieves pain. When we have negative thoughts, noradrenaline (a stress hormone sometimes referred to as norepinephrine) is dispersed. Below are some additional things that occur when we have negative and positive thoughts.[1]

Negative thoughts
- Slow down brain coordination
- Make it difficult to process thoughts or find solutions
- Hinder creative ability
- Decrease activity in the cerebellum
- Impact the left temporal lobe (fear factor), affecting mood, memory and impulse control

Positive thoughts
- Synapses (areas connecting neurons) increase dynamically
- Increase mental productivity by improving cognition
- Intensify ability to pay attention, to focus
- Improve ability to think and analyze incoming data
- Improve ability to solve problems quicker and enhance creativity

We all have visceral (gut) reactions to things that include fear, worry, anger, and sadness, but it does not mean that we have to live with chronic fear, worry, anger, or sadness. We are in charge of our emotions. We choose every feeling in all circumstances in our lives. No person or any life condition can make us feel a certain way unless we allow it. The key is to not react to normal fear, worry, anger, or sadness, for it is when we judge and react to these normal feelings that they are amplified.

Depression is often dependent upon our rapt attention to it. It is like looking at the sky on a cloudy day and forgetting that there is a sun and a beautiful blue sky above the clouds.

Negative thinking stops us from seeing and experiencing positive outcomes, even when they happen. It's as if there's a mental block filtering out all the positive things in our lives and only letting in information that confirms negativity all around us. Be very mindful of your tendency to do this so you can change this habit.

When we consistently focus our attention on something other than our depression, it recedes or disappears. We are free to direct our thoughts the same way we direct the cursor on our computer to tell it what to do. When most of us think of tasting a lemon we salivate. Salivation is a biochemically based physiological reality that exists in the body just as depression is a biochemically based physiological reality.

We don't have to cut out our tongue to stop salivating. We just have to stop thinking about lemons. Thoughts cause salivation and thoughts can "un-cause" salivation. Likewise, thoughts can cause depression and thoughts can "un-cause" depression.

We don't have to ignore our feelings, but we don't have to suffer from them either. When we shift our thoughts of depression to new thoughts and new behaviors, it creates new feelings; less stressful feelings. When our stressful thoughts stop, our brain is no longer in a state of alarm and good feelings can once again return.[2,3]

I invite you to look at the work done by Dr. A.B. Curtiss who helps people with depression using a technique called "Directed Thinking" which is designed to change neural programming in the brain by changing harmful thought patterns.[4]

In SELF Magazine, Dr. Curtis said the following: "Neuroscience studies show that feelings of depression occur in a more primitive part of the brain. Cognitive thinking occurs in the neocortex, a more developed area. By stimulating the neocortex, you can prevent your mind from focusing on your sadness. It's a trick you may use already, if you've ever worked through a bad mood by playing the piano, immersing yourself in a novel or throwing your energy into cooking up a feast. By giving your brain a break from thinking only depressed thoughts, you stabilize your mood. It isn't easy and most severely depressed people can't think themselves out of it. But most people find once they learn to direct their thoughts away from depression, those feelings slowly disappear."

How social media may fuel depression

Have you ever played the social media comparison game? If you have, you are not alone. Most people at one time or another have gotten caught up in what I call a "comparathon," where they measure the happiness and success of their lives with others based on what they see in posts on various social media. Often, people feel they don't measure up to the seemingly full and happy lives of others, which can cause changes in mood.

Numerous studies have shown the negative effects of social media (as well as the positive, so there are pros and cons), especially with people who already live with anxiety and depression.

Social media is often the place where there are pictures and videos of family and friends living as if they don't have a worry in the world. People often depict living what appears to be a pretty normal life and involved in more activities than you. This can further aggravate depression because you feel like you are missing out, but there is good news...

...what we all know and often forget is that the lives that many people display on Facebook, Twitter, Instagram, etc., don't tell the whole story. It is a microscopic view of their lives. For some people, it is as exciting and fun as they illustrate. For many others, it isn't as fun and easy going as we interpret. Everyone has challenges, some of whom hide them very well and only show the fun things in their lives. This gives others a skewed perception of reality.

Don't get me wrong, there are lots of very happy people living their lives, having a ball and portraying it on social media exactly as it is, but there are also many who give this appearance when it doesn't exist. For many, social media is an escape from their own painful reality.

Behind many of the "happy" images, we don't see or hear about financial problems, marriages breaking up, kids struggling in school or into drugs and alcohol, health issues, depression, stress, anxiety, worry, fear...the list is endless. Many people who seem to have the perfect life often live with the same things that challenge or haunt the rest of us. We are not alone in any of our worries or concerns by a long shot. If you are human, you have issues…simple as that. Do your best to get rid of any envy you may have. You are just as worthy as anyone else.

Further, if you are involved with online support groups where people talk about problems they are having, this can cause you to worry that it may also happen to you. If you are an empathetic person, you may also take on the burden of others. This being the case, balance your time on social media and the outside world.

As a life/health coach, I work with people who have chronic health conditions, anxiety, depression, weight issues, stress, work/life balance, relationship issues, etc., and many of them become more unhappy and unhealthy because of what they see on social media.

Social media induced depression does not discriminate; it can affect anyone at any age. It is especially challenging in the winter months when people are stuck indoors and for those who have Seasonal Affective Disorder (SAD), which causes a shift in moods.

With all of this in mind, the next time you are looking at pictures and videos of others on social media and feeling depressed about your life because it isn't you in those images, remember that this is just a small window into their lives. For most, there are challenges behind all the "happy" smiles so please do not view everything you see on social media as the whole story. In fact, you may be happier than the people you perceive as "living the life."

HOWEVER, to contradict everything I just said since my focus is primarily on the negative impact of social media (I think social media also has positive attributes), I suggest practicing "letting go." Be happy for others and all the things they are doing in their lives and for sharing it with us; acknowledge them for the fun moments they enjoy. This is a much healthier way to process what we see. Sharing in each other's happiness and joy will help us all feel better. Even if what people display is not be the whole story, big deal; share in the happy moments because we all have them. Just keep things in perspective so you don't get too down when you decide to compare your life with someone else.

Going on an information diet
We are all of course aware of diets for food, but what about diets for other aspects of our life, such as those that feed our emotional health? I wonder

how many of us really think about the "obesity" of information being thrown at us all day long and how much our brain is required to process. More specifically, how the instant message world of information we live in impacts our psychological health, which I touched on above.

It is so easy to hop on Facebook, Instagram, Pinterest, Twitter, Snapchat, etc., and have an hour or more go by as if no time seemed to pass at all. All the while, receiving and sending text messages, watching television, talking to others in the room, and maybe even listening to music as well. We also have an endless number of TV stations from which to choose, and if you don't have cable there are tons of streaming services such as Netflix, Hulu, Amazon Prime Video, YouTube TV, and Sling TV, among many others.

I often think how hard it must be for the younger generations that grow up with our current technology where they have rarely been exposed to delaying gratification, a very important tool to have throughout life to cope with difficult challenges and things not always going as we expect or plan. Because of smartphones, information and entertainment are just a click away. Now, probably more than ever, it is near impossible to find peace of mind, so much so that younger generations may not know what real peace of mind is, and sadly, the older generations are forgetting what it feels like.

When we look at the statistics, depression and anxiety are on the rise in all age groups, and research shows that there is a link to the overconsumption of information and the speed at which we receive it. One of the major factors with instant information is that the brain gets hits of dopamine more often than it is wired to handle. The problem with this is the rise and fall of emotions.

For example, if you post something on social media and it gets a lot of likes, shares, retweets, etc., and when you get a notification of a new message or comment, it probably makes you feel good. It is like being on a drug in terms of the pleasure centers of the brain that light up. It is also a similar response as Pavlov's dogs that salivated at the sound of a bell because they were trained to get the reward of food. Some people do not care how many "likes" a post gets, me being one of those people. They post things because they think it might be of interest to others without any care if people click "like" or "love" or one of the other reactions that are available on various social media. Others will literally count their "likes" and "loves" etc., and value their post, and themselves, based on the number of interactions.

This is one reason we keep the phone nearby and check it so often; because it feels good and because we are attached (or addicted in some cases) to needing to know what is happening all the time. But what happens when there is a slow day of activity in our social media circles? For many people, there is an empty, sad feeling. Worst case scenario is depression, which is all too common.

When technology fails, we aren't just inconvenienced. When technology goes down and slows down, life goes down. Relationships stop and laughter is silenced. Some of us don't know what to do with ourselves.

It is no secret that many of us are addicted to our phones and they truly are very helpful. We have just become so reliant on them for everything. "Phones" (they are actually computers that we can also use as a phone) have become a source of transportation (Google Maps and rideshare apps), an online shopping center, a weather service, an arcade, a dating service, and a source of connection. They are also a big source of DISCONNECTING from ourselves and reality, which is the main problem in my opinion. I recognize that this is not a problem for everyone because many people feel better when they are away from their phones because of the peace and quiet. However, I think this is the exception and not the norm.

Most of us would do well to learn how to better, and more often, sit with ourselves in a place of peace and let life take care of itself. But we feel the need to have our finger on the pulse all the time, and this can be a great source of anxiety. The ironic thing is that there really isn't too much we are missing. We just have the illusion that we are because most of us are constantly on the lookout for new information and entertainment.

A study by Asurion, a global tech protection and support company, found that the average person struggles to go little more than 10 minutes without checking their phone. Of the 2,000 people surveyed, 1 in 10 check their phones on average once every four minutes. The survey found that 31 percent feel regular anxiety at any point when separated from their phone and 60 percent reported experiencing stress when their phone is off or out of reach. Just how crucial our phones are becoming comes in the revelation that 4 in 10 Americans would rather lose their voice for a day than lose their phone for 24 hours.

Other studies show that we check our phones on average 40-80 times a day. The higher number of use is for the younger generations, but the older generations are beginning to mirror these traits. While those ages 18 to 24 have the highest ownership of smartphones and usage, people 55 years and older have accounted for the strongest growth during recent years.

We need to learn to disconnect to reconnect in a different way. Our brain can't process all the information we demand of it. I need to rephrase that; I think our brains are the real supercomputers and not computers or phones, but we do not train our brains as much as we used to because we rely so much on technology where everything is done for us. As mentioned, anxiety and depression are on the rise, which to me is in large part due to the obesity of information we consume daily and not using our brains nearly enough to be more creative and resourceful. Information is controlling us versus the other way around.

If you think your anxiety, depression, and other moods are from an over-consumption of information or an addiction to your phone, begin making yourself only look at it a certain number of times of day and challenge yourself to leave it at home when you go out. It is hard and takes a lot of discipline, so start easy by leaving it in a different room in your house. If you go outside for a little while, leave it inside. On occasion, leave it at home when you go out for a short run of errands. See how it makes you feel.

If you are highly anxious or sad, this is an indication that you may need a diet from your phone. I know for some of you, maybe a lot of you, just the thought of not having the phone with you causes anxiety and sadness. If just the thought of it does this, that may indicate a bigger problem and more reason to put yourself on a diet. In a nutshell, we need to find more things to do that do not require our phones. Find peace just being with yourself and those around you.

Managing depression

The stigma that depression carries drives many people to hide it, try to tough it out, or self-medicate with alcohol and drugs. To effectively treat/manage depression, it is important to seek care from a licensed mental health professional and get a correct diagnosis and treatment plan.

Many treatments for depression are available and typically include a combination of therapy and medication. Other ways to reduce depression, in addition to all that was previously mentioned in this chapter, include getting adequate sleep, eating a healthy diet consisting of an abundance of fruits, vegetables, proteins, and healthy fats, social support, stress reduction, massage, acupuncture, yoga, qigong, tai chi, etc.

Other lifestyle changes that may help include getting into a regular routine, setting goals, taking on new responsibilities, reframing negative thoughts, questioning the truth about your current beliefs, doing new things, and being socially active. It is not necessary to implement all of these things at once. Find one or a few things that work and then implement others as needed when you are ready.[5-11]

Regular exercise has also been shown to increase the effectiveness of multiple organs that are critical for mood regulation. Exercise has also been shown to have an anti-inflammatory benefit. This is important because inflammation is a driver of depression.

Combining music with exercise is also effective for battling depression. According to a Cleveland Clinic research study, listening to upbeat music can ease symptoms of depression up to 25%. Music can also help people feel more in control of their pain and less disabled by their condition.[12]

Tips for coping with depression
- Get help as soon as symptoms of uncontrollable sadness appears.
- Learn about your condition so that you can better manage it. Don't be afraid to ask for help. If you believe your medication is causing depression, speak with your doctor about alternative treatments.
- If possible, stay involved in activities you enjoy and learn new skills.
- Maintain a daily routine as best you can.
- Keep your support network active. Whether it is friends, family, church, golf, tennis, or other social activity; connections to others are helpful to fight depression and isolation.
- Take proper care of yourself. Eating well, exercising, and quitting smoking and drinking can reduce the risk of depression and reduce negative effects of chronic illness.
- Become more involved with your health and your treatment decisions.
- Maintain emotional balance to cope with negative feelings.
- Maintain confidence and a positive self-image, understanding that you are no less of a person because of your challenges.
- Get involved with support groups.
- Do for others, especially when you are feeling down.

References

1) How does positive thinking affect neuroplasticity? Association of California School Administrators. Retrieved January 18, 2021 from:
https://content.acsa.org/articles/how-does-positive-thinking-affect-neuroplasticity

2) www.healthcentral.com, Retrieved January 14, 2014 from:
http://www.healthcentral.com/depression/c/84292/112118/depression/

3) www.depressionisachoice.com, Retrieved January 14, 2014

4) Curtiss, A.B. *Depression Is a Choice: Winning the Battle Without Drugs.* (2001). Hyperion; New York, NY.

5) www.cdc.gov, Retrieved October 29, 2013 from:
http://www.cdc.gov/pcd/issues/2005/jan/04_0066.htm

6) www.clevelandclinic.org, Retrieved October 29, 2013 from

7) www.beyondblue.org.au, Retrieved October 29, 2013 from:
http://www.beyondblue.org.au/resources/for-me/men/what-causes-anxiety-and-depression-in-men/serious-health-events-and-chronic-illness

8) www.webmd.com, Retrieved October 29, 2013 from:
http://www.webmd.com/depression/guide/detecting-depression

9) www.spasmodictorticollis.org, Retrieved October 29, 2013

10) www.infodystonia.com, Retrieved October 29, 2013 from:
http://www.infodystonia.com/post/32254759204/living-with-dystonia-disability-distress-and-despair

11) www.helpguide.org, Retrieved January 26, 2014

12) Good, M., Siedlecki, S. (June 2006). Listening to music can reduce chronic pain by up to 21 per cent and depression by up to 25 percent. Journal of Advanced Nursing. Vol 54. Issue 5. 553-562. Retrieved October 29, 2013 from:
http://www.jbmusictherapy.com/wp-content/uploads/2010/11/Seniors.pdf

Chapter 12
Managing anxiety

Anxiety is the apprehension, uncertainty, and fear one feels when he or she is anticipating a threatening event or situation, whether the threat is real or imagined. Anxiety is not the same as fear. There are subtle differences.

Fear is an emotional response to a known or definite threat; something realistically intimidating or dangerous. It is an appropriate response to a perceived threat. Anxiety, on the other hand, can occur when there is no present threat. It is a reaction or over-reaction to a situation that is subjectively seen as dangerous. It is often accompanied by restlessness, fatigue, problems concentrating, and muscle tension. Put simply, it is an unpleasant state of inner turmoil often accompanied by nervous behavior. However, the two are related, as fear can cause anxiety and anxiety can cause fear.

Anxiety is actually a normal human emotion that everyone experiences at times. Many people feel temporarily anxious or nervous when faced with a problem at home or work, before taking a test, making an important decision, etc. For people with anxiety disorders, worry and fear are constant and overwhelming, which can be crippling. They can cause so much distress that it interferes with a person's ability to lead a normal life.

While the person living with it may realize their anxiety is taking over, they may have difficulty controlling it which can significantly impact their day-to-day living. There are many types of anxiety disorders that include panic disorder, obsessive compulsive disorder, post traumatic stress disorder, social anxiety disorder, specific phobias, and generalized anxiety disorder.

Anxiety can reduce or eliminate self-confidence, especially if you also deal with disability, job loss, marital problems, chronic pain, etc. Anxiety can cause us to excessively worry, sometimes to the point of paranoia.

When discussing anxiety and fear, it is important to mention structures in the brain called the basal ganglia. The basal ganglia are a set of large structures towards the center of the brain that surround the limbic system (structures in the brain that deal with emotions and memory). They are involved with setting the body's anxiety level, forming habits, modulating motivation and drive, mediating pleasure/ecstasy, and steadying fine motor movements. This is particularly interesting to me because I live with a movement disorder. I have also lived with anxiety and fear during the period of time I have had this health condition. Clearly there is a connection.

If the basal ganglia are overactive, people are more likely to be overwhelmed by stressful situations and have a tendency to freeze or become immobile. They often live in chronic fight or flight. In my life coaching practice, practically every client with a chronic health condition also has an issue with anxiety. This is why I stress throughout this book the importance of mind-calming activities (prayer, meditation, mindfulness, breathing, progressive muscle relaxation, visualization, etc.) for optimal health. The basal ganglia and other brains structures need to be properly trained using these tools so they are better equipped to modulate movement, anxiety, fear, and moods. This learning is called neuroplasticity.[1]

Panic attacks

Panic attacks are the sudden onset of intense anxiety. They are characterized by feelings of great fear and apprehension, and are often accompanied by heart palpitations, shortness of breath, sweating, and trembling. Panic attacks are usually accompanied by avoidance, anticipatory anxiety, and worrying about the consequences of a panic attack.

Heightened apprehension to the point of panic or terror striking when no threat is present is an inappropriate response to the environment. If your attempts to avoid fear begin to dominate your life, please seek professional help. Treatments include medication, stress reduction techniques (breathing re-training, physical exercise, guided meditation, progressive muscle relaxation), and cognitive behavioral therapy (and other forms of therapy that your doctor deems appropriate).

I know all too well what panic attacks are like. I used to have them frequently. One of my former triggers for a panic attack was driving, even close to home (I also panicked in other settings like the grocery store). I used to especially panic at a red light if I was not the first car at the light or didn't have a way to turn off the road. I felt like I was going to have a heart attack or pass out. My heart would pound and my hands would sweat. I was claustrophobic. I would also feel very weak and my legs and arms would tremble. My breathing also became shallow and my chest was heavy. I would also feel light-headed and dizzy. This was such a confusing thing for me to experience, as I used to drive all over the country for work and never thought twice about it.

After a few years, I had to do something. I did not want to live like that anymore. I had to force myself to deal with the anxiety if I wanted to live a fuller life outside of my home. I knew I had to face my fears head on.

For the next couple of weeks, I put myself in situations that created anxiety and panic. I purposely drove in congested areas of town during afternoon rush hour where I was certain to get caught at red lights and slow-moving traffic. Previously, if I saw that I was not going to catch a green light at an intersection, I would turn off the road, make a U-turn and then catch the green light from another direction. As long as I kept the car moving, I could avoid or reduce panic. What I now realize is that I was still panicking; just in a different way. I was running, keeping the fear alive in me, with the illusion that I was defeating it.

Within two weeks of purposely exposing myself to heavy traffic and red lights, my panic attacks ended. It was a process, but I managed to overcome them in a shorter period of time than expected. I overcame something in two weeks that I lived with for over 2 years.

I then approached my next driving fear which was going over bridges. Anytime my field of vision expanded to wide open spaces, which is typically what happens on bridges, along with being up high, panic would set in. Just as I did with heavy traffic and red lights, I chose to face this anxiety head on by driving over a bridge we have in town that takes you over a river. I avoided it for years, even as a passenger.

The first few times I drove over the bridge by myself I was dizzy, my hands were dripping wet, and my body was trembling. I also felt like I was floating on top of my seat as if I were not part of the car, and like the car was not touching the road. I had white knuckles from gripping the steering wheel so hard. It was like being on a scary roller coaster, but I was literally just driving straight and steady at only about 40 miles per hour.

I did my best to focus on the music I had playing in the car. I specifically chose it to distract me. It took less than a minute to get over the bridge, but it seemed like 20 minutes. I had such a feeling of relief to be safely on the other side, but then I had to return!

Worrying about the return trip, I missed my turn around exit. I found myself on a highway travelling at speeds I hadn't driven in 10 years. My anxiety skyrocketed trying to keep up with other cars. I finally came to the next exit and had to park for a little while to calm down before I got back on the road to head back.

Anxiety crept back in when I got back on the highway and onto the bridge again. When I got across safely, I wanted to get home immediately where I felt safe. Instead, I stopped myself and did some slow, rhythmic breathing, turned around, and drove back over the bridge again.

Even though I had just done it, I was not satisfied with how I felt. I was concerned that the high anxiety I experienced would prevent me from coming back, so I felt I had to do it again to prove to myself that it wasn't a fluke. The second time was a little better, so I went home after I was done, proud of my accomplishment. I then did the same thing every day for the next week.

Each time I was on the bridge and the highway I had anxiety, but it was less and less every day. My confidence grew when I saw that I had nothing to fear which gradually reduced my anxiety. After about a dozen times over a period of a week, I no longer had anxiety driving on this bridge or any other bridge. Nor did I have anxiety being on the highway. In between trips to the bridge, several times a day in the comfort of my home I visualized myself successfully traveling over the bridge. I believe this daily visualization practice added to my success.

I now had much more confidence to do things I previously feared, as well as try new things. I began doing other things I was avoiding which opened my world and made life interesting and exciting again. Instead of worrying about all the bad things that might happen before I did an activity, I started to look forward to them. A huge burden was lifted and I was living again.

Fear is a liar

Fear and anxiety make it so we are afraid to live fully. We become afraid of the thoughts and feelings we have, most to none of which are based on logic or reality. The longer we allow our mind to keep playing the same broken record of the lies that fear plays in our head, the more we believe the lies and live in a self-imposed prison.

An elephant can be tethered by a thread if he believes he is captive.
If we believe we are chained by habit or anxiety, we are in bondage.
- John H. Crowe -

My approach to tackling fear and anxiety might not be the right approach for you. We must find the best way to manage our fears and anxiety that are unique to our situation. However we choose to do it, it is important to test our boundaries and reevaluate our limitations (and limiting beliefs) to avoid over-protecting ourselves and missing out on the richness of life. Asserting control over our lives by putting anxiety into perspective can give us a tremendous sense of accomplishment and confidence, two things that are missing when we have a life filled with worry.

The key to switching out of an anxiety state is to fully welcome and experience all of the uncomfortable feelings and allow time for them to pass. Let them come. Let yourself feel all of it. Then breathe and let your rational mind enter. Speak to your anxious thoughts with that rational mind, understanding that these are just harmless thoughts. Do not judge them as good or bad. Just let them come and let them go. They have no meaning unless we give them meaning.

I want to share two more experiences where anxiety reared its head. It was my first time on an airplane (2016) after not flying for 15 years. When the plane left the gate to taxi to the runway, I felt my heart race, my palms get sweaty, and churning in my stomach. Out of fear, I began physically resisting every single bump and turn and jostle the plane was making by holding onto the armrests and seat in front of me. We hadn't even left the ground yet.

Recalling how I dealt with my driving anxiety and knowing how tightening my body and holding onto the seat for dear life was going to make the anxiety worse, as well as increase the tension in my body, I knew I had to let go. Rather than resist the turns and bumps, I let my body go with the movement of the plane. I also focused on my breathing, telling myself that I was safe. The more I did this, the more at ease I became. I was literally able to go from almost having a panic attack to being as calm as I used to be when I flew on a regular basis years ago. The key for me was non-resistance to everything I was thinking and feeling, and doing my best to trust that I would be safe, and I was. Each leg of the trip proved to be easier and easier.

The other experience I want to share was several years ago when I had to have an MRI. I am very claustrophobic and extremely uncomfortable having this test. I requested an open MRI, but even an open MRI is a pretty enclosed space. I was nervous before they put me into the machine, and once I was in it, it got worse. Recalling how I dealt with previous fears and anxiety, I went into my little tool bag of anti-anxiety tricks and they helped a little. What helped me most, again, was letting go and rather than look at this machine as a scary place, I let my mind get completely lost in the amazing technology of it.

I first went to a place of incredible gratitude for the person who invented it and how amazing it was how they were able to come up with technology to see things in the human body to help people get better from horrible health conditions and how fortunate I was that it was available to me to help me with my problem at the time (an ear/head issue).

I then got lost in complete awe and curiosity about how this amazing machine worked. I listened to all the sounds it made and pictured what it was doing. Before I knew it, the procedure was over. Believe it or not, it was kind of fun. In the back of my mind, I also knew that I could ask the technicians to take me out at any time, so there was no real reason to have any fear in the first place.

I was so proud of myself and then not long after I got home, the phone rang. Perhaps to test my resolve, it was the hospital telling me they made a mistake and did not get one of the images they needed, so I had to go back the next morning and do it all again!! I had a moment of nervousness, but that immediately dissipated. I went back the next day without any fear and did the entire procedure again. For me to get through it, twice, I had to change my mindset to change the experience that I was having. I had to stop letting my mind fool me into being fearful of something that was not dangerous.

I also had to make sure I did not get angry at the technicians for making a mistake that forced me to return the following day. I knew that would not do me any good whatsoever. I had to accept and forgive so I could be at ease, which I have become much better at in recent years and has served me well. I discuss specific examples of this in detail in various parts of the book.

Accepting anxiety helps it disappear. Fighting it will make it worse. The acronym, AWARE, from the book *Anxiety Disorders and Phobias: A Cognitive Perspective*, by Aaron Beck and Gary Emery, is a helpful reminder for how to cope with anxiety.

A: Accept the anxiety. Welcome it. Don't fight it. In other words, if we have an emotional reaction to our anxious feelings, we increase those feelings which moves us further away from being at ease. We need to stop and recognize our feelings without judging our feelings. Emotional reactions to anxiety create panic.

Replace your rejection, anger, and hatred for what you are feeling with acceptance. By resisting, you are prolonging the unpleasantness of it. Instead, flow with it. Don't make it responsible for how you think, feel, and act.

W: Watch and Wait. Look at your anxiety without judgment. It is neither good nor bad. Become detached from it. Remind yourself that you are not your anxiety. The more you can separate yourself from the experience, the more you can view it as a third-party observer.

Even though there is a powerful urge to run away to try and escape anxious situations, postpone that decision for a little bit. Stay in the situation. Don't tell yourself you can't leave. Keep that option open so you don't feel trapped, but remember that you don't need to run away to get relief. Let relief come to you.

A: Act with the anxiety. Act as if you aren't anxious. Function with it. Slow down if you have to but keep going. Breathe normally. If you run from the situation your anxiety will go down, but your fear will remain or get worse. If you stay, both your anxiety and your fear will eventually go down.

R: Repeat the steps. Continue to accept your anxiety, watch it, and act with it until it goes down to a comfortable level.

E: Expect the best. What we fear rarely happens. Recognize that a certain amount of anxiety is a normal part of life. Understanding this puts you in a good position to accept it if it comes again. You are familiar with it and know what to do with it. This is similar to how I approached the experience with the MRI that I described above.

Please understand that AWARE is a practice. Our brains are wired to run from things that cause us pain and discomfort, so it is much harder to do in real life than I am describing. It is something to be mindful of every day so it becomes more of a way of life rather than a technique we use only once in a while. Our mind is amazing. We can use it to our advantage or to our detriment.

Here are some questions to ask yourself about your fear and anxiety:

- What fears do I have that prevent you from taking part in different activities?
- What beliefs do I hold onto that create self-fulfilling prophecies?
- To what extent have I challenged your boundaries?
- How willing am I to take a step, however big or small, towards overcoming a fear?

The damaging effects of fear

Fear is probably the single most damaging, debilitating, detrimental energy we have. It interferes with our healing process and our well-being in every area of our life. We cannot thrive when we are controlled by fear because fear stresses our immune system and clouds our thinking. Facing fears may feel uncomfortable, but taking action allows the body to release the tension it has built up. Conquering fear could be the saving grace to our mental and physical health.

Something I used to do was purposely drive down random roads in town and explore the area or go into a store even if I didn't need anything (driving and being in stores were panic inducing as previously mentioned). I would either browse around or pick up a few things. I needed to be around other people in random places and exposed to the speed at which the world was moving. This was a big part of me being able to break free from being isolated with fear for so many years from a world that had become a scary place for me.

One of my favorite acronyms for FEAR is, "Face Everything and Rise." Sadly, for too long I was afraid to face my pain from dystonia, but more than anything, the loss of the life I once knew, so I followed a different acronym for FEAR: "Forget Everything and Run." This approach didn't help matters at all.

There is a great line in the movie, *We Bought a Zoo,* with Matt Damon. Damon's character, 'Benjamin Mee,' is having a conversation with his son about fear and courage. It was in the context of how he first met his wife, but it applies to anything in life where we experience fear or apprehension. Damon's character said, "sometimes all you need is twenty seconds of insane courage. Just literally twenty seconds of just embarrassing bravery, and I promise you, something great will come of it."

He's right. Feel the fear, whatever it is, and do it anyway. It will quickly dissipate, allowing us to move forward with confidence. The more we avoid what we are afraid of, the scarier it becomes; the bigger the monster we create in our minds.

Bravery is not being without fear.
Bravery is having fear and walking through it.

A student once asked his old yogi master how he maintained such peace of mind and physical well-being. "Oh, my son," the yogi smiled, "you only see the outside of my life. Inside my mind it is as if two powerful dogs are always waging war with each other." "Wow," said the student. "what do the dogs fight about?"

The Yogi answered, "One is always leading me to a better life; good health, strong energy, creativity, wonderful relationships, and constant joy and peace. The other is always leading me away from that wonderful place, to a horrible place that is its opposite. He has only one method, but it is a very powerful one. He leads me to fear. Once I am afraid, I cannot move. I am stuck and I can only spend my energy worrying and being upset or trying to prevent what I am afraid of. This dog causes me much suffering."

"Tell me, Master, which dog most often wins?" The yogi sighed, paused, then smiled and replied, "Whichever one I feed."

Too many of us complicate our lives by feeding the wrong dog, preventing us from living a fulfilling life because we are afraid. Be assertive and push through fear so you live on your terms. The anticipation of what might happen is almost always worse than what we are worrying about.

Breaking free from anxiety induced isolation

Anxiety can often lead to isolation, as it did to me. Being around others can be challenging because there is a belief that no one can understand our problems. We may feel so different and uncomfortable that we think others can see what we feel. In other words, we may feel completely unstable on the inside and have our minds fool us into thinking how we feel manifests on the outside where people can see it. This is not the case, but when we feel anxious, it is hard to not want to do everything possible to avoid people.

Some people can also be rude, or what may seem rude, when they look at us and/or ask questions or make comments. Much of the time it comes from a place of curiosity, care, and an attempt at understanding, but if we are anxious about how we look and feel, it can seem like people are being judgmental.

I know because I lived like this for many years when I had intense fear and anxiety that led to isolation. It was too stressful being around people because I was very self-conscious about my physical and mental health. It eroded my self-confidence. However, I think our efforts make us stronger in many ways. The awareness that we are living quite well despite great challenges can be a catalyst for boosting self-confidence, if thought of this way. This is how I began to think of it and it helped tremendously.

I cannot stress enough the importance of learning to become comfortable where you are uncomfortable. We must dig deep to avoid isolation. Human interaction is very important to our well-being. If only once or twice a week you meet with friends or volunteer in your community, for example, it can do wonders for your mental stability.

When is the proper time to face our fears?
In Chapter 9, I discussed a back injury I suffered while at a basketball game and how I worked through it. What I did not mention was that it was so scary that I worried I might hurt myself again if I went to another game. Thankfully, my rational mind told me that if I continued with this mindset and avoided going to another game, worry would turn to fear, fear would turn to panic, and panic would turn into complete avoidance.

Not wanting this to happen, I took advantage of the next opportunity to go to a game. The team had only one home game remaining, so if I didn't go to this one I would have to wait a whole year wondering and worrying if I would have the courage to go to a game next season. This much time allows our anxious, worried minds to get creative, often thinking and believing things that are not true or real. In other words, our mind is really good at making things seem worse than they really are (this is why I previously said that fear is a liar). Not wanting to experience this, I knew it was important for me to go to this game.

As the time was approaching to leave for the game, I was of course a little nervous and cautious because the previous time when I hurt my back was clearly etched in my mind, but I am happy to report that I got through it without a problem. I actually felt good at the game and afterwards, and I felt more confident by realizing, again, that one or more bad experiences does not mean all future experiences will yield the same result.

In my mind, I HAD to go in order to gain the assurance and confidence that the back injury incident was a unique, one time experience and that it would probably not happen again. I had to do it so I could trust that I would be okay so I didn't create a habit of apprehension I might bring to other things in my life.

This is the thing about fear. It has a sly way of sneaking in the back door and paralyzing us from doing things because it rips away our confidence in an instant. We MUST not allow it to take over, and instead move on and face our fears when they happen, or shortly thereafter.

As I shared earlier in this chapter about my direct approach to driving anxiety, I completely understand that there is more than one approach to solving a problem. I also understand that facing fear can be very difficult for most people and it takes time and lots of practice and patience, and there are many techniques.

I think the most important thing to understand about fear is that it is normal and we all experience it. What we do with it next is the most important step, because often when we experience a painful incident, anxiety, panic attack, or some other uncomfortable/painful situation, we tend to avoid that particular place, event, or whatever it might be. This can create more anxiety in our lives, which then creates more overall fear in other areas of our lives, which then creates more overall stress that prolongs suffering.

I think the sooner we can face whatever we are afraid of, the easier and more quickly we can exercise that fear out of our mind and body, specifically our memories, which is often subconscious and can lead to anxiety disorders if left unattended.

The body keeps the score and it holds memories and connections to past trauma of any kind, even if it is subconscious. Connecting with it and not being fearful of it is a very powerful way to process it and transcend it. Practicing the art of mindfulness and self-care is invaluable in this process. Another way of saying it is that fear and anxiety can become habitual and we need to create new behaviors to produce new outcomes, which means creating new habits of thinking.

The long and short of my message is to not allow fear to linger. This will more than likely worsen the fear and give it more power over us, which may keep us stuck in the fight/flight/freeze mode where we become immobilized.

A well-known quote that I believe is attributed to Eleanor Roosevelt says that "we should do one thing every day that scares us." I agree. The Dalai Lama has a similar quote with a line added that says, "you have nothing to lose but fear itself." Eleanor's husband, Franklin D. Roosevelt said, "the only thing we have to fear is fear itself." I believe all of them to be correct.

In no way have I overcome all my fears. I still have plenty, but I understand them differently than I once did so my relationship with them has changed, which has provided me with more peace of mind and the courage to face them. I know for a fact that this has a direct, positive impact on my physical symptoms of pain and dystonia. My life is very different now from that overly anxious, panic ridden person, but it took a lot of work as I describe throughout this book.

I encourage you to do something every day to help you get out of this horribly uncomfortable, helpless place. One baby step at a time, and for anyone who is in this dark place, you know that a "baby step" is actually a giant leap. Take those leaps by breaking down your very big and complex problems into smaller, more manageable pieces.

Releasing ourselves from fear is an unbelievably liberating experience. If we don't appropriately manage our fears, they will come to surface over and over in all areas of our lives. Please don't be like me and became so isolated and secluded that you forget what it smells like outside!

If we continue to think and act the same way,
we will continue to get the same results.
We must be willing to think and
act differently if we want to change.

Tips for coping with anxiety

- Recognize false alarms. A rapid heartbeat does not mean you are having a heart attack. It's your body's natural response to arousal. Many thoughts and sensations that we interpret as cues for concern or panic are just background noise. Notice them and let them pass.
- Repeat your worry until you are bored. Face your fear head on and repeat it over and over until it no longer bothers you.
- Allow time to pass. When we worry, everything can feel like an emergency. This is all about anxious arousal, which is temporary. Every feeling of panic comes to an end, every concern wears itself out, and every so-called emergency evaporates.
- Purposely make your anxiety worse. When you try too hard to control your anxiety, you only heighten it. Instead, exaggerate it and see what happens. This is similar to getting over my fear of red lights and heavy traffic. I purposely put myself in the worst traffic possible. When I was able to deal with the worst, I could drive anywhere with more ease. This is also one of the ways I dealt with my OCD. It is called Exposure and Response Prevention (ERP).[2]
- Eat a balanced diet of healthy carbohydrates, proteins, and fats. Avoid caffeine, sugar, and white flour products. Physical and emotional health are impacted by our nutrition.
- Distract yourself with work and fun activities.
- Deep breathing and progressive muscle relaxation.
- Prayer, meditation, visualization
- Counseling, life coaching.
- Exercise regularly.

References
1) Amen. D. *Change your brain change your life*. (2015). Harmony Books; New York, NY.
2) International OCD Foundation. Exposure and Response Prevention (ERP). Retrieved on February 21, 2021 from https://iocdf.org/about-ocd/ocd-treatment/erp/

Chapter 13
Coping with physical pain

Most of this book focuses on emotional pain so I wanted to devote a specific chapter to physical pain. All of us have experienced pain in our lives, and if you live with a chronic health condition where pain is one of the attributes, you know full well how it can change your life. Most people can relate to acute pain or some form of temporary limitation when they are sick, but life offers a whole new set of challenges when the condition is chronic, particularly for those who were once in good health. As Bonnie Prudden said, "pain, not death, is the enemy of mankind."

Although I just made a distinction between temporary pain and chronic pain, and this section refers primarily to chronic pain, this chapter is applicable to anyone. This is because pain of any kind can impact every aspect of our lives, whether it be temporary or chronic, or mild or severe. Pain is the great equalizer when it affects one's quality of life.

Acute pain
Acute pain is of sudden onset and usually results from something specific such as an injury, surgery, or infection. It is immediate and usually of short duration. Acute pain is a normal response to injury and may be accompanied by temporary anxiety or emotional distress. The cause of acute pain can usually be diagnosed and treated.[1,2]

Chronic pain
Chronic pain, ranging from mild to severe, is continuous pain that can persist for weeks, months, years, or even a lifetime. In other words, beyond the time of normal healing. The cause of chronic pain is not always evident, although it can be due to many conditions such as arthritis, fibromyalgia, peripheral neuropathy, movement disorders, low back pain, etc.[1,2]

Chronic pain can often interfere with quality of life, as it tends to permeate every aspect of our lives. Losing one's identity, abilities, and choices that many often take for granted is the reality of chronic pain. It can be a life altering experience. While life is ever evolving for each and every one of us, adapting to a life filled with pain and debilitation (mental and/or physical) is a situation that offers many challenges. You are almost always being tested to the limits.

When I developed dystonia in 2001, for the first few months I had little to no pain in my neck or back. Over a period of about 8 months my pain increased exponentially to the point that I could barely function (as mentioned in Chapter 1). It felt like there was a power drill continuously driving into the base of my skull which radiated down my neck into my shoulders. It was a miserable existence for years.

I didn't know pain like that was possible. It was similar to how it feels at the exact moment of injury, such as a sprained ankle, stubbed toe, or jamming a finger; the feeling at the exact peak moment the injury occurred when you could feel your breath taken away. Unlike those instances where the pain subsides in a short period of time, the pain from dystonia never left. It was like I was experiencing that peak moment of injury over and over without ever getting a break. Imagine the feeling of a Charley horse (painful muscle cramp/contraction in the hamstring or calf) that never goes away. This is how dystonia feels for a lot of people, in whatever part of the body affected by their form of dystonia. For me it is in my neck and back.

As Maggie Phillips writes in her superb book, *Reversing Chronic Pain*, the common denominator for people in pain is the longing for relief and a permanent end to pain. We hold out hope for a magic bullet, which is essentially an all or nothing approach. When those hopes go unmet, we are often plunged into the depths of despair, making it difficult to remain optimistic.[3]

As humans, we don't just have physical pain; we agonize over painful memories, uncomfortable emotions, and difficult self-evaluations. We worry about them and engage in all kinds of activities to avoid them. We do not merely value feeling better. We value a productive life much more than simply a lack of suffering. We want to feel well and make the best of our time.[3]

A comment about the word "suffering"; ironically, even though I titled the book, *Beyond Pain and Suffering*, I do not use the word suffering very often. Instead, I use the term "living with" or "experiencing" when I refer to different health issues and general life challenges. Suffering is a word that can be dangerous to our mental health when not used correctly.

My use of it is to explain a part of the human condition. Too many people I know use it as an identity, which I think is detrimental. It is a perspective which feeds the victim mentality that we need to get away from so we can better learn to live life to the best of our ability given any circumstances. For example, many people I know refer to themselves and others as a "dystonia sufferer." I see no reason to default to this classification simply because I/we have this specific health condition; and it is not unique to this health condition. "Sufferer" is used to describe someone who has any health condition, which is an assumption because there are people who have a health condition who do not characterize it as a suffering experience or characterize themselves as suffering people. Therefore, we need to stop using it as a noun as if everyone falls into this category.

I experienced a lot of horrible symptoms of dystonia that literally stopped parts of my life. At my worst and even my best, I fell into the trap of using the word suffering too much which was counterproductive to a healthy mental state. I became a victim, and a bitter one at that.

Calling myself a sufferer makes me feel like a suffering person, even when I began to get healthier. Calling myself a sufferer made me more attached to my unwell feelings, as well as to my "suffering," which was legitimate suffering for a long time. Thinking this way negatively impacted every aspect of my life. It validated my existence which made me feel better about my "suffering," but it didn't make me feel better about my life. It made me feel worse. It validated my miserable existence and confirmed that my problems defined who I was.

I don't deny suffering. I just characterize it differently so it doesn't wear me down or depress me. We must remember that every word we use sends a message to our brain that can impact our emotional and physical health, so we must choose our words carefully. We must also use them in proper context with what we are truly experiencing.

Changing the words to "living with" or "experiencing" helped me get out of the dark hole I was in. It also helped/helps me be proactive versus reactive and emotional about tough times. I now describe myself as a healthy, functional, compassionate, hard working person who lives with a condition called dystonia. It is not my life. It is a part of my life. I know how horrible the mental and physical pain is for many health conditions to where it can often seem like your entire life, but if we change our words and reframe our perspective, it lessens the grip it has on us.

Effects of chronic pain

People with chronic pain not only live with unrelenting sensation of pain, but they may also have trouble sleeping, become depressed, experience anxiety, and have difficulty making decisions. Not only does chronic pain interfere with daily activities, research shows that chronic pain may actually damage the brain and destroy brain cells. Chronic pain has also been linked to high blood pressure.[4]

Researchers have reported that brain activity in patients with chronic pain is different from those who do not have chronic pain. In a 2008 study at Northwestern University, Feinberg School of Medicine, investigators identified a clue that may explain how long-term, chronic pain could trigger other pain-related symptoms. The study was supported by the National Institute of Neurological Disorders and Stroke (NINDS).[5]

In a healthy brain, all regions are in a state of equilibrium. When one region is active, the others quiet down. In people with chronic pain, the prefrontal cortex, the location for cognitive, emotional, and behavioral functioning, is always active. When this region is stuck in full throttle, neurons can change their connections with other neurons or die prematurely.

It was hypothesized that these changes make it more difficult for people to concentrate, solve problems, make decisions, or be in a good mood. A person in chronic pain is impaired in a similar manner to those who are multi-tasking without ever getting a break.[5,6]

Another common problem for people with chronic pain is an inability to sleep. Areas of the brain responsible for sensory stimulation are also responsible for controlling our sleep and wake cycle. When there is overstimulation, it makes it difficult for the brain to rest.

Another symptom frequently experienced by those in chronic pain is anxiety. Researchers observed that patients in chronic pain have reduced brain activity in the areas of the brain that control the human response to pain. They believe that reduced control over pain signals causes the brain to become extremely vigilant in anticipating future pain. This "on edge" feeling helps explain the heightened levels of anxiety frequently experienced by those living with chronic pain.[6]

Researchers also believe that reduced control over pain signals contributes to depression. It causes increased emotional reaction to future experiences of pain which contributes to a sense of hopelessness in being able to overcome pain. This research is consistent with other research that has found that people who are depressed have reduced ability to control their emotional state. It also supports studies indicating that 30 to 60 percent of patients with chronic pain also develop depression.[6]

Pain management

There are many ways to treat/manage chronic pain including, but not limited to, surgery, medications, nutrition, acupuncture, chiropractic, massage therapy, cranial sacral therapy, physical therapy, behavior modification, biofeedback, prayer, meditation, and rest/relaxation therapies. Another important component to pain management involves regulating your daily schedule so that you have the right balance of activity, rest, social interaction, quiet time, and energy-giving activities.

When choosing your method of pain relief, an interesting fact to keep in mind (which was also discussed in Chapter 3) is that neutral or positive sensory messages travel through the nervous system faster than painful messages. For example, soothing sensations travel up to seven times faster than sharp or burning pain. This means that if soothing sensations and painful sensations reach the "pain gate" at the same time, the pleasant sensations will prevail, blocking the slower, painful ones.

One of the main ways of reversing the course of pain is to find what creates consistently reliable pleasant body experiences that compete successfully with pain. This might include massage, acupuncture, a good movie or book, quality time with family and friends, sex, meditation, prayer, exercise, and music; whatever you find to be a pleasant experience.[3]

I am still in pain, but not as bad as it once was. People often ask me what helps most, which is hard for me to answer because I do so many things and have done so many things. For me, one or two things isn't enough to break the cycle of pain, adrenaline, pain, anxiety, pain, lack of sleep, pain, racing mind, pain, depression, pain, etc. This is just one example of a pain cycle a person might experience.

Many things at different times have helped me with pain over the years including medications, nutrition, vitamins/supplements and specific herbs like ginger root and turmeric, massage, exercise and stretching, topical lotions, acupuncture, CBD oil, Oska Pulse (PEMF device), trigger point tools, ice, heat, TENS unit, meditation, music, dancing, abdominal work, swimming, sleep and plenty of rest breaks during the day.

On the emotional side: healthy relationships, stress management, not being so hard on myself, saying "no" without guilt, confronting and overcoming anxiety and depression, doing meaningful activities, breathing and mindfulness activities, hobbies, taking on projects to feel a sense of accomplishment, relationships that make me laugh but are also deeper than surface level, and most importantly, how I think about things and process life events which is what much of this book is about. I also do my best to remove toxicity from my life, be it people, the environment, my thoughts, or what I put in my body. I also avoid noxious stimuli that overwhelms my nervous system (certain lights, sounds, environments), and how much I push myself beyond the boundaries that my body can handle.

I know this list is long, and there is more that I do, but all of this has become part of my lifestyle so it is not as daunting as it may seem. Also, by making it a lifestyle and not bemoaning the fact that I need to make it a lifestyle to feel as well as possible, is paramount to my well-being. The other point I want to make is that I address my health with more than just physical treatments. I also focus on emotional and social aspects of my life, which is something doctors and patients too often neglect as part of their care.

What I feel is most important to stress and emphasize is that the way I have been able to get improvement, and lasting improvement, is years of daily dedication to all the things I mentioned. I also needed to learn to accept my situation and make the most of it. I had to get rid of the intense anger, resentment, shame, blame, depression, anxiety, and every other negative emotion for my body to begin to heal. I still slip and have bad days physically and emotionally, but I don't let them overtake me because I trust that the things I do every day will keep me on the right track. Trust is a big part of our ability to cope and move closer to a state of healing.

Ultimately for me, a significant change in lifestyle and accepting that lifestyle are the keys to my ability to better manage my pain and other symptoms. I have also decided to enjoy every day to the fullest to the best of my ability no matter what is going on in my life. I make a conscious decision to make the best of every moment I have.

Describing your pain

There is no medical test that can measure or convey the level of pain one is feeling. We can only describe our pain. To provide an accurate description of your pain, it may be helpful to share answers to the following questions with your doctor:

- Where is the pain located?
- How long have you had pain?
- Does the pain come and go or is it persistent?
- What makes the pain better or worse?
- What medications or treatments have you tried for the pain?

A convenient way to organize questions and answers about pain is to think of the letters of the alphabet from **P** through **T**.

P: What **Provokes** my pain? What **Palliates** or relieves my pain?
Q: What **Qualities** does my pain have? For example, is it burning, aching, electric shock-like, sharp or dull?
R: What **Region** of my body is involved with pain?
S: What is the **Severity** of my pain? Mild, moderate, or severe?
T: What **Time of day** is my pain worse or is it independent of time and more activity related?

Pain scale

When we visit the doctor, we are usually asked to rate our pain level on a scale of 1-10 (1 being no pain and 10 being the worst pain possible). I think this scale is too subjective. Pain is relative to the individual, so using a generic scale can be misleading. Furthermore, I can't recall a doctor or nurse ever asking what those numbers specifically mean to me, so how can they tell what my pain level really is? The numbers mean something different to everyone.

For example, what I consider to be a 4 or 5 someone else might consider an 8 or 9. I have become more tolerant to pain so I might assign lower numbers than someone with the same kind of pain who is less tolerant. Much of my pain is also activity/task dependent so my pain level on the 1-10 scale doesn't accurately depict what I experience because it fluctuates. It may be more or less when I am with the doctor which doesn't reflect my overall pain condition.

My treatment or treatment plan has never changed no matter what number I write down. There were a couple times I purposely wrote down 1 or 10 for every answer on the pain scale just to see what the doctor would do. They never even noticed!

It makes me wonder why the current pain scales are used, particularly for patients who have chronic pain that is so variable. If we are being treated for an acute injury or other ailment for which there is an expected recovery, I can better see the benefit of this pain scale because it is actually measuring progress towards a desired goal of recovery or cure. In chronic pain conditions, the rules for "recovery" are different because there is rarely a clear or quantifiable end goal in sight.

Taking all of this into consideration, it would probably be wise to create your own personal pain scale to better communicate with doctors about how you feel. The number 1, or "no pain at all," is the only number that is quantifiable. At the other extreme, 10, or "pain as bad as it can be," is relative to what a person perceives as the worst pain possible for them. Before dystonia, my worst pain possible paled in comparison to the pain that came with dystonia. In other words, my pain scale, or perception of pain, has changed over the years.

I prefer to assign a descriptive word, phrase, or picture to each number to describe my pain. I also like to assign activities to the different numbers. For example, a 2-3 might mean that I am having a great day and am able to do x, y, z activities with more comfort than on a day I rate a 5-6. A 7-8 pain day means I am in shutdown mode and have to lie down most of the day and a 9-10 means that I want to die. Some days can be so random that I fluctuate between a 1 and a 10.

A word of caution regarding that last description- as true as it may be to want to die because of the pain we are in at the moment, we have to be very careful what words we use. If we say we are in so much pain that we want to die, it might be misconstrued as a psychiatric condition, a cry for help, or a perceived suicide threat. It puts doctors in a position where they are required to alert the appropriate authorities. Unless you really mean it, explain that your pain is such that it is near impossible to function at the moment and that the pain is currently intolerable; not that you actually want to kill yourself.

Instead of a standard 1-10 pain scale, create a personal scale that accurately paints the picture of your pain. You are different than every patient who walks into a doctor's office so be creative when communicating with your doctor.

Finding peace amidst the pain

As just discussed, we all perceive pain differently. Also, the way we emotionally process pain and how that pain impacts our lives is different from person to person. It is my belief that the way we respond to pain (physically or emotionally) can have a significant impact on how well we cope with pain, and even determine the level of pain we experience. This is because pain is an emotional experience in the brain. In other words, if you hurt your back, you actually feel the pain in the brain. Not in the back itself.

With physical and emotional pain, the same areas of the brain are activated. Pain is not a sense, like touch, sight, or hearing. However, the neural, blood, and immune pathways between brain and body are tagged with body location information, which is why we "feel" or link pain to a body part.

Because pain is primarily an emotional experience, we often have an emotional reaction to it when it occurs, such as worry, anger, fear, sadness, helplessness, depression, and anxiousness. None of these emotions are pleasant and the human brain is wired to either fight against or run from these adverse feelings or situations, also known as the fight or flight response.

This is a healthy response to have in the short term when we are in danger, but if we live in this state all the time, it creates chronic stress which is very unhealthy, as shared in Chapter 7. It is very common for people with things like pain and long-term health conditions, financial distress, relationship issues, etc., to live in a highly stressed body. This makes it very difficult for the body to perform optimally and for it to heal. Chronic fight or flight (also called sympathetic dominant, referring the sympathetic branch of the autonomic nervous system) can also cause thinking to become cloudy, making it difficult to concentrate and make rational decisions.

Fight or flight is an important built-in mechanism in the body, but we have been conditioned to live like this when we are not supposed to. We have been taught to run from or resist things that don't feel good, instead of feeling things that are unpleasant. If we can learn to resist less and allow ourselves to feel more of what we experience, rather than run from what doesn't feel good, it can have a very beneficial impact on our health. When we learn to "sit with" problems, this helps them recede or resolve, and disengages the fight or flight stress response. We also come to learn more about ourselves and better understand our pain and suffering (mindfulness), which will hopefully teach us how to offset or reduce future pain and suffering.

If we instead allow the fight or flight response to always kick in, it becomes habitual and over time, this may manifest into or prolong physical and/or emotional illness. The less we understand and relate to what is happening to us leads to chronic stress that keeps all forms of pain alive in the mind and body, and we never learn to break the cycle.

To "sit with" or accept painful feelings/problems means not trying to hide, avoid, or deny what we are feeling. It means taking on the totality of the experience and not having an emotional reaction to the experience. This is counterproductive to working through the experience. As mentioned, pain itself is an emotional experience. Adding emotions, or a reaction, to the existing emotions, amplifies the pain.

In order to resolve feelings such as grief, anger, and resentment, and embrace joy and happiness, we have to really feel these things in the body. This is why it is so helpful to sit with pain and develop a new relationship with it. No different than you would with another person during conflict resolution. Doing this may hurt for a little while because we are not used to it, but it can offer relief and the emergence of a new perspective about ourselves and others, and a different experience of pain; which, hopefully of course, is less pain. Sitting with the pain can also help reduce its intensity and even help it pass more quickly.

If we can consciously and mindfully avoid an emotional reaction to pain on top of that which is automatic, the more tolerable the pain will be in the moment and long-term. Too many of us in pain experience an emotional and physical cycle like the following... we have pain, then fear, adrenaline production, anger, then more pain, fear, adrenaline, pain, etc. This cycle, or something similar, keeps pain alive and constant until we intercept or break the cycle and learn to sit with the pain differently than we have been. We need to change our emotional reactions/responses to create new outcomes, and the only way to build the neural pathways in the brain necessary to change our perception of pain (neuroplasticity) is to change our habits, judgments, and memories of painful life experiences.

Putting pain into perspective

This year marks the 20th anniversary when devastating chronic pain from dystonia took over my life. Within months after my first symptoms, I went from a very active, social, athletic person to a pile of meat on the floor rolling around in pain all day. Dystonia blindsided me, turning my world completely around.

As I shared previously, I didn't have good days or bad days back then, or even parts of days that were okay enough where I could do things around the house or outside the house to run an errand, enjoy a meal with friends, or just go to a movie. I was literally floor ridden and only got up to go to the bathroom or get something to eat, which I often brought back to the floor to eat lying down because being upright for any length of time was excruciating.

The pain from the involuntary muscle spasms and contractions, and my head being locked in a turned position, forced me to give up almost everything from the life I was living. I could barely do the most basic of daily tasks. It was heartbreaking.

After years of working through the physical and emotional pain and finding numerous things to help me better manage my symptoms, which is still a daily requirement for me to be as functional as possible, it is a far cry from the person I was before dystonia, but a far cry from me at my worst, which is how I measure my progress. I don't compare myself today to the person I was before dystonia. To me this is unrealistic. I measure my life now to my toughest times to see how far I have come.

I encourage you to do the same because when we look at the past and grieve the old us for too long, it only brings sorrow. I can compare the person I was before dystonia to the person I am now and see how different life is, and easily become sad. There is no point to this because I was crushed with a brutal, life altering health condition, so the only fair measurement, from my perspective, is how far I have come from the devastation of that life change.

The biggest challenge for most of us is learning to emotionally deal with pain. The pain is horrible for sure, but the anxiety, depression, fear, and isolation are in the front seat along for the ride.

The first thing I had to do was learn to accept that life was different. Not that it would always be different, but to be present in the moment and accept that it was different from before. I then had to learn to be present with my pain, rather than run from it or try to mask it. This was such a huge step in my ability to cope, because running from pain, emotional or physical, does not make it go away. It can sometimes make it worse.

Allow yourself to acclimate to all events and situations without resistance. Resistance to anything in life increases its power over us. If we can learn to stop resisting what is, it leads to comfort in uncomfortable situations. We learn to accept what is happening in the moment, without panic, worry, fear, or anger. This then leads to easier acceptance of other life changes and challenges.

The following poem is called The Felt Sense Prayer (anonymous). It describes the many ways we attempt to avoid all sorts of physical and emotional pain. It also highlights how recognizing pain and accepting it can increase self-knowledge and improve self-care.

I am the pain in your head, the knot in your stomach, the unspoken grief in your smile. I'm your high blood pressure, your elevated blood pressure, your fear of challenge, your lack of trust. I'm your hot flashes, your fragile low back, your agitation, and your fatigue.

You tend to disown me, suppress me, ignore me, inflate me, coddle me, condemn me. You usually want me to go away immediately, to disappear, just back into obscurity. More times than not, I'm only the most recent notes of a long symphony, the most evident branches of roots that have been challenged for seasons.

So, I implore you. I am a messenger with good news, as disturbing as I can be at times. I am wanting to guide you back to those tender places in yourself, the place where you can hold yourself with compassion and honesty. I may ask you to alter your diet, get more sleep, exercise regularly, breathe more consciously.

I might encourage you to seek a vaster reality and worry less about the day-to-day fluctuations of life. I may ask you to explore the bonds and the wounds of your relationship. Wherever I lead you, my hope is that you will realize that success will not be measured by my eradication, but by the shift in the internal landscape from which I emerge.

I am your friend, not your enemy. I belong. I have no desire to bring pain and suffering into your life. I'm simply tugging at your sleeve, too long immune to gentle nudges. I desire for you to allow me to speak to you in a way that enlivens your higher instincts for self-care.

My charge is to energize you, to listen to me with the sensitive ear and heart of a mother attending to her precious baby. You are being so vast, so complex with amazing capacities for self-regulation and healing. Let me be one of the harbingers that lead you to the mysterious core of your being, where insight and wisdom are naturally available when called upon with a sincere heart.

References
1) www.medscape.com, Retrieved August 19, 2013 from:
http://www.medscape.com/viewarticle/465355_2
2) http://www.medicinenet.com, Retrieved on August 29, 2013 from:
http://www.medicinenet.com/script/main/art.asp?articlekey=40842
3) Phillips, M. *Reversing Chronic Pain.* (2007). North Atlantic Books: Berkeley, CA
4) www.conquerchiari.org. Retrieved August 19, 2013 from:
http://www.conquerchiari.org/subs%20only/Volume%203/Issue%203(3)/Chronic%20Pain%20Hypertension%203(3).html
5) Paul, M. (2008) Chronic Pain Harms the Brain. Retrieved September 2, 2013 from
http://www.northwestern.edu/newscenter/stories/2008/02/chronicpain.html
6) www.wellescent.com, Retrieved September 2, 2013 from:
http://wellescent.com/health_blog/the-damaging-effects-of-chronic-pain-on-the-brain

Chapter 14
Coping with emotional pain

Living with a challenge or any form of adversity is often accompanied by painful emotions such as fear, worry, anger, sadness, frustration, and despair. Some days you may wonder if it is possible or even worth getting out of bed. Other times you may wake up with energy and excitement to take on the day. Since each day is so different and can be an emotional roller coaster ride, it is important to make thoughtful choices about your daily activities so you can do all you can and want within the scope of your abilities.

Before continuing, I want to briefly discuss the word "coping" because the meaning and application of it may differ from person to person, and there are a lot of different coping strategies. According to researchers and psychologists, coping means to invest one's own conscious effort to solve personal and interpersonal problems, in order to try to master, minimize or tolerate stress and conflict; to struggle, face, and deal with responsibilities, problems, or difficulties.[1-3]

Here are some words and phrases for coping that might make this word/concept more tangible: managing, enduring, facing, battling, confronting, getting through, surviving, dealing with, getting a handle on, looking after oneself, weathering the storm.

Coping with daily challenges
The key to coping successfully with the challenges of life is to acquire the right mixture of practical skills and mental attitudes. By combining these, you can promote a positive, realistic approach to your life. Maintaining a positive attitude may seem inappropriate or even infuriating when you are in physical and/or emotional pain and exhausted. However, there are certain attitudes and beliefs associated with people who cope well with adversity:

- Live for today; one day at a time; not in the past or the future.
- Treat problems as challenges to overcome.
- Take pride in your achievements in overcoming challenges.
- Accept the problem and reject "why me?" questioning.
- Take responsibility for your circumstances and don't blame others.
- Be willing to use all available resources for help.

Being organized, setting realistic goals, and prioritizing activities will go a long way to helping you cope well on a day-to-day basis. Decide what is really important and what can slide. Then live your life as fully as you can. Don't try to do too much and don't feel guilty for tasks not completed:

- Allow flexibility and extra time in your plans.
- Find things you enjoy and find the time to enjoy them.
- Get your routines organized and written down.
- Do your most difficult tasks at the time of day you feel best.
- Recognize that your capacities may vary. What is possible one day may not be another.
- Seek help as soon as you feel unable to cope.
- Schedule rest and quiet time.

To stay as healthy as possible, watch for warning signs. Stop and rest as soon as you begin to feel tired or pain coming on. Learn to read your body and its messages. Keeping a journal of physical symptoms, emotions/feelings, and activities will help you better understand your body and its patterns.

If you have a health condition, keeping a symptom journal will help you better explain your condition to your doctor so he or she can most appropriately treat you. We go through so much that it is often difficult to remember things unless we write them down.

Our challenges can become so exhausting that they damage self-image, leading to stress, anxiety, withdrawal from society, isolation, and depression. You may become anxious and uncertain about the future, worrying about your physical health or financial difficulties down the road. For some, emotional issues can be just as significant as physical symptoms, if not more.

It is not uncommon to experience feelings of denial, anger, worthlessness, resentment, and loss of control as you come to terms with your challenges. The first step in avoiding or reversing emotional health problems is to accept these feelings as part of the process and reject any negative judgments you may be having about them. You are entitled to feel all of it.

Be very careful to not beat yourself up for what you are feeling and what you are going through. We tend to be our worst enemies by being overly critical of ourselves. A careful examination of your life will show that you are a valued person with lots to offer. Positive, reasoned self-talk can help you overcome negative thinking.

- Don't blame anyone for your problems.
- Define success as taking good care of yourself.
- Enjoy small pleasures when you recognize them.
- Know that you are not defined by what you can or cannot do.
- Know that your value and worth have not decreased.

Becoming self-empowered

Remember that you are the only one with unique self-knowledge about your challenges and how they impact your life. You are the one who can and should make the major decisions about your life. Only you know how you feel at any given time, what you are capable of, and what your boundaries are. Don't allow feelings of guilt push you into doing something you know your body will pay for, either during or afterward.

Be careful about being a people pleaser. It often means jeopardizing your health for the sake of others, an attribute that may be a great source of stress. Set boundaries! Others can adapt to you. It is important to remember that we teach people how to treat us. If we allow others to take advantage of our good nature, they will do just that. Make it clear that you have needs as well.

Be sure to find doctors you can trust if your problem requires the care of a doctor and don't forget that your doctor works for you. Do not let their busy schedule force you out of the office before you feel he or she has met all your needs. Together, you and your doctor can map out the best plan for your care, but you must be involved.

Make wise decisions about your priorities. On your best days you may find you can do more things with relative ease. Other days, a single task might wipe you out for the rest of the day or even several days thereafter. Plan ahead so you can prepare yourself prior to an activity and rest time afterwards if necessary.

Take personal time for yourself, whether to relax or have fun. Don't forget how important it is to let go and enjoy life. It is far healthier to focus on all you can do versus all the things you find too difficult or cannot do. Dwelling on problems can make us forget how to have fun. There is joy all around us and ways to let go of fear and anxiety, and other problems.

Take a walk in the park. Go to a movie, concert, play, or sporting event, if you are able. Treat yourself to a massage or other way of pampering yourself. Remove toxic people from your life. Do whatever you can to create peace in your life.

Learn how to ask for help without guilt. We all need help. Let someone else take care of cleaning the house or shopping. Let friends or family members take care of your kids every now and then so you can get some rest. When you feel well enough, pay the favor forward.

Everything is survivable. You can still have a high-quality life regardless of any problem. Do whatever it takes to make it work. You can get through the hard times and come out on top. Just keep in mind what's really important in your life and then go for the fullest life possible. It's yours to live, one day at a time.[4]

Self-love
Heal yourself by refusing to belittle yourself. Choose to stand out, to do what you know in your heart is right at this moment. Choose to appreciate yourself for who you are, accepting yourself entirely and sincerely. Make self-love a daily ritual.

The only challenge greater than learning to walk a mile in someone else's shoes is learning to walk a lifetime comfortably in our own. When we are genuinely comfortable in our own skin, maybe not everyone will support us, but we won't care because we have chosen to be true to ourselves and are living an authentic life.

In the end, loving ourselves is about enjoying our life, trusting our feelings, taking chances, losing and finding happiness, and learning from the past so we continue to grow and feel a sense of meaning. Sometimes we simply have to stop worrying, wondering, and doubting, and have faith that things will work out; maybe not exactly how we planned, but just how it is meant to be.

Relationships and communication
A big part of emotional health are healthy relationships, some of which we have to work harder at than others. Most people I know who do not have the health condition I have, or something similar, too often take for granted the many things they can do that I once found so easy as well and also took

for granted. This caused me great frustration and anger, which changed or ended some relationships, but I am now okay with this because I understand that we only know what we know.

Since we only know what we know based on our own unique experiences, no one can ever fully relate to us and can never completely understand what we are going through. By the same token, we can never entirely understand what another person is going through either. Therefore, I choose to be understanding and compassionate and hope others do the same.

There is a big difference between "understand" and "understanding." This is discussed in more detail in Chapter 20. To understand is to know everything about what someone else is going through. To be understanding is to acknowledge another's challenges and be considerate and supportive.

For relationships to be successful and satisfying, be it a marriage, friendship, family, work relationship, or any other, we must embrace the above reality. As much as we want to be understood, others do as well, so we must be prepared to give others what they need and be willing to ask others what we need. In a nutshell, it is all about shared kindness, compassion, patience, and empathy.

An acronym to remind us how to communicate with one another in all situations is **THINK**.

T Is it **True**?
H Is it **Helpful**?
I Is it **Inspiring**?
N Is it **Necessary**?
K Is it **Kind**?

Are we too serious?
Please remember Rule #6. If you have ever read the book, *The Art of Possibility*, by Rosamund Stone Zander and Benjamin Zander, you know what this means. You may have also seen this in other places. For those unfamiliar with Rule #6, here is an excerpt from the book:[5]

Two prime ministers are sitting in a room discussing affairs of state. Suddenly a man bursts in, apoplectic with fury, shouting and stamping and banging his fist on the desk. The resident prime minister admonishes him: "Peter," he says, "kindly remember Rule Number 6," whereupon Peter is instantly restored to complete calm, apologizes, and withdraws.

The politicians return to their conversation, only to be interrupted yet again twenty minutes later by an hysterical woman gesticulating wildly, her hair flying. Again the intruder is greeted with the words: "Marie, please remember Rule Number 6." Complete calm descends once more, and she too withdraws with a bow and an apology.

When the scene is repeated for a third time, the visiting prime minister addresses his colleague: "My dear friend, I've seen many things in my life, but never anything as remarkable as this. Would you be willing to share with me the secret of Rule Number 6?" "Very simple," replies the resident prime minister. "Rule Number 6 is 'Don't take yourself so damn seriously'." "Ah," says his visitor, "that is a fine rule." After a moment of pondering, he inquires, "And what, may I ask, are the other rules?" The prime minister responds, "There aren't any."

When I first heard this story, I realized how seriously I took many things, including myself, and made a point of remembering Rule #6 as much as possible. I began to look more at the folly of life and laugh and smile more which made a huge difference in my level of joy. Think of something right now that is bothering you and/or weighing heavy on your mind. How can you think about it differently so it isn't such a stressful burden? Are you doing all you can to take care of it or allow it to take care of itself? Can you let go of your anxious, angry, frustrated feelings and find a way to perhaps laugh at the intense energy you are giving it? Not that it is funny per se, but can you find the silliness and humor in the nonsensical, time-consuming, randomness of challenges that pop into your life from day to day so they don't wear you down more than it is worth?

We tend to be our worst enemy by taking ourselves and so many things way too seriously. Have some fun and let go of the many worries you hold onto. It is not worth it and most of what we worry about is out of our control anyway. Time is short and none of us are getting off this merry-go-round alive. Enjoy yourself.

Many things in life are serious and need our attention, but there is no reason we can't approach everything with a little more lightness. Rigidity and seriousness only make things more painful. We all know this. We just don't practice it enough. When was the last time you laughed and could not stop;

one of those belly laughs that kept you laughing on and off all day long? You probably felt pretty good that day. Within humor is great peace.

Benefits of laughter
- Decreased muscle tension - laughter exercises the diaphragm, contracts the abdominals and also works out the shoulders, leaving the muscles more relaxed.
- Improves sleep.
- Increases endorphins.
- Distraction - laughter takes the focus away from pain, anger, guilt, stress, and negative emotions.
- Change in perspective - our response to stressful events can be altered by our reaction to them. Humor can give us a more lighthearted perspective, making stressful events less threatening.
- Socially beneficial - laughter connects us with others and is often contagious.

Laughter is also thought to effect physiological functions such as lower blood sugar levels, healthier arteries, reduced stress hormones, and a stronger immune system.

Where to find laughter
- Rent a movie or go to a movie or comedy club.
- Tell jokes. Learn some if you don't know any.
- Go to a party or have friends over for a party or game night.
- Spend time around babies and animals.
- Watch something funny on television or the computer. There is no shortage of opportunities to laugh all over the place, whether in person or in front of a screen. A stroll through YouTube videos can keep you laughing for hours.

Benefits of smiling
- Improves immune function. When we smile we are more relaxed.
- Helps us stay positive.
- Lowers blood pressure.
- Relieves stress.
- Lifts the face and makes us look (and feel) younger.
- Makes us feel and appear more confident.
- Smiling makes us attractive and more appealing to others. People are drawn to us when we smile, just as we are drawn to them.

Frowns, scowls and grimaces push people away, but a smile draws them in.

- Smiling improves our mood. Smile the next time you feel down. There's a good chance your mood will change for the better. Smiling can trick the body into helping you change your mood.
- Smiling is contagious. When someone is smiling, they lighten up the room and change the moods of others.
- Smiling puts others at ease and makes them more comfortable. Take flying for example. When there is heavy turbulence, a smile from another passenger or a flight attendant always puts me at ease.

I know how difficult it can be to laugh and smile when times are tough, but sometimes this is when we need to laugh and smile the most. Even just the act of forcing a laugh or smile has benefit. Some studies have shown that we can gain the positive effects of forced laughing and smiling just as much as the real thing. The brain does not know how to distinguish between real and fake laughs and smiles.

With this in mind, force a smile and a laugh more often if it doesn't come naturally. It certainly can't hurt. You might even find that forced expressions of joy lead to real smiles and laughter. Plus, if you bring more laughter into your life, you will most likely help others around you laugh more. By elevating the mood of those around you, you can reduce their stress levels and perhaps improve the quality of social interaction you experience with them, reducing your stress even more.

Since we don't have much of a choice about how life is going to work out or when we will make a mistake, I think it is very helpful to joke about it rather than beat ourselves up. There is no point in making matters worse by torturing ourselves and avoiding the obvious.

Happiness isn't a state, it's a skill. It's the skill of knowing how to take what life throws your way and make the most of it.
- Gary Null -

If something is frustrating or upsetting, realize that you can look back on it and laugh. Think of how it will sound when you tell others down the road, and then see if you can laugh about it now. You may find yourself being more lighthearted and sillier, giving yourself and those around you more to laugh about. Despite whatever pain you are experiencing, approach life in a more joyful way. You'll find that you are less stressed about painful events.

Tools for emotional health[6]
A good way to approach these tools is to take one or two at a time and put them to practice every day until you have them mastered. Then focus on new ones. Eventually, they will become a part of your lifestyle to such an extent that they require little to no thought.

- Get outdoors and spend time surrounded by nature.
- Exercise if you can. Modify activities for your ability level.
- Get involved with groups that give you a sense of belonging.
- Engage in activities that give you a feeling of accomplishment.
- Create new ways of doing things you enjoy that may have become difficult.
- Do not argue about things that are not productive.
- Avoid people who cause you stress.
- Find rewarding things you can do to increase your self-image/esteem.
- Don't waste time worrying about what could have been. The past is over. Focus on the present moment.
- Simplify your goals.
- Pamper yourself.
- Eat well. Nutrition and moods are linked.
- Keep busy learning new things.
- Stop feeling guilty for what you can't do and praise yourself for what you do get done.
- Set boundaries. It will be make it easier to say "no" without guilt.
- Don't compare yourself to other people.
- Don't give up your aspirations and goals. Make them more realistic.
- Accept, trust, and love yourself no matter what is wrong.

If you have a health condition

- Take charge of your health. Make informed decisions about your body. Be smart, if not smarter than your doctor about your condition.
- Seek out the best medical care you can that fits your specific needs. Don't give up until you find the health care team that fits you best.
- Keep a folder of all your medical treatments.
- Keep a journal of how you feel, noting any changes in symptoms and mood.

- Have a list of friends and family you can call for support when needed, as well as emergency numbers for your doctors and other medical personnel.
- Avoid isolation. When we lose connection with others it can intensify depression, helplessness, loneliness, and fear.
- Connect with a support group in your area or online. Share your experience with others and learn from them. Everyone has something to offer.
- Accept help when it is offered and ask for help when you need it.
- Find comfort in your discomfort. A happy life is not contingent on our health status.

References

1. Weiten, W. & Lloyd, M.A. (2008) Psychology Applied to Modern Life (9th ed.). Wadsworth Cengage Learning. ISBN 0-495-55339-5.[page needed]

2. Zeidner, M. & Endler, N.S. (editors) (1996) Handbook of Coping: Theory, Research, Applications. New York: John Wiley.

3. Dictionary.com. Retrieved January 29, 2021 from: https://www.dictionary.com/browse/cope4) Serdans, Beka. Adapted from "Coping with Illness", Care4Dystonia

5) Zander, R., Zander, B. *The Art of Possibility.* (2000). New York, NY, Penguin Putnam

6) Modified from: DMRF, Dystonia Dialogue, September 2013, p. 22 and Dystonia International Support Group on Yahoo

Chapter 15
Self-care and healthy lifestyle strategies

Living well requires that we be disciplined in taking good care of ourselves. Some people rely solely on their doctors for their well-being. Unfortunately, except for suggestions, doctors can't do much for us beyond providing treatments. We must do more for ourselves. We are ultimately responsible for our well-being which is done by practicing self-care. With effective self-care we can monitor our health and make whatever physical, behavioral, and emotional changes necessary to maintain a high quality of life.

When it comes to the state of health in our country, we really need to look at the statistics to grasp just how dire it is to take better care of ourselves. According to the National Center for Chronic Disease Prevention and Health Promotion (NCCDPHP),[1] 6 in 10 adult Americans have a chronic disease and 4 in 10 adults have 2 or more chronic diseases. According to The National Council on Aging, approximately 80% of older adults have at least one chronic disease and 77% have at least two.[2]

The NCCDPHP reports that the key lifestyle risks for developing a chronic disease are tobacco use, poor nutrition, lack of physical activity, and excessive alcohol use. This is where we have control, as lifestyle can help prevent, reverse, or reduce the extent to which we suffer with an acute or chronic health condition.

Take diet/nutrition for example. Many diseases are correlated with weight and the fact that over 70% of the US population is overweight or obese speaks directly to this problem. This is a shocking statistic we really must take to heart because some of the most prevalent chronic diseases (alcohol related health diseases, heart disease, diabetes, arthritis, obesity, stroke, lung disease, and kidney disease) are heavily promoted by diet and lifestyle, ALL of which we are 100% responsible. When I say ALL, I am referring to diet and lifestyle, which is completely in our control. Our lifestyle can either decrease or increase these jarring statistics, so we must become more self-disciplined in our choices. We can't rely on anyone else to practice self-care for us and based on where money is spent, the health care system is not interested in prevention.

Chronic diseases account for 75% of the money our nation spends on health care, yet only 1% of health care dollars are spent on public efforts to improve overall health.[2] This is a very sad state of affairs and something that really brings to light just how unhealthy our population is and where the focus of health care is...treating diseases rather than preventing them, which amounts to big money for the medical establishment. We must take back control, and this is done by becoming self-disciplined in our lifestyle choices so we can enjoy vibrant lives and not rely on anyone else for our well-being.

Education

An important component of self-care is being educated. In fact, self-efficacy, the belief in our ability to accomplish a specific behavior or achieve a health goal, is an underlying theory of patient education. Studies show that when we increase our knowledge about our health and the care we receive, it improves clinical outcomes. Increased self-care and self-management also reduces hospitalizations, emergency department use, and overall managed care costs.

Studies also show that educated patients are more compliant and satisfied with treatments across a broad range of conditions and disease severities, resulting in a significant improvement in health behaviors and health status. Being well educated also improves coping skills because our involvement gives us greater control over the decisions made about our health.[3-6]

Self-care for me includes eating well, exercise, quality sleep, stress management, massage, listening to music, resting by the pool, beach, or my yard, meditation, prayer, avoiding toxic people, refraining from activities that overtax my body, taking breaks from my computer and phone, being out in nature, reading inspirational books, watching my favorite movies and TV shows, and spending time with people who lift me up.

There are so many of us that have the right self-care intentions, but don't practice enough. We might say all the right things and do the exact opposite. We hope to experience growth but resist change. We want less stress, yet we indulge in drama. We long for better relationships, and then refuse to trust anyone. In other words, what we say we want and what we actually do with our time are disconnected.

I have been able to implement many self-care activities throughout my day, mainly because I have made them part of my routine and lifestyle. However, it wasn't always easy. I had to first try different things to see what might help and then do them daily, without guilt. That was the sticking point...guilt! I felt guilty for taking time for myself until I realized just how helpful it was for my health and how much better it made me for others. If you struggle with guilt or anything else that prevents you from self-care activities, I want to share an idea that might be different than how you have approached self-care in the past.

A starting point for making self-care more of a priority

Far too often, we only utilize self-care activities and behaviors when we find the time. In other words, we fit it in around everything else. This doesn't make much sense when we think of it in the context of other things, because if we want something badly enough, we find a way to get it or do it. If someone with a great track record had a great investment opportunity for you, you would clear your schedule and seriously research it. If you got a call that would let you pursue your dream career, you would do anything to say yes. You would quit everything else. But self-care seems less urgent and less important; something you might get around to later when you find the time.

What I think is maybe a better approach is to pick one self-care activity that you implement every single day and schedule everything around that activity. It's the opposite of how most of us do it. It could be the same self-care activity every day or a different one every day of the week. Whatever it is, commit yourself to that ONE self-care activity, which makes it a priority versus something you get to when you can fit it in.

I know how cliché it is to say this, but we have to take care of ourselves in order to take care of everything else in our lives and everyone else in our lives for whom we are responsible. It's also cliché to use the following example, but it is a great metaphor for life: when we are on an airplane, we are always told in case of an emergency to first secure our oxygen mask before helping others. This is what more of us need to be doing in our everyday lives.

Determine that one self-care activity or tool that will help you feel better or that you want to do and implement that one thing into your life to see how it makes you feel. Not just how the self-care activity makes you feel, but how you feel about making self-care more of a priority. From there you can determine what next self-care activity you can implement. The important step for many of us is to first get comfortable practicing self-care, so take it slowly. There should be no guilt or shame for anyone to do what they need to take care of themselves.

Something else to keep in mind is the value of resting. It is important for better productivity, and if we don't schedule time for rest, our body will schedule it for us - and that will not be pleasant rest.

I like to be active, but I also like and need to rest because of my health condition (dystonia). As mentioned earlier, for years I felt guilty resting during the day because I felt like I was wasting time and being lazy. I was not comfortable doing what I perceived as "nothing." It was not until I changed how I looked at it and realized that doing "nothing" is a form of self-treatment and care that is vital to my health. I now schedule it into my day and call it "purposeful resting" because it serves an important need.

When I realized the benefit of my self-care activities and by renaming them to things such as "purposeful resting" and "self-treatment," the guilt went away. I am now more comfortable doing these things because I value how much they improve my life. What I also discovered is that it is during these periods of time when most of my ideas for things that I write about, videos I make, and all sorts of other projects that I am involved with come to me; not when I am sitting at my computer working. It is during my downtime, which makes these hours of doing "nothing" my most productive. I find I can accomplish more and be more effective with my work when I take this personal time. I need a clear mind to gain perspective and tap into my creative side. Not when there is a lot of "noise" around me.

If you are struggling with taking time to care for yourself, whatever that means to you, change how you look at it and/or what you call it; similar to the way I do with "purposeful resting."

> *When you're good to yourself, you're being good to everyone around you because when you feel good, you'll only react well to other people.*
> *At the same time, it's very easy for you to do things for other people when you know that other people are just an extension of yourself.*
> - Anita Moorjani -

Listening to our body
Our body is always talking to us. Pay attention. Listen to what it is telling you. With practice, you will begin to notice subtle signs that things are improving, getting worse, or something might just be more on or off than usual a particular day. Use these cues to restructure your thoughts and behaviors.

When you notice something starting to feel worse than usual or something different than you are used to, take a moment and assess the situation. Ask yourself what you need right now to feel better. Communicate with yourself. Even do it aloud if that helps. Do you need to lie down, put ice or heat on a painful area, exercise, meditate, pray, or talk to someone? Do you need to go somewhere to change your environment? Take a break from everyone and be alone? Get in some good exercise? It could be anything and over time, you will begin to know what you need to keep your health better balanced. The important thing is following through with what your body tells you and being consistent with what helps.

If you notice a pattern of feeling better for a period of time during the day or perhaps several days on end, take note of it by writing it down. Figure out what you did or did not do that helped you feel better. When you journal, it is important to include positive things as well as things that are bothering you. When we have a problem we are really struggling with, it is easy to focus on all the things wrong with us which can make journaling counterproductive. Work hard to acknowledge the good things by writing about them as well. They are very important to our mental health.

> *Our bodies have voices. They are often drowned out by*
> *the constant babble of the world we create for ourselves,*
> *but they are there waiting and willing to tell us what they need.*
> *Most often subtle and quiet, the voices get louder as we refuse to listen.*
> - Dr. Judith Petry -

Exercise/movement
Exercise or "movement" is an essential part of healthy living, which makes sense because our bodies are designed to move. Movement, of any kind, improves circulation, reduces blood pressure, promotes weight loss, improves sleeping patterns, reduces stress, relieves symptoms of depression and anxiety, increases muscle strength, improves joint structure and joint function, and helps manage pain, among other things.

There are so many forms of exercise and movement that it is not possible to say what would be right for you. Everyone has different abilities and interests. For those who have health/physical limitations where you are unable to exercise on your feet, there are exercises designed for sitting in a chair and even lying down. The key thing to remember is that some form of movement, whether you are sitting, standing, or lying down, is the most important thing.

Through trial and error (I prefer saying "trial and success"), I find stretching, light weight work, walking, and stabilization/balance exercises to be most beneficial for me. Strong muscles support and nourish bones and joints and hold them in good alignment. Weak muscles are more prone to injury. I also enjoy biking around my neighborhood and swimming in a pool on occasion. I modify my posture when I ride and swim so I don't aggravate my back and neck which are already compromised from dystonia.

Finding what best suits you is the key. Tailor it to your needs. There is no cookie cutter approach to exercise. Do whatever you enjoy and remember, movement is the key!

Sleep and why it is so important

Another very important part of self-care and a healthy lifestyle is adequate sleep. Without enough sleep, we are not physiologically able to withstand the rigors of a regular day, let alone an especially difficult day or extended period of time where life is kicking us extra hard.

Rest and sleep help relax muscles and reduce pain, among other things. Unfortunately, many people these days have difficulty sleeping. This comes as no surprise considering how challenging it is to relax with the hectic world we live in, especially now with all the technology where it is hard to unplug. Many people have to use over the counter or prescription sleep aids.

Sleep requirements vary; 6-8 hours is sufficient for me and I also take rest breaks throughout the day if I am able. If I can take a quick nap as well, it helps keep my mind and muscles calmer, and gives me more energy. There is a great book about sleep I recommend called, *Why we sleep,* by Matthew Walker.

There are so many benefits to sleep. When we are sleeping, our body releases hormones that help repair cells and control the body's use of energy. During sleep, the body is also doing most of its detoxification. Researchers have also discovered that sleep plays a critical role in immune function, metabolism, memory, and learning. Chronic lack of sleep is linked to colds and flu, hypertension, diabetes, heart disease, mental health, and obesity.[7]

Sleep is also necessary for our nervous system to work properly. Too little sleep impacts concentration, memory, and physical performance. If sleep deprivation persists, mood swings may develop. Sleep gives neurons that are used while we are awake a chance to shut down and repair themselves. Without sleep, neurons may become so depleted in energy that they begin to malfunction.[7]

Tips for better sleep[8-10]
Boost melatonin production
Melatonin is a hormone in the brain that helps regulate other hormones and maintains the body's circadian rhythm. When it is dark, our body produces more melatonin. When it is light, the production of melatonin drops.

When it is time to go to bed, turn off your computer and television. Light from these devices suppresses melatonin production and television can stimulate the mind rather than relax it.

If you must use a light at bedtime, for reading for example, do not read from a backlit device (such as an iPad). Choose a light source such as a bedside lamp. Use a low-wattage bulb so you can avoid bright lights. Make sure the room is dark. Cover electrical displays, use curtains or shades to block light from windows, and wear a sleep mask to cover your eyes.

Increase light exposure during the day
Remove your sunglasses in the morning and let sunlight hit your face. Try to take work breaks outside, exercise outside, and walk during the day instead of at night. Also let as much light into your home and workspace as possible.

Sunshine affects the brain via the interaction of the chemicals melatonin and serotonin, as well as vitamin D. When sunlight hits your eyes, your optic nerve sends a message to the pineal gland in the brain that tells it to decrease its secretions of melatonin until the sun goes down again.

The opposite happens with serotonin, a hormone connected with feelings of happiness and wakefulness. When we are exposed to the sun, our brain increases serotonin production. When sunshine touches our skin, the body produces vitamin D, which helps us maintain serotonin levels.

When melatonin and serotonin production are properly balanced, we feel energized during the day and a slowing down during the dark hours. Some find vitamin D supplements helpful for maintaining this hormonal balance, especially during the colder months when we spend more time indoors. For some people, a lack of vitamin D can lead to physical and mental health problems, such as Seasonal Affective Disorder (SAD) and other mood imbalances. Most standard bloodwork includes a vitamin D test. If not, you can request it to determine if you fall within the therapeutic range.

Stick to a sleep schedule
Maintain a regular bedtime and wake time schedule. A regular wake time in the morning strengthens the circadian function and can help with sleep onset at night.

Pay attention to what you eat and drink
Don't go to bed hungry or full. Also limit how much you drink before bed to prevent trips to the bathroom. Avoid nicotine, caffeine, and alcohol. The stimulating effects of nicotine and caffeine can wreak havoc on quality sleep, and even though alcohol might make you feel tired, it can disrupt sleep.

Create a bedtime routine
Establish a regular, relaxing bedtime routine each night to tell your body it is time to wind down. This might include taking a warm bath or shower, reading a book, or listening to soothing music. Relaxing activities ease the transition from wakefulness to drowsiness.

Make your bedroom more sleep friendly
Make your bedroom reflective of the value you place on sleep. Check your room for noise, light, temperature, or other distractions, including a partner's sleep disruptions such as snoring. Keep your room temperature 70 degrees Fahrenheit or less. Consider using shades that darken the room, a sleep mask to cover your eyes, earplugs, recordings of soothing sounds, and a fan or other device that creates white noise.

Make sure your bed allows enough room to stretch and turn comfortably. Experiment with different levels of mattress firmness, foam or egg crate toppers, and pillows that provide appropriate support. If you share your bed, make sure there is enough room for two. If you have children and/or pets, set boundaries for how often they can sleep with you or have them sleep in their own space.

Include physical activity in your daily routine
Regular physical activity can help you fall asleep faster and enjoy deeper sleep. Find a time to exercise that works best for you. Shortly before bed is usually not the best time of day as it can cause you to be too energized to fall asleep.

Reserve your bed for sleeping and sex
Use your bedroom only for sleep and sex to strengthen the association between bed and sleep. Take work materials, computers, and televisions out of the bedroom. If you only use your bed for sleep and sex, when you go to bed, your body gets a powerful cue: it's time to either nod off or be romantic.

I hope this information leads you to better sleep. Many of these suggestions have significantly improved my quality of sleep. If you still have trouble falling asleep, maintaining sleep, awaken earlier than you wish, don't feel refreshed after sleep, or suffer from excessive sleepiness during the day, please consult your doctor.

Basic nutrition
Nutrition is probably one of the most controversial, confusing, and emotional topics next to politics. We are bombarded with so much information that it can be difficult to really know what is best to eat. My suggestion is to adopt the simple approach my brother developed called The DeFlame Diet, which is what I do.

My diet consists primarily of chicken, pork, fish, eggs, and an abundant amount of vegetables, as well as fruit and nuts. I choose to exclude grains, legumes, dairy products, flour, refined sugar, and refined oils for the reasons in upcoming paragraphs. This is my preference; it need not be the same for you. My focus is general health maintenance by eating a diet that is as anti-inflammatory as possible to ward off pain and other unwanted health problems. I also take a variety of nutritional supplements that include a multivitamin, magnesium, vitamin D, vitamin C, vitamin B3 (niacinamide), probiotics, zinc glycinate, fish oil, iodine in the form of kelp, coenzyme Q10, MSM (methylsulfonylmethane), GABA (gamma-Aminobutyric acid), L-Lysine, and ginger root.

I encourage you to read my brother's book, *The DeFlame Diet: DeFlame your diet, body, and mind,* for more information about diet and inflammation, and various easily tracked inflammatory markers that we need to keep in the normal range. Examples of some of the important markers include body weight, waist/hip ratio, BMI, glucose levels, lipids, vitamin D, and C-reactive protein.

While most people choose to be omnivores, a DeFlame Diet can be vegan, omnivore, or carnivore. The key for all three is to avoid the overconsumption of refined sugar, flour, and omega-6 oils. Corn, sunflower, safflower, cottonseed, peanut, and soybean are the primary sources of refined omega-6 oils. Shockingly, refined sugar, flour, and omega-6 oils make up almost 60% of the calories consumed by the average American.

Examples of these calorie sources include cereal, bread, pretzels, chips, desserts, soda, sweet tea, donuts, French fries, salad dressing, and most packaged foods. Eating a little bit of these calories is typically not a big deal for most people, which means people do not necessarily have to give them up completely, as I choose to do. The problem is that these "foods" make up the majority of calories consumed by Americans, which leads to obesity, related chronic diseases (cancer, heart disease, etc.), depression, anxiety, and chronic pain.[11]

This means that most people eat themselves into a state of chronic pain and then look for treatments to reduce their pain, which in many cases does not work because pain treatments are typically not able to overcome the painful inflammatory state created by the overconsumption of refined sugar, flour, and omega-6 oils. I will briefly comment on these calories in the paragraphs below.

Sugar and flour
Approximately 40% of all calories consumed by Americans come from refined sugar and flour. When we overeat these calories, there is a dramatic rise in blood glucose after a meal. The body cells exposed to such high levels of glucose begin to release an excess of inflammatory chemicals. This happens every time we overeat these calories, which is why I never eat sugar and flour products.

This is why people with the metabolic syndrome and type 2 diabetes who have high fasting levels of glucose typically always feel unwell, because they live and sleep in a hyperglycemic state. In other words, they live in a state of chronic inflammation that will not turn off until normal glucose levels are achieved. Approximately 25% of the entire adult population in

America has the metabolic syndrome, which is a pre-diabetic state. For people 60 and older, over 40% have the metabolic syndrome.[11] For those unfamiliar with the metabolic syndrome, it is a cluster of conditions that includes high blood pressure, high blood sugar, excess body fat around the waist, and abnormal cholesterol levels that increase the risk of heart disease, stroke, and diabetes.

One of the many problems with sugar is that it forms free radicals in the brain's membrane and compromises nerve cells' ability to communicate. This could have repercussions in how well we remember instructions, process ideas, and handle our moods. Sugar also causes premature aging. When sugar travels into the skin, its components cause nearby amino acids to form cross-links. These cross-links jam the repair mechanism and, over time, leave you with premature wrinkles.[11]

The primary challenge people face when they try to give up refined sugar and flour calories is that they are emotionally attached to these foods because they taste good. Substance-abuse researchers have performed brain scans on subjects tasting sugar and found that the brain lights up in the same regions as it would in a drug addict or an alcoholic with their drink of choice. Dopamine, the reward chemical, spikes and reinforces the desire to have more. In other words, sugary foods turn on our brain's pleasure centers in a fashion that resembles addictive drugs like cocaine.

My suggestion is that if you choose to eat sugar and flour, do it with strong mental focus and disciplined mindfulness. Eat only condiment sized portions and force yourself to stop even if your tastebuds and emotional brain nudge you to eat more.

If you think about it, drastically reducing sugar and flour consumption is consistent with our biological needs. For the majority of human existence, there was no such sugar and flour available. We were endowed with a sweet tooth so that we would consume natural sugars contained in foods, such as fruit. With the advent of processed sugar cane, our adaptive sweet tooth turned into somewhat of a curse, causing us to crave foods that cause our body to create inflammation, pain, and chronic disease.

Grains
Grains and grain products include rice, amaranth, barley, rye, millet, bread, pastries, pasta, cereal, crackers, chips, pizza, and pretzels to name a few. All grains are whole grains prior to going through the refinement process.

There is a popular misconception that whole grains should be a regular part of our diet because they are so nutritious. This is only true if you compare the nutrient value of whole grains to refined grains. However, when you compare the nutrient value of whole grains to vegetables, fruits, potatoes, and beans, a different story emerges.

In general, the recommendation to eat whole grains is based on the false premise that whole grains are the best dietary source of fiber. In reality, the best sources of fiber are fruits, vegetables, nuts, and seeds (such as chia seeds). Understand that the way to compare dietary fiber levels is to compare foods based on calories and not cups as you can see in Table 1 below.

Notice that two cups of cooked oatmeal provide far more calories compared to two cups of broccoli. To compare two cups of oatmeal to broccoli, you have to eat at least six cups of cooked broccoli to equal out the calories consumed from both foods. And when you do that, on a caloric basis, broccoli delivers more fiber, AND the same holds true for most vitamins, minerals, and other nutrients, which are not included in Table 1.

Table 1 - Fiber density - vegetables and fruit versus grains and beans

Food and amount	Calories	Fiber (g)
Bread		
4 pc white bread	320	4
4 pc whole wheat bread	280	8
Whole grains		
1.5 cups medium grain, cooked brown rice	327	6
2 cups cooked oatmeal	332	8
Vegetables		
6 cups cooked broccoli	324	36
3 heads romaine lettuce	318	39
Fruit		
3 large apples	348	15
5 navel oranges	345	15
3 bananas (7.5")	354	9
Potatoes		
2 large sweet potatoes (360 g)	324	12
1 large white potato (299 g)	281	6
Beans		
1.5 cup cooked lentils	345	24
1.5 cup cooked red kidney beans	338	20

Nuts		
Almonds (2 oz)	362	6
Cashews (2 oz)	310	2
English Walnuts (2 oz)	366	4
Macadamia (2 oz)	406	4

Based on the information in Table 1, if someone has concerns about getting adequate fiber, they should consider eating beans. Only 1.5 cups of cooked lentils provide 3 times the fiber as two cups of oatmeal and legumes are also a greater source of vitamins and minerals compared to whole grains.

The information in Table 1 is from my brother's book, *The DeFlame Diet: DeFlame your diet, body, and mind.* He used a website called NutritionData.com to create the information in Table 1. You can check nearly any food you eat to identify calories, fiber, vitamins, minerals, and even omega-6 and omega-3 fatty acids. If you utilize NutritionData.com or a similar website, make sure to correlate the portion size and calories to identify nutrient values based on caloric intake. REMEMBER, this is because it takes more than 6 cups of broccoli to approach the caloric content in just 2 cups of cooked oatmeal. When we eat vegetables based on caloric content, one can feel quite full without eating substantial calories and gaining weight.

Gluten
Gluten is a protein found in wheat and related grain species, including barley, rye, spelt, and kamut. Gluten gives elasticity to dough and provides a chewy/gooey texture that is most notable in pizza. Gluten can also be found in condiments, salad dressings, soups, processed meats (cold cuts, hot dogs, sausages, etc.), ice cream, reduced fat products, gravy and cream sauces thickened with flour, soy sauce, hydrolyzed vegetable protein, yeast extract, malted drinks, beer, ale, gin, and whiskey.

About 1% of the population has celiac disease, which is an autoimmune type of disease that is stimulated by the consumption of gluten. About 5% of the population cannot tolerate gluten because they suffer from what is called non-celiac gluten sensitivity. People with celiac disease and gluten sensitivity can manifest very diverse symptoms, such as abdominal pain and bloating, diarrhea, constipation, joint/muscle pain, headaches, anemia, depression, eczema, chronic fatigue, and various neurological problems.[11]

I do not have celiac disease or non-celiac gluten sensitivity AND I still avoid gluten because it is found in grains, which are the least nutrient-dense whole foods as I described in the previous section. On the rare occasion that I eat foods that contain gluten, I only eat them in condiment-sized portions. Since gluten may promote a host of unwanted health conditions, all of which can exist without digestive problems (making some unaware if they have gluten sensitivity), it is in our best interest to avoid foods containing this substance even if we don't fall into the 1-5% category mentioned in the previous paragraph.

In recent years it has become popular for people to go "gluten free." What this means for a lot of people is that they don't really change the foods they eat. Instead, they eat the same foods that had the gluten removed or not added during production; mostly these are foods that are still unhealthy for other reasons. To truly go gluten free, we need to eat foods that never had gluten in the first place.

Water consumption
Drinking plenty of water to keep the body hydrated is critical. Water plays an important role in digestion, blood circulation for carrying nutrients and oxygen to cells and removing toxins, regulating body temperature, protecting the movement of joints, and helping metabolize fat. A widely accepted standard for daily water consumption is to divide your weight in half and drink that many ounces of water. For example, at around 190 pounds, I consume about 100 ounces of water day (a little over 6 pints). I have re-usable water bottles with different ounce measurements that help me accurately determine how much water I consume daily.

Changing how we eat
It is widely accepted that refined sugars, sugar substitutes, white flour and white flour products, refined omega-6 oils, too much alcohol, caffeine, preservatives, and foods with a high glycemic index should be avoided in general. Glycemic index refers to how fast and how much a food raises blood glucose levels. Foods with higher glycemic index values raise blood sugar more rapidly than foods with lower glycemic index values, which can promote chronic inflammation when eaten in excess as discussed. Because of how addicting many of these foods are, it is difficult for many people to remove them from their diets.

A good way to go about changing the way we eat the calorie sources mentioned above is to slowly replace bad foods with good foods. It may take time to adjust, so allow yourself the time you need. Also change the way you shop. It is best to shop the perimeter of the grocery store because this is where all the healthy, fresh foods are located. Make this a new habit. Aside from a few things, the aisles are where they stock most of the foods we want to avoid. Shop the perimeter of the store to find the best foods. This will also condition you to think more about healthier foods to help you to make better choices. Also remember that we are responsible for the food in our homes. If we don't buy it, we don't eat it, so keep it away if possible.

For many, eating is an emotional activity, as it is often a coping mechanism or an escape from physical or emotional pain in search of comfort. This is not a behavior reserved just for people overweight or obese. It is a reality for most people. However, as a frame of reference regarding weight, approximately 70% of the US population is overweight or obese, which represents a state of chronic inflammation from the overconsumption of refined sugar, flour, and omega-6 oils, as well as a lack of exercise/movement. This is a serious problem.

Food does more than fill our stomachs; it also satisfies feelings. When we quench those feelings with comfort food, it can be a very satisfying companion. However, most comfort foods are unhealthy which will cause overeating because they increase cravings for sugar, salt, and fat laden foods.

If you are an emotional eater, you may find yourself using food as a reward when you are happy and craving sweets or unhealthy snacks when stressed. By eating healthier, we can reduce cravings for these foods and then begin to seek or crave healthy foods, such as fruits and vegetables versus chips and ice cream, for example. This is a liberating experience. Exercise is also very helpful for reducing cravings.

It typically takes a few days to a few weeks for the body to eliminate cravings. If you are dedicated through those initial days/weeks, you might be surprised how little a previous food/craving has over you. It is a very empowering feeling to be in control! To learn more about this, please see another book by my brother entitled, *Weight loss secrets you need to know: Why your brain, body physiology, emotions, and primordial drives want you fat and what you can do about it.*

I am the model on the cover of that book. My brother wanted me on the cover because I lost 150 pounds and have kept it off since 2007, and I was able to do this despite suffering with a severe case of dystonia and pain that compromises my physical activity. So, if I can do this, mostly anyone can, which means that you can do this too.

Eating well is vital because a stressed-out body and mind (which most of us have) needs nutritional support. The literature is vast in this area. Good nutrition can give us more energy, reduce our risk for diseases, reduce inflammation and pain, and help us lose weight and/or maintain a healthy weight. It may also help reduce physical symptoms of a health condition, and a great way to do this, as previously mentioned, is to eliminate sugar, sugar substitutes, refined oils (corn, safflower, sunflower, peanut, etc.), fried and processed foods, caffeine, soda, and alcohol from our diets.

If you are unsure if what you are eating is causing problems with your physical or mental health, eliminate something from your diet for a couple weeks and see if you notice a difference in how you feel. Try this with a variety of foods and food groups. Monitoring the results of bloodwork is also helpful.

Changing how we eat requires us to change the way we think about eating, so we need to ask ourselves some important questions. Are we eating to satisfy cravings or to satisfy hunger? Are we eating foods that make us feel good emotionally or physically? Are the foods we eat causing unwanted health problems? Is what we eat going to be healthy in the long term or disease promoting? Your answers to these questions will determine what kinds of food to fill your plate.

How I lost 150 pounds

Prior to the onset of dystonia in 2001, I lived an active, healthy life involved in many sports and activities. When dystonia hit, chronic pain caused me to be very sedentary and I no longer took proper care of my body like I used to. I began eating fatty foods and drank beer to numb the pain. While I did not eat dessert type foods, I consumed lots of fatty meats, cheeses, pasta, fried and processed foods, pizza, bread, sandwiches, crackers, and chips.

I went from an athletic 190 pounds in 2001 to around 340 pounds in 2006. At around 240 pounds, I was put on blood pressure medication for hypertension. Ironically, prior to developing dystonia and gaining weight, I was a high-level athlete in several sports and partner in a nutrition education company! What was I thinking you might ask; simple, I wasn't thinking because I was in too much physical and emotional pain to care what I was doing to myself. I needed to find a way to cope and for me it was food and alcohol.

I was never overweight my entire life, let alone obese, so it was a new experience for me. I was very self-conscious. It felt like everyone was looking at me and judging me (I was probably judging myself more than others were judging me). I think people looked at me more because of my weight than they did my dystonia, even though dystonia caused me to have distorted body postures that attracted attention.

Whatever the case, it was not an appealing combination. I felt and looked awful, but in all honesty, I really didn't know how I looked because I rarely looked in the mirror and avoided having pictures taken. I regret that now, but I didn't want to see my exterior because it was a reflection of how unhappy I felt on the inside. It was also a reminder of the pain I was in that was the main contributor to gaining all the weight. Because of my embarrassment and shame, I retreated from the world as much as I could and lived a very isolated life for years.

As mentioned in Chapter 1, in December 2006, 5 1/2 years after my dystonia began, I caught a stomach virus. During those two weeks, I spent all day in bed and the bathroom. It was one of the greatest blessings because I was too sick to engage in self-destructive activities. Not being able to eat any solid food or drink alcohol turned my life around. Being so idle gave me time to think about what I was doing to myself and what I could do to change.

While I was sick, I lost a little weight and my dystonia ever so slightly improved (probably from all the resting and changing my destructive habits), allowing me to be a bit more active when I got better. I knew that this was my opportunity to make lifestyle changes. If I did not take advantage of this opportunity, I was potentially facing life threatening health problems.

I took it very slowly and began walking a little each day and returned to a healthy way of eating by following practices I ignored for over 5 years. I started by walking to the end of my driveway and back for a couple weeks. Then about 100 yards to the end of my street and back. Every week or so I would go a bit further. I eventually got the strength to walk 2-3 miles twice a day and lost most of my excess weight in 10 months. It was an incredible feeling! I also focused my attention on a very targeted movement therapy program for my dystonia symptoms and achieved about 75% improvement within a year.

Unfortunately, I pushed the envelope and walked too much, aggravating my dystonia to the point of injuring my back. I had to stop walking completely. The pain on the entire upper right side of my body was so bad that I was unable to even hold a pen in my hand to write. When I stopped walking, my weight was 210 pounds, but by eating well I continued to lose weight. I eventually got down to 180 pounds and currently, at 6′ 2″, I weigh 190 pounds.

It has been almost 15 years since I stopped exercise walking and I have not wavered from 190 pounds (compare my 2007, 2014, and 2021 pictures at the end of the chapter to see how little difference there is post weight-loss). I find it both interesting and important to note that I continued to lose weight months after I stopped walking, which I attribute to eating well. I mention this because there are people with health problems or time limitations who are not able to be as active as they would like, which does not mean they cannot maintain a healthy weight. If you are someone who loves to exercise but eat poorly or not as well as you could, to help put nutrition and exercise into perspective, we cannot out-exercise poor nutrition, so please be mindful of what you put in your body. It's the only one you have. Treat it well.

I still don't do much aerobic exercise and am able to maintain my weight. I might walk, bike, or swim a little on occasion and do light weight bearing exercises a few times a week, but I mainly do exercises that target my dystonia. Flexibility and strength are very helpful for me, but I have to be careful with what I do and how much I do so I don't aggravate my symptoms. Too much or too little activity can be detrimental, so it is a delicate balance.

While it is possible to lose weight and maintain a healthy weight by eating properly and being moderately active, we should try and do some form of aerobic exercise. Listen closely to your body and do what is best for you and your specific situation.

As mentioned previously, I primarily eat fresh fruits and vegetables, meats, fish, eggs, and raw nuts. I do not eat dairy, grains, pasta, bread, cereal, crackers, chips, desserts, fried or processed foods, sugar or sugar substitutes, and all I drink is water. This way of eating may sound extreme, but it only sounds extreme because we have become so accustomed to eating poorly.

I don't like to call what I eat a "diet" because it is more of a lifestyle. The distinction between diet (temporary) vs. lifestyle (long term) is very important. Calling what we eat a "diet" often creates expectations and pressure, which can be self-defeating and result in failure.

We need to use terminology that triggers the right attitude towards food because if we change how we look at eating, we can change what we eat. When we change what we eat, we can change how we feel. When we change how we feel, we make more thoughtful choices about what we put in our bodies, resulting in better weight management and overall health promotion.

While the years of being overweight were very painful, I am grateful I went through the experience. I now have a much better appreciation for how food and drink can become our best friends. I better understand the emotions that cause people to eat poorly and overeat, and how it feels to have a negative body image and be self-conscious around others. I also understand how people can escape this self-imprisonment and live a healthier, happier, higher quality life.

If you want to change your eating habits, you can totally revamp your diet or take baby steps by making small changes at a time. Then build on each step to a healthier you. We all travel this road differently, so find what works best for you and put it to practice.

References
1) National Center for Chronic Disease Prevention and Health Promotion (NCCDPHP). Retrieved on January 8, 2021 from:
https://www.cdc.gov/chronicdisease/resources/infographic/chronic-diseases.htm
2) National Council on Aging. Retrieved on January 8, 2021 from:
https://www.ncoa.org/news/resources-for-reporters/get-the-facts/healthy-aging-facts/
3) Gold DT, McClung B. Approaches to patient education: emphasizing the long-term value of compliance and persistence. Am J Med. 2006 Apr;119(4 Suppl 1):S32-7. Retrieved on November 15, 2013 from:
http://www.ncbi.nlm.nih.gov/pubmed/16563940

4) American Family Physician, Retrieved October 18, 2013 from:
http://www.aafp.org/afp/2005/1015/p1503.html
5) Bodenheimer T, Wagner EH, Grumbach K. Improving primary care for patients
with chronic illness. JAMA. 2002;288:1775–9
6) Whitlock WL, Brown A, Moore K, Pavliscsak H, Dingbaum A, Lacefield D, et al.
Telemedicine improved diabetic management. Mil Med. 2000;165:579–84
7) www.clevelandclinic.org, Retrieved September 3, 2013
8) www.helpguide.org, Retrieved September 3, 2013
9) www.curiosity.discovery.com, Retrieved September 4, 2013
10) www.sleepfoundation.org, Retrieved September 3, 2013 from:
http://www.sleepfoundation.org/article/sleep-topics/healthy-sleep-tips
11) Seaman, D. *The DeFlame Diet: DeFlame your diet, body, and mind.* (2016). Shadow
Panther Press.

2003

2005

2007

2014

2021

Chapter 16
Think better to live better

Mind-Body connection

Every feeling we have affects some part of our body. Even if we are doing everything "right" (exercising, eating well, managing stress, etc.), our emotions can impact how we feel physically. To achieve emotional balance, it is necessary to uncover and express emotions such as anger, resentments, frustrations, and fear, and replace them with forgiveness, love, joy, and hope. Chronic negative emotions will negatively affect our health.[1,2]

Some scientists are reluctant to embrace this mind-body paradigm. One of the factors is that you cannot see or measure emotions inside the body. However, just because we do not have the technology to see the mind-body connection does not mean it is not real. Those who have a health condition know first-hand that there is a connection.[1,2] Recall what I mentioned earlier about my friend who gets a headache when she gets a text from people who cause her stress. Just the mere sight of their name causes a headache before she even reads their message, and she does not have an underlying health condition.

While the mechanics of mind-body links are still being unraveled, it is known that our thoughts and emotions do play a role in our experience of physical pain and may play a role in the development of chronic disease. In a study published in the Proceedings of the National Academy of Sciences, researchers in Finland showed that emotions tend to be felt in the body in ways that are generally consistent from one person to the next, irrespective of age, sex, or nationality. For example, those suffering from depression will often experience chest pains even when there is nothing physically wrong with their heart.[3]

"Our data show bodily sensations associated with different emotions are so specific that, in fact, they could at least in theory contribute significantly to the conscious feeling of the corresponding emotion," says Dr. Lauri Nummenmaa, Professor at Turku PET Centre and Department of Psychology, University of Turku, Finland. From an evolutionary perspective, "emotions developed as a way to draw organisms either away from trouble or towards positive, pleasurable events."[3]

Consider the words and descriptions we use to describe how we feel. Is your "head spinning" with everything you have to do and you find yourself with dizzy spells from time to time? Is discomfort in your stomach trying to give you wisdom about something your intuition knows on a "gut level?" Maybe work is not going well and there are things you "don't want to hear." Could there be a connection between this and the tinnitus (ringing in the ears) that you've been experiencing lately?

These subtle language clues may offer insight and help you view your health in a new and unique way, and you may feel your body moving forward or "stepping out" into new levels of wellness and vitality.[4] For more on the mind-body connection, please see the book, *You Can Heal Your Life*, by Louise Hay.

Affirmations
After mentioning Louise Hay, it is fitting to include a section on affirmations because a great portion of her work centers around this topic.

Most people have probably heard the saying, "change your thoughts, change your life." There is great truth to this. There are chemicals produced in the body when we have different thoughts and emotions. When we are joyful, chemicals are produced that are beneficial to the body. When we are angry or sad, chemicals are produced that are harmful to the body.

Consider the power of a placebo. It is not the pill, medicine, or procedure that does anything. It is the person's belief in the specific treatment that does the healing. When the mind thinks healthy thoughts, the body finds it easier to be healthy.

Affirmations are positive, specific statements that can condition the subconscious mind to develop a more positive perception of ourselves. Affirmations can help us change harmful thoughts and behaviors and accomplish goals. They can also help undo damage caused by negative things we repeatedly tell ourselves (or what others repeatedly tell us) that contribute to a negative self-perception.

If you believe the phrase "you are what you think," then life circumstances truly stem from thoughts. However, we cannot rely purely on thoughts. We have to translate thoughts into words and eventually into actions in order to manifest our intentions. This means we have to be very careful with our words, choosing to speak only those which work to our benefit and cultivate our highest good.

Affirmations are like exercises for our mind that can rewire our brain. Look at them the same way as repetitive exercises that improve your body's physical health. Positive mental repetitions can change our thinking patterns so that we begin to think and act in a new way. They play an integral role by breaking patterns of negative thoughts, negative speech, and negative actions.

The spoken word is very powerful. When we say "I can't," the energy of those words will repel against us. If we say "I can" and "I will," we are better able to manifest what we desire.

Write down the areas in your life you want to work on or behaviors you want to change. For each, come up with a positive, present-tense statement you can repeat to yourself several times a day. It is important that your affirmations are credible, believable, and realistic. Below are some examples of affirmations. Even if some of them are not true at the moment but how you want things to be, say them. We can manifest anything with the right mindset. Choose one or two that resonate with you, or make up your own, and put it to memory. Use it often so you hear the words over and over.

Affirmations
- My ability to conquer challenges is limitless.
- I am free of pain and free of fear.
- My only work is to relax and breathe.
- Everything that is happening now is for my ultimate good.
- Though these times are difficult, they are only a phase of life.
- I am at peace with what has happened, is happening, and will happen.
- I sleep in peace and wake in joy.
- Every day in every way I am getting healthier and feeling better.
- I love and care for my body and it cares for me.
- My body is a safe and pleasurable place for me to be.
- I am in control of my life and health.
- I value my time and energy.
- My mind is calm and peaceful.
- I allow myself to play and enjoy life.
- My body is strong and healthy.

- My body is flexible.
- Every cell in my body is alive with health and energy.
- My body has a remarkable capacity for healing.
- I am full of energy and vitality.
- Every day is a new day full of hope, happiness, and health.
- I am perfectly healthy in body, mind, and spirit.

Affirmations should use positive language and clearly express what you desire. It is important to use affirmations with "I," "I am," and "I will" statements, affirming that you will use your abilities to achieve your goal. Close your eyes, shut out the rest of the world, and repeat the words, thinking what they mean to you. Feel the emotions that the affirmations evoke.[5-9]

Life can be distracting so it is easy to forget our affirmations or forget saying them. Leave reminder cards in various places. Use index cards or post-it notes to write your affirmations and put them where you will see them, such as the kitchen table, refrigerator, bathroom mirror, car dashboard, desk drawer, purse or wallet, or computer monitor.

An affirmation I came up with that I say often is: "My mind is clear and calm. My body is balanced and strong. My heart is loving and pure." These are all areas where I feel the need to focus my attention to achieve balance in my life. The more I repeat this, the more it becomes part of my everyday life, positively impacting everything I do. There have been many times when my body and mind have been restless and I recited this affirmation over and over, while visualizing how each word feels, and I have fallen asleep. This I how powerful our words and images can be.

Developing a positive mindset is one of the most powerful life strategies at our disposal. With positive affirmations and visualization, it is possible to transform our life and our health and renew joy and passion.

Mindfulness

The words "mindfulness" and "mindfulness meditation" are talked about a lot these days. It is becoming a common practice for many as a means to find peace of mind. A simple definition of mindfulness is, "a practiced skill of non-judgmental awareness and acceptance of our present-moment experience, including all of our unwanted thoughts, feelings, sensations, and urges."[10]

Mindfulness teaches us to accept all of our unwanted internal experiences as a part of life, regardless of whether they are "good" or "bad." As meditation teacher James Baraz says, "mindfulness is simply being aware of what is happening right now without wishing it were different; enjoying the pleasant without holding on when it changes (which it might); or being with the unpleasant without fearing it will always be this way (which it won't)."

The first time I heard about mindfulness was when someone suggested I look into the work done by Jon Kabat-Zinn to help me get through a difficult experience. Jon is Professor of Medicine Emeritus and founding director of the Stress Reduction Clinic and the Center for Mindfulness in Medicine, Health Care, and Society at the University of Massachusetts Medical School. The program he developed with his colleagues is called Mindfulness Based Stress Reduction (MBSR). His practice of yoga and studies with Buddhist teachers led him to integrate their teachings with those of Western science. He teaches mindfulness meditation as a technique to help people cope with stress, anxiety, pain, and illness.

Jon has written several books and created audio programs that provide great information for integrating mindfulness into your life. The program I suggest, especially for those new to meditation, is *Mindfulness for Beginners*.

In this two CD program, Jon gives a great overview of what mindfulness is all about and also provides several mindfulness meditation exercises that you can begin practicing right away. Among the great books he has written, I highly recommend *Full Catastrophe Living*, which is relevant for anyone going through any adverse life condition.

Jon felt that the phrase "the full catastrophe" (in reference to a comment made by the character Zorba in the book and movie, *Zorba the Greek)* captures something positive about the human spirit's ability to come to grips with what is most difficult in life and to find within it room to grow in strength and wisdom. Facing the full catastrophe means finding and coming to terms with what is most human in ourselves. There is not one person on the planet who does not have his or her own version of the full catastrophe.[11]

"Catastrophe" here does not mean disaster. Rather it means the poignant enormity of our life experiences. It includes crises and disaster, but also all the little things that go wrong that add up. The phrase reminds us that life is always in flux, that everything we think is permanent is actually only temporary and constantly changing. This includes our ideas, our opinions, our relationships, our jobs, our possessions, our creations, our bodies... everything. Thus, practicing mindfulness helps us more effectively and joyfully live in the moment no matter what is going on around us or inside of us.[11]

Jon defines mindfulness as, "paying attention, on purpose, in the present moment, as if your life depended on it, non-judgmentally." This is one of my favorite descriptions of mindfulness. It is easy to understand, making it easier to put into practice. Jon continues, "mindfulness is basically just a particular way of paying attention. It is a way of looking deeply into oneself in the spirit of self-inquiry and self-understanding."[11]

Mindfulness is not something one masters overnight. It is a journey that requires effort, commitment, and dedication. While mindfulness may provide relatively rapid relief to one's distress in certain situations, it is perhaps better conceptualized as a long-term shift in perspective that allows us to better manage the complexity of human psychological experiences. Like learning a new language, mindfulness takes time and patience to master, and ongoing effort to remain fluent.[10]

Living mindfully allows us to stay in the present without worry about the future or regret about the past. It also allows us to relate more skillfully with difficult bodily sensations, feelings, and thoughts without becoming overwhelmed by them.

The practice of mindfulness meditation helps us remain in the present moment where life is actually happening. Remember that there are only two days in the year that nothing can be done about. One is called yesterday and the other is called tomorrow. ENJOY THIS MOMENT BECAUSE THIS VERY MOMENT IS YOUR LIFE. Even if you are going through a tough time, be present with it and work with it to get through it. It will pass, so focus your attention on finding all the good in this moment. This is where mindfulness is so helpful because it keeps our hypervigilant mind from racing out of control.

Mindfulness meditation techniques
As mentioned above, the primary focus of mindfulness meditation is to observe your thoughts and feelings without judging them good or bad. The intent is to create a sense of stillness or "no thought." The point is to do

nothing but focus your attention on one thing by bringing it to the center of your awareness. This might be your breath, a sensation you feel in your body, an object, a sound, or a particular intention (or thought) you set for yourself. Make it as simple as possible. The goal is maintaining a calm awareness, allowing thoughts and feelings to come and go. Mindfulness meditation can be practiced anywhere, anytime, and for any length of time. Below are a few examples.

Breathing
- Sit or lie in a comfortable position. The object is not to fall asleep, but to "fall awake."[11]
- Focus only on your breath. Breathe in and out without forcing it.
- Observe how air comes into your body and how you release it.
- Observe how your chest or stomach rises and falls.
- If a distracting thought enters your mind that takes you away from your breath, accept it for what it is and let it pass. Put the center of your attention back on your breath.

Continue the process for as long you would like. For beginners, it might be only a couple minutes before your mind becomes too distracted and you lose focus on your breath entering and leaving your body. This is okay. The time you can sit in meditation will increase with practice and vary depending on the circumstances of that particular day. It is not so much the amount of time you spend meditating, but the quality and effectiveness of your practice.

Regarding breathing, the first thing you might want to do is allow yourself to breathe normally and then count how many seconds your in-breath is and how many seconds your out-breath is. This is your natural breathing rhythm at rest. There are many different breathing techniques for different purposes, but as a general rule, whenever you notice you are not in your natural breathing rhythm or when you feel the need to focus on your breath (perhaps in a stressful or anxious situation), tap into your natural breathing rhythm by actually counting what you previously practiced.

Counting
This is a variation of the breathing exercise, but also an exercise in concentration.
- Close your eyes and VERY SLOWLY count to ten.

- If your concentration wanders to anything but counting, start back at number one.
- When you reach ten, start over and repeat until you get the desired result, whatever that might be for you.

This practice sounds easier than it is. At first, it may go something like this: "One...two...three...this isn't so hard...oops, I'm thinking. Start over." "One...two...three...what do I want for dinner tonight? Start over." "One...two...three...four...now I've got it. I'm really concentrating now...oops. I did it again. Start over."

It's okay if your thoughts interfere. Don't beat yourself up. This happens to all of us. That is why meditation is called a practice. Even if you are only able to get to the number three or four before thoughts intrude, you have begun the process and are on your way. In fact, your awareness that this is happening is a practice in mindfulness in and of itself, so be proud of your efforts. The key is to not resist thoughts. Let them come and let them go.

Something you can also do is visualize each number to help keep your attention. For example, you can give each number a color, shape, movement, feel, and taste. Use your senses to bring the number to life so you can increase your awareness. You can also choose one number and focus solely on it. Remember that the purpose of these exercises is to clear your mind of clutter and simply be in the moment focused on one thing.

Conscious observation
This technique requires the use of an object. Any random object will do. In Jon Kabat-Zinn's program, *Mindfulness for Beginners*, he uses a raisin.
- Sit or lie in a comfortable position.
- Hold the object in your hand.
- Don't study it. Just observe it for what it is.
- Bring to awareness how it looks, feels, smells, and perhaps tastes. Do this without analyzing how you think it should look, feel, smell, or taste. Allow it to be just as it is and observe all of its unique attributes.
- Continue until you feel a sense of calm come over you.

These are just a few of examples of many mindfulness meditation practices. The interesting thing about them is that they seem so simple but can be quite challenging at first. Also, many of us incorrectly think that meditation requires lots of time, a special location, a special pillow to sit on, etc. Meditation can be practiced anywhere, anytime of the day. It can even be done with movement. I believe that we are in a meditative state whenever we are so focused on a task that we are not aware of anything else around us. Athletes call this being "in the zone." When "in the zone," athletes usually perform at their best.

In the movie, *For Love of the Game*, Kevin Costner is a pitcher for the Detroit Tigers. The movie shows him pitching at Yankee Stadium with a loud and boisterous crowd. Every time he looks at the catcher for the signal for the next pitch, he says to himself, "clear the mechanism." When he does this, all the noise in the stadium silences and all the people and other things around him become a blur. The only thing that he can see is the catcher's glove. This, to me, is an example of being in the zone and what I believe to be a meditative state. It should be noted that getting into a state like this requires practice. If you try meditation a few times and do not feel like it does much for you, you might not have given it enough practice. It requires repetition to learn how to do it and reap the reward.

Sometimes when I am working at the computer, I will sit back for a couple minutes and work on the breathing exercise I mentioned above. If I am waiting in line at the store, I might focus my attention for a minute or two on an object, be it something in my cart, a picture or word on a magazine, or a sign on the wall, and practice the observation meditation.

The more we practice, the easier it becomes, with the result being more mental calmness in our lives. With enough practice, you will do it and not even know it. Instead, you will feel an overall sense of peace in all aspects of your life because mindfulness has become part of your life. This is the goal.

Letting go
A main component of all meditation is letting go of the past and the future and just being present in the moment. It is important to remember that we have the power at any time to let go of the things that are bothering us. It is a choice and mindfulness meditation is very helpful in teaching our mind to become more disciplined to have the thought(s) we want. When we let go, we realize that we can go with the flow and not attach to what we want or push away what we don't want. We can just "be" with whatever is going on. Even when we are hit with an unexpected circumstance or event, we don't have to react with hypervigilance. We can remain calm throughout, and meditation is an incredible tool to help in this regard.

Someone once asked me a simple, yet profound, question when I was in the middle of something causing me great stress: "Do you want to be right or do you want to be happy?" I chose to be happy over being right. I was fighting so hard to be right and to be understood that it literally made me physically sick. Even though I may have been right, it did not matter because the other person saw it a different way so fighting them proved pointless. Their perspective was different and I couldn't do anything to change it.

My anger about this situation used to cause me physical and emotional pain. Already living with both, it made no sense to remain attached to a battle I couldn't win. In order to heal from the hurt of the situation, I had to release the white knuckle grip I had on trying so hard to make things right. I was allowing the actions of others contribute to my pain by not taking responsibility for myself. I had to remind myself that I was in control of how I respond to what others say and do, and that no one can make me feel a certain way unless I give them permission. When I stopped giving them permission, I began to feel better in all aspects of my life. It was also during this time when I focused a lot on mindfulness which helped me through it.

When you find yourself in situations such as this, talk to yourself. Ask yourself how relevant something someone says or does is in the grand scheme of things. Is it something that will bother you five or ten years from now, or even just a week, a month, or 6 months from now? Probably not, so release it now (let it go) so you can stop needlessly suffering.

To further describe what letting go means, I want to share a short piece from The Minimalists:[12]

Letting Go Is Not Something You Do

Letting go does not require a trip to Goodwill or a purchase from The Container Store. Letting go is not something you do. It is something you stop doing.
You stop pretending everything is precious.
You stop clinging to toxic relationships.
You stop acting like busy is a good thing.
You stop posturing as if achievements make you, you.
You stop thinking new habits will solve the problem.
You stop trying to "fix" everything.
You stop turning to breaking news for information.
You stop mistaking information for understanding.
You stop polishing the facade of success.

You stop chasing happiness.
No matter the fixation, be it possessions, people, or prosperity,
attachment is always suffering…Always.
When you let go of attachments, you pick up freedom, peace, equanimity.
But if you hold on, you'll get dragged.

Get lost

I sometimes say this to my coaching clients in a joking fashion because one of the biggest challenges for most of us is letting go of control and turning off the world to put their mind to rest. This can be accomplished many ways (meditation, yoga and other exercise, martial arts, walking/running, hobbies, and anything else where we are "in the zone"). For me, one of the best places to soothe my soul is in nature. I love the outdoors because it is the ultimate place to get in tune with our senses.

Take time to feel the sun on your face, the rain on your skin, the feel of the grass on your bare feet, watch the branches on a tree sway in the wind, notice a bird, butterfly, dragonfly, or a bee work and play in their surroundings. Smell the air, feel and listen to the wind, touch a tree, the dirt, the grass, the leaves, or anything you can physically grasp. Rather than run from the rain, stand in it and let the water shower over you.

Every sense is activated by nature which can really help us get more in tune with our body and feel more grounded. In fact, there is a practice called "grounding/earthing," which refers to contact with the earth's surface electrons by walking barefoot outside to transfer the energy from the ground into the body.

If you ever saw the movie *Pretty Woman*, recall the scene where Julia Roberts and Richard Gere are in the park and Julia removes Richard's shoes and socks so he can walk barefoot in the grass (he is a compulsive worker). Later in the movie, after he feels he has lost Julia and is also struggling with his business ethics, he does this on his own to feel what he felt when he was with her and gain perspective about his life.

There is a quote that says, "sell your cleverness and purchase bewilderment." In other words, get out of your thinking mind and just become bewildered, or lost, in your surroundings. Turn off your phone, close your computer lid, and "get lost." For me, something like a spider web, a bird's nest, the way a squirrel stores and hides nuts, watching a bird soar in the sky, watching water shimmer on a pond, lake, river, or ocean, the way branches on a tree grow, etc., all bring an awe-inspiring experience into my mind and body that offers great peace. These are also wonderful mindfulness activities.

According to Psychology Today,[13] studies show that taking breaks and allowing our mind to wander can help our brain retain information, refocus, gain fresh perspective, and make new connections between ideas. One study out of the University of British Columbia shows that mind wandering increases brain activity in the Default Mode Network (DMN), which deals with complex problem-solving. The DMN is system of connected brain areas that show increased activity when a person is not focused on the outside world. Just think of the eureka moments that occur while we're engaged in the most mundane of tasks, be it showering, driving to work, walking the dog, or doing the dishes.

A mindfulness technique to find peace from stress and pain

I have a client who suffers with a movement disorder, which is accompanied by chronic pain. He was sharing a situation where he was feeling stress, anxiety, and pain, and then how he mindfully focused on taking one deep breath and how much that one breath helped to calm him down in that moment. This reminded me so much of the research and work that I have done in the areas of trauma, stress and stress management, the power of breathing, and how it all relates to our physical health.

After our conversation, one of the main thoughts that came to me is how many of us live our lives with a sense of urgency. In other words, many of us have a hard time sitting with ourselves or sitting with our pain or anything unpleasant. What I mean by "sitting with," as I mention several times in this book, is not running from or emotionally reacting to or fighting things that we may not like about our situation in life. When we run or emotionally react, we initiate the fight or flight response which keeps stress levels high with adrenaline pouring out in bucketloads, which negatively impacts the symptoms of whatever problem we are experiencing.

Let's use people with anxiety as an example. Even when they are at rest, their mind is always going. I know this from personal experience, as someone who once suffered from severe anxiety and panic attacks. My mind was constantly racing. It still does at times. Eventually I realized that I had to learn to sit with my discomfort (be comfortable with what was uncomfortable). I had to learn to be okay with what I viewed as not okay. I had to learn to put my mind in pause mode to reduce the adrenaline running through my body.

To try and make it easier for me (and others) to find a sense of peace in the moment, I came up with a very quick and easy way to get into a better head space when we feel urgency, anxiety, and the need to rush around. As a side note, there was a time when my anxiety was so constantly ramped up that I literally could not sit for a few minutes without feeling this unbelievable urge to move around.

When I feel like the train is running off the track, so to speak, I say to myself, PAUSE. BREATHE. RESET. It stops me in the moment to keep me from running further off the track. It sounds so simple, and it really is. That's why I like to use it when I don't have time to fully meditate or do breathing exercises. It's amazing how just that 10 second PAUSE, BREATHE, RESET practice can totally change how I'm feeling in the moment.

The power of the pause is such that it can literally change your day and put you into a totally different mindset. The power of the breath is too long to go into here, but suffice to say, breathing has health benefits such as detoxification, it releases tension, relieves emotional problems, relaxes the body and mind, massages organs, strengthens the immune system, improves posture, improves digestion, balances the nervous system, boosts energy, improves cellular regeneration, and elevates moods, to name just a few.

Many people I speak with wake up in the morning with a sense of urgency and anxiety. This is a great time to practice PAUSE. BREATHE. RESET, and then begin your day. We have all probably heard the saying, "I got up on the wrong side of the bed today," to describe why someone is having a bad day. There is some truth to this because the way we start our day can often determine the kind of day we will have. It is probably best to start the day in a place of peace, so allow yourself that extra time to go into that place of peace. For some it is easy and for others it is a challenge. As with anything, it takes practice, so please practice this mindfulness technique, or others, if you are challenged in this area. It can have profound health benefits.

So, the question we should all be asking ourselves at this point is, "how often should I pause during the day; a moment, a minute, a half hour, an hour, or longer?" The answer is as often and for as long as you feel you need. Most of us probably don't do it as much as we need. Our lives can often feel like we are on a hamster wheel doing the same monotonous things or always have a feeling of trying to catch up. Just waiting a few minutes for something to warm up in the microwave can feel like hours to some of us. Tell yourself to PAUSE. BREATHE. RESET in these moments and whenever you feel out of control. It literally takes seconds to do, but the benefit can last hours when practiced on a regular basis.

I encourage you to try it and see how it makes you feel. You can do it anywhere at all that you feel the need to pull back. You can be at a traffic light or traffic jam, stuck in a long line at the store, or running around doing ten things at once. It is also helpful when your mind is racing, even at rest in the comfort of your home and you feel a sense of urgency, and for when you are experiencing pain, sadness, anger, or remorse. This is why I love this tool because it is so easy and quick, and great for "in the moment" anxiety.

Let go of what has happened.
Let go of what may come.
Let go of what is happening now.
Don't try to figure anything out.
Don't try to make anything happen.
Relax, right now, and rest.

Another approach to meditation is called RAIN, originally coined by Vipassana teacher Michele McDonald. RAIN stands for Recognize, Allow, Investigate, and Nurture.

Recognize what is happening.
Allow the experience of life to be just as it is.
Investigate with interest and care.
Nurture with self-compassion.

The following is from Psychology Today[14] which expands upon this:

R = Recognize: Notice that you are experiencing something, such as irritation at the tone of voice used by your partner, child, or co-worker. Step back into observation rather than reaction. Without getting into the story, simply name what is present, such as "annoyance," "thoughts of being mistreated," "body firing up," "hurt," "wanting to cry."

A = Accept (Allow): Acknowledge that your experience is what it is, even if it's unpleasant. Be with it without attempting to change it. Try to have self-compassion instead of self-criticism. Don't add to the difficulty by being hard on yourself.

I = Investigate (Inquire): Try to find an attitude of interest, curiosity, and openness. Not detached intellectual analysis but a gently engaged exploration, often with a sense of tenderness or friendliness toward what it finds. Open to other aspects of the experience, such as softer feelings of hurt under the brittle armor of anger. It's OK for your inquiry to be guided by a bit of insight into your own history and personality, but try to stay close to the raw experience and out of psychoanalyzing yourself.

N = Not-identify (Not-self): Have a feeling/thought/etc., instead of being it. Disentangle yourself from the various parts of the experience, knowing that they are small, fleeting aspects of the totality you are. See the streaming nature of sights, sounds, thoughts, and other contents of mind, arising and passing away due mainly to causes that have nothing to do with you, that are impersonal. Feel the contraction, stress, and pain that comes from claiming any part of this stream as "I," or "me," or "mine" - and sense the spaciousness and peace that comes when experiences simply flow.

As Tara Brach explains, "RAIN invites a shift in identity. It helps transform an angry, blaming person into a tender presence that gently holds whatever is going on. The whole fruit of our path and practice is to wake up from who we thought we were, which is usually separate and deficient in some way, and to rest in the vastness of heart and awareness that is our true nature."[15]

Prayer

Along with meditation, prayer is an important aspect of self-care for me. It helps quiet my mind and bring me closer to a higher power that I believe emanates all of us and all that surrounds us. Connecting to that higher power can be incredibly challenging when we have adversity in our lives because we can become so attached to our pain and suffering.

We do self-health checks all the time and we wonder and worry if we will be able to sleep, go to work, take care of the kids, pay the bills, go grocery shopping, etc. Being so body identified can make the remembrance of

God/Spirit/Source much more challenging. Prayer and meditation can help keep us balanced so we are not so controlled by our wandering thoughts.

The following quote comes from the book, *A Course in Miracles,* by Helen Schucman, which ties all of this together: "The memory of God comes to the quiet mind. It cannot come where there is conflict. For a mind at war against itself remembers not eternal gentleness. Let all this madness be undone for you, and turn in peace to the remembrance of God, still shining in your quiet mind."[16]

Quiet your mind by turning off the computer, phone, television, and radio. Go outside where you can listen to the sounds of nature or find a quiet place in your home or elsewhere that you feel at peace. Many people are uncomfortable NOT having noise (actual noise, drama, checking the phone constantly, watching the news, engaging in intense conversations, etc.) in their lives all the time because it means they have to deal with themselves and their problems. Technology is an especially great escape from reality. However, facing reality is the only way to battle and overcome what ails us. Seek out a quiet mind through prayer, meditation, or whatever brings you inner peace.

Sometimes we get angry when our prayers are not answered. Perhaps they are being answered and we are just looking at it the wrong way. When we pray for something or ask for something, we may not get exactly what we pray for. Instead, we get the opportunity to be what we pray for. You may recognize the following from the movie, *Evan Almighty*.

Morgan Freeman, who played God in the movie, said, "if someone prays for patience, you think God gives them patience or does He give them the opportunity to be patient? If he prayed for courage, does God give him courage, or does He give him opportunities to be courageous? If someone prayed for the family to be closer, do you think God zaps them with warm fuzzy feelings, or does He give them opportunities to love each other?"

Perhaps this is a better way to look at it... if we pray for courage, we the get the opportunity to be courageous. If we pray for love, we get the opportunity to be loving. If we pray for patience, we get the opportunity to be patient. If we pray for money, we get the opportunity to make money. If we pray for health, we get the opportunity to be healthy. Life is all about opportunity and it exists everywhere. Sometimes we just need a little more faith that everything is going to work out fine and things might not be revealed to us the way we anticipate. Going into silence helps us better see our answered prayers.

References

1) www.mercola.com, Retrieved January 30, 2014 from:
http://articles.mercola.com/sites/articles/archive/2014/01/30/eft-mapping-emotions.aspx?e_cid=20140130Z1_DNL_art_1&utm_source=dnl&utm_medium=email&utm_content=art1&utm_campaign=20140130Z1&et_cid=66919168&et_rid=413180808

2) Retrieved on February 25, 2014 from:
http://www.pnas.org/content/early/2013/12/26/1321664111

3) www.usnews.com, Retrieved January 30, 2014 from:
http://www.usnews.com/news/articles/2013/12/30/study-finds-emotions-can-be-mapped-to-the-body

4) Totten, Mindy. Retrieved on June 17, 2014 from: www.MindyTotten.com

5) Retrieved on February 25, 2014 from: http://www.huffingtonpost.com/dr-carmen-harra/affirmations_b_3527028.html

6) Retrieved on February 25, 2014 from: http://www.vitalaffirmations.com/

7) Retrieved on February 25, 2014 from: http://www.wikihow.com/Use-Affirmations-Effectively

8) Retrieved on February 25, 2014 from:
http://www.mindtools.com/pages/article/affirmations.htm

9) Retrieved on February 25, 2014 from:
http://www.healyourlifetraining.com/affirmations/positive-affirmations-for-health

10) Quinlan, K. Mindfulness for OCD and Anxiety, Retrieved June 30, 2014 from:
http://www.ocdla.com/blog/mindfulness-ocd-anxiety-1920

11) Kabat-Zinn, J. *Full Catastrophe Living*. (1990). New York, NY. Delta

12) Millburn, JF., Nicodemus.R. Letting Go Is Not Something You Do. The Minimalasts. Retrieved February 20, 2021 from:
https://www.theminimalists.com/stop/

13) Hanson, R. Let it R.A.I.N. We need to reduce what's negative and increasing what's positive. Psychology Today. May 2014. Retrieved on December 30, 2020 from:
https://www.psychologytoday.com/us/blog/your-wise-brain/201405/let-it-rain

14) Davis, J. In Praise of the Idle Mind. Psychology Today. September 2019.
Retrieved on February 22, 2021 from:
https://www.psychologytoday.com/us/blog/tracking-wonder/201911/in-praise-the-idle-mind-0

15) Miller, A. Buddhist psychotherapist and "RAIN" champion Tara Brach.
Retrieved December 29, 2020 from https://www.lionsroar.com/shining-a-light-buddhist-psychotherapist-and-rain-champion-tara-brach/

16) Schucman, H. *A Course in Miracles*. (1976). New York, NY. Viking: The Foundation for Inner Peace

Chapter 17
The power of hope

Living with adversity of any kind is sometimes reminiscent of the plight of Sisyphus, a king from Greek mythology. Sisyphus was king of Ephyra who was punished for chronic deceitfulness and condemned to an eternity at hard labor. His punishment was to roll a massive boulder up a hill until he reached the top. However, right before he reached the top, the boulder rolled all the way down and he had to repeat the task over and over. If you are struggling with something, this might sound like what you experience on a daily basis. It can be utterly frustrating and exhausting.

Although it may often feel like you are rolling a boulder up a hill only to have it roll back down and crush all your efforts, in the face of all your challenges, is it not an accomplishment to even get the ball rolling up the hill? I think so. Adversity challenges us in ways that we probably never imagined possible. These challenges make each accomplishment more rewarding. With this perspective, we realize that our adversity does not diminish our value as a person. In many ways it enhances our value.

If you have ever seen the movie, *The Shawshank Redemption*, which I mention a couple of times in this book, picture the moment when 'Andy Dufresne' (played by Tim Robbins) escaped from prison after crawling through a 500-yard sewage pipe. He came out on the other end where he fell into a stream with the rain pouring down on him. He tore off his shirt and raised his arms to the sky as a sign of freedom and triumph after being wrongfully incarcerated for nearly 20 years.

Just like Andy Dufresne, you will have days when you feel like you are trapped in a prison cell. There will also be days when you feel as he did when he reached the other side of the sewage pipe and was free. Savor these moments. Remember these feelings. Write about them in your journal. Talk about them. Celebrate them. Figure out what you did or did not do that made you feel better. Do whatever you can to leave an imprint on your mind about how you felt so you never forget. We all have the ability to go back to that place in our minds anytime we choose to get that same relief and peace. Visualization is a very powerful tool.

No matter your situation or dark hole you might be in, hope never dies. You can always get out. You do not have to live in the mental and emotional world of fear and loneliness that is like the prison cell and sewage pipe.

When you get knocked down, you can get back up. If you have done it before, you can do it again. It does not matter how many times you get knocked down, as long as you keep getting up and keep going. Strength is not defined by how powerful you are but how persistent you are. The only person standing in the way of everything you want to be is you.

Just like Andy Dufresne said in the movie, "there are places in this world that aren't made out of stone. There's something inside that they can't get to, that they can't touch; that's yours; hope. Hope is a good thing, maybe the best of things, and no good thing ever dies." Remember this as you live your life. Just because today may be a challenging day, there is always the gift of tomorrow.

How hope changed my life
Hope is a simple word that can mean so much to anyone going through a difficult time. It can mean the difference between giving up and hanging on. It can mean a tiny smile in the face of a devastating diagnosis. It is one word with no true definition — hope can mean anything you want.

I know this first-hand, having lived with dystonia for almost 20 years. At its most severe, my pain and other symptoms were so bad that I didn't feel like I had any quality of life or hope for one at all. I could barely function. I wanted to give up, but something kept me going... it was hope! Hope that I would eventually find tools to help my pain and change my life around from the 180 turn it took where I lost the ability to do almost everything. Hope that there was something to relieve my pain; something to relieve my depression; something to comfort my sorrow. Every day I wanted to end my life, but every day I also knew there was more out there for me to do with my life, which made me hang on.

I realize now, 20 years later, that the something I was looking for was hope, and I had it the whole time. I just didn't feel it moving through me until around year 5 of my diagnosis when I decided to learn with all my strength how to gain greater control of my symptoms and overall health, and dedicate my entire life to it. Not just to help myself, but others as well if possible. This is why I wrote my first book and this book, as well as continue to write articles, blogs, make videos, speak, and do podcasts. I do all I can to educate and raise awareness about the nature of living with adversity, above and beyond just health problems.

Two years after making the shift to dedicate my life to health, I began to share my story to let others know they were not alone and that hope was real. It was also the year I lost 150 pounds that I had gained since the onset of my symptoms. Two years later, I became certified as a professional life coach to directly help people on a regular basis, and then wrote my first book, *Diagnosis Dystonia: Navigating the Journey*. This, keep in mind, is from a guy who literally rolled around on the floor all day in pain for years.

I mention these accomplishments because I was at the end of my rope and was able to make a new life for myself, and you can too. It's about turning our problem upside down or "turning our mess into our message," as Robin Roberts said. I got to where I am now because of hope and never giving up, and it is because of hope and never giving up that I intend to continue improving upon the person I am every day.

What can help us remain hopeful and optimistic is to know that everything in life will not go as planned and that this is okay (see Chapter 21 for the section called, *Learning to be okay with what we view as not okay*). Sometimes not getting what we want or think we need is often a good thing, since there is often something greater on the horizon to fill its place. We just need to be more patient.

We must accept that life has obstacles, roadblocks, negative emotions, and circumstances that will derail our plans. Knowing this can help remove burden and worry, helping us better flow with life rather than resisting it. We must realize that life is not pure sailing, but an adventure full of valleys and victories. Consider the words of Helen Keller, an amazing inspiration in so many ways: "Although the world is full of suffering, it is also full of the overcoming of it."

If you think about it, most of us already have hope. Even the most pessimistic person has a glimmer of hope or they wouldn't keep going. Sometimes we are afraid to believe things can improve because it seems easier to doubt when pummeled with problems. This was how it was for me in my darkest days.

When your life is over, would you rather have spent your time believing you had some control over the state of your existence or would you rather have spent that time wondering or living in regret? It is not the amount of time we have in life, but how we spend that time. Eventually our days will come to an end, so use every penny of your life account, so to speak, on the highest quality of joy you can.

After writing this, I realized that much of it was in line with the ancient Greek philosophy of Stoicism. Stoicism sets out to remind us how unpredictable the world can be and how brief our moment of life is. It teaches us how to be steadfast and strong, and in control of our emotions.

There is a Stoic exercise and mindset for making the best out of anything that happens: this is to treat each and every moment, no matter how challenging, as something to be embraced, not avoided. To not only be okay with it, but to love it and be better for it. Just like a fire needs oxygen to burn, obstacles and adversity can become fuel for our potential, if we choose to view it this way.

When we look for opportunities in misfortune, we see options which can get us more enthusiastic about life and help calm our mind. This is critical because we cannot live in a healthy body and mind if we are riled up all the time about things that are not important or out of our control. Remember, the only thing we can control is our response to life events. Not life events themselves.

To summarize this section, I want to share a few quotes:

The road that is built in hope is more pleasant to the traveler than the road built in despair, even though they both lead to the same destination.
- Marion Zimmer Bradley -

Every difficulty in life presents us with an opportunity to turn inward and to invoke our own submerged inner resources. The trials we endure can and should introduce us to our strengths. Dig deeply. You possess strengths you might not realize you have.
- Epictetus –

Hope is important because it can make the present moment less difficult to bear. If we believe that tomorrow will be better, we can bear a hardship today.
- Thich Nhat Hanh -

Chapter 18
Finding meaning and purpose

What gives life meaning and purpose differs from person to person. However, I believe the one thing that holds true for most of us is that we want to live a life where we give value and feel valued. We want to follow our passion and interests that serve the highest purpose within us. There is great virtue in any endeavor where we choose to invest our time, if done with the right intentions and motives. The key component for finding and living a life with meaning and purpose is being true to ourselves and not compromising our beliefs, interests, opinions, thoughts, or feelings for the sake of others. It is our conviction to what we think and do that creates what we want in our lives.

Patanjali, the father of meditation and yoga, said the following: "when you are inspired by some great purpose; some extraordinary project; all your thoughts break their bonds. Your mind transcends limitations, your consciousness expands in every direction, and you find yourself in a new, great, and wonderful world. Dormant forces, faculties, and talents come alive, and you discover yourself to be a greater person by far than you ever dreamed yourself to be."

What this quote is saying is that when we become enthusiastic about life, it does wonders for not just our physical and mental health, but our entire lives. Nothing stands in our way when we have passion and enthusiasm. The word enthusiasm comes from the Greek word enthousiasmos, meaning "the God within." Over time the meaning of enthusiasm came to mean "craze, excitement, strong liking for something."

We can have enthusiasm for almost anything, from sports to cooking to reading and writing to teaching...anything. Enthusiasm breeds passion and when we have passion for something, we are inspired to transcend all boundaries. Live passionately and I promise you will find meaning and purpose, and ultimately a much happier life.

In several lectures I heard Dr. Wayne Dyer give, he shared the following story about finding meaning in our lives by being true to ourselves. He talks about happiness, but any feeling or aspiration can be inserted.

There once was a kitten in an alley chasing his tail around. Along comes an old alley cat that stops to watch the show for a while. Finally, the alley cat asks the kitten, "Why is it that you chase your tail?" Proudly, the kitten states, "I have just returned from Cat Philosophy School where I have learned two things. The first thing I learned is that happiness is the most important thing. The second thing is that happiness is located in my tail. I have determined that if I can just get a grip on my tail, I will have a hold on eternal happiness."

The old alley cat, wise beyond his years, laughs a little, "I am not as fortunate as you have been. I never attended Cat Philosophy School, but I have also learned that happiness is the most important thing and that it is indeed located in my tail. But what I have discovered is that if I chase after it I will never be able to reach it. Rather, if I just go about my business doing what it is I want to do, happiness will follow me everywhere I go."

As Henry David Thoreau said, "If you advance confidently in the direction of your OWN dreams, and endeavor to live the life which YOU have imagined, you will meet with a success unexpected in common hours." This is what the old alley cat was telling the kitten; if you follow your dreams and passions, happiness (his tail) will follow wherever you go. You don't need to chase it.

Adversity in life does not mean our lives lack meaning and purpose. Perhaps having adversity is to better fulfill our purpose because of all it teaches us. At least please be open to this possibility. Look within. Perhaps your adversity was the blessing in disguise to open your eyes to something you have been unable to see. The less we fight and the more we explore, the better our chances that something will be revealed. We are all here for a reason or we wouldn't be here at all. Be good to yourself and be patient with yourself, especially during the worst of life's storms. And unlike the kitten in the story above, stop chasing your tail. Live an authentic life by being true to yourself and let your "tail" find you.

Obstacles or opportunities

Life is ever evolving so it is important to remember that the storms in our lives do not last forever. As mentioned several times, opportunity exists in everything. Granted, the opportunities, or silver lining, can often be hard to find when we are going through tough times, but it exists. If we change our thinking around a little, the good fortune will reveal itself.

I believe the greatest opportunities in life are available to us when we are going through our darkest hours. We experience a wide range of emotions and feel at a crossroads. We feel lost. We can choose to let it take us down or we can look at this "in limbo" state as the starting point to find direction.

As I shared in my story in Chapter 1, I lost everything I was doing with my life when I got very sick with dystonia. Since then, I have greatly improved my symptoms, I lost 150 pounds, became a certified professional life coach, and authored a book that was recognized all over the world, and now a second book that you have in your hands. I also edited and published 5 other books for another author. I have been on international radio shows and podcasts and featured in various pain and neurology magazines. I have also been asked to speak at national conventions. I have achieved other things as well, but the point is that I went from literally living on the floor rolling around in pain for years wanting and waiting to die, to someone who has made a new life for himself.

It is very rare for me to talk about myself like this. It makes me uncomfortable. I am only sharing it to illustrate the point that it doesn't matter how deep our despair. We can always find a way out if we look for opportunities to turn our mess into a message, for ourselves and others.

I had to get lost before I could find myself. I had to lose all purpose in life to find my purpose, which I now know is to continue my personal growth and to teach and help others. I believe this is the purpose for all of us and we all do it in our own special ways. I just needed the gift of substantial adversity to show me my way.

As Napoleon Hill wrote in *Think and Grow Rich*, "one of the tricks of opportunity is that it has a sly habit of slipping in by the back door, and often it comes disguised in the form of misfortune or temporary defeat. Perhaps this is why so many fail to recognize opportunity."

As much as your challenge(s) in life have taken away parts of you, how often do you acknowledge how it has helped you grow as a person? How about the things it has taught you about yourself and others; how you have had doors close and others open that would have never otherwise been opened; met people and grown in ways you never would have otherwise? Instead of focusing on all the things you can no longer do or what has been lost, how often do you take time to appreciate all you have and can do?

While we most certainly need to grieve and vent at times (and I do and it feels good when I need to), we need to spend more time answering these questions and think more about how adversity has changed, or can change, our lives in positive ways. I am not saying, "oh, just be positive" in a passing, matter of fact kind of way. I am saying it with first-hand experience and knowledge about how damn hard it is to be in the pits of hell and how practicing proactive thinking can make life much easier on ourselves, even if we are in this mindset for just one minute a day. Just one minute a day of being open to the possibility that there is meaning in our pain and suffering. We can all spend one minute a day in this place, and I promise you that the time will increase the more you practice.

A journey of a thousand miles begins with a single step.
- Lao Tzu -

Complaining about anything is very easy and actually requires no effort, no matter the issue. We can all very easily go to that well and fill many buckets of things to complain about, but how many buckets do you fill with all the good that has come from your challenges? Not many because we don't do it enough, but if we took the time, we might be surprised just how much good there is in all our lives. This is where practicing gratitude can be life transforming.

I am not saying it is easy. It requires us to truly look deep inside to find those things. This is one of the gifts of adversity. It forces us to become mentally and physically tough. It forces us to look within and grow.

I have heard stories from so many people who made the effort to find the good fortune in their lives and are better people as a result. Many have come from some harrowing situations and triumphed by never giving in and finding new ways of living to help them adapt and accept their situation. Their stories teach me, humble me, motivate me, and help me question my perspectives so I can live a more productive life.

No matter your situation in life, some days are harder than others, and I believe the days I am being tested the most are when I am meant to learn the most. It might not be that day, but a day or two after (maybe longer) when I reflect on the experience and what it taught me. BUT, in order to learn, we must choose to look at the situation to find the meaning; not something many of us are wired to do. We are wired to avoid and ignore the bad days and move on when we feel good.

There is nothing wrong with this, but what happens when we are hit with bad days again? What did we do the previous times to help us better prepare for the upcoming tough days? If nothing, then we probably won't have the tools to effectively cope with tough times. This is one of the many lessons we can learn from our difficult days.

All of this begins with changing our inner and outer dialogue about the struggles of life. It can do wonders for our emotional well-being and helps us remain hopeful in the present moment and about our future, during good times and bad.

Some people are not at the point where they can look at adversity from this perspective, and that is okay. There was a time I couldn't imagine there was anything positive about my struggles in life. In time, starting with one minute a day, my mindset has changed. While I have lost certain things in my life, as we all have, I have also gained many things. This reminds me of the quote by Robin Williams in the movie *Patch Adams* when after losing the love of his life he said, "I've lost everything. But I've also gained everything." He didn't let the death of his beloved stop him from passionately pursuing his dream to become a doctor. It made him even more passionate. In his loss, he learned more about the power of his life and those around him, all of whom made a significant impact on each other.

I believe we are far luckier in so many ways than people who never lived with adversity. The things we endure make us stronger and help us gain new appreciation and wiser perspectives about things. BUT, we have to be open to learning in these tough situations. Focusing on how to peacefully cohabitate with your challenge/adversity versus angrily listing all the ways it has ruined your life is the way to find peace and joy. To further illustrate this point, I want to share a poem written by a friend of mine.

How would you know to experience the true pleasures of life if you've never experienced the pain? Sorrow and suffering of any kind, in time, reveal an exquisite beauty; a secret that is meant to be found.
Life is worth living.
When you learn to embrace the pain and accept what is, THAT is when life will begin. Just when you think you can't take it anymore, When you are ready to give up, don't! That is when the change is about to arrive. If you feel your life has fallen apart, rebuild from the ground up. That is the beauty in being broken.

I don't think she meant that we are broken, although when she wrote this, she may have felt broken, as I am sure many of us have at times. My take is that many of us live life not appreciating all we have until it is gone. If we have something (like a health challenge) that reduces our ability to do many of the things we once enjoyed, it should remind us how nothing should be taken for granted and to live life to the fullest all the time.

When I feel particularly unwell or "broken," the words of this poem help me better enjoy the good days and cope better on the not so good days. Each rough day provides me time to reflect and an opportunity to rise a stronger person.

The most compelling part of this poem for me is when she says, "when you are ready to give up...don't! That is when the change is about to arrive." This could not be truer from my perspective. The less we fight against and instead embrace what is, opening ourselves up to all possibilities, the better chance our lives will be transformed for the better.

Think of a time when you felt in limbo about your life or were at a crossroad and not sure what to do. You might be there right now. How does it feel? More than likely you feel lost and confused, but here is the catch that most of us don't embrace enough, if ever; the best way to find ourselves is when we are lost. Picture yourself literally standing at the center of an intersection with crossroads. You have 4 directions you can go (more if you go in between the crossroads). If we look at it this way, crossroads means we have options, not roadblocks.

We can always rebuild no matter how much things have fallen apart. The pieces may not go where they once did, but that is okay. We have to trust that it is okay. Things may not be how you want them to be, but maybe this is where the pieces are supposed to be. To be happy, we must make adjustments and find new things in our lives that fit in with the new us. This is how we effectively adapt. Everything in life is determined by how we think about things so if we change the way we look at things, the things we look at change, just like the crossroads I mentioned above.

Instead of recognizing the opportunities that lie within our "misfortune," as mentioned above, we often get angry and become closed minded. Some even feel vengeful, as if the world is out to get them. It is imperative that during these times we persevere, open our minds, and really pay attention.

It is then that we realize that life is happening for us, not to us. As Zig Ziglar said, "you cannot tailor make your situation in life, but you can tailor make your attitudes in those situations." This perspective helps us remain hopeful in the present moment and about our future.

We have to stop saying life shouldn't be this way or that way; it should be this way, because it is this way! We have to stop resisting what is, move forward, and make great things happen. I promise that yelling at your problem will not fix your problem.

With this in mind, I made a promise to myself a long time ago. I said, "I do not know why this health issue happened to me and I lost everything, but I do know one thing for sure; something great is going to come from it because I refuse to go through this for nothing." I first heard this from author and motivational speaker, Sonia Ricotti. I carry this thought with me every day. It is most helpful on days when I feel like throwing in the towel.

Train yourself to be thankful for closed doors. They often guide us to the right door. Be thankful for what you have and you will end up having more. Don't start your day with broken pieces of yesterday. Today is a new day to start fresh. Every day is another chance to change your life. Wake up, say thank you for the opportunities of the day, and take that first step out of bed. Let the rest of the day fall into place.

> *When the Japanese mend broken objects, they aggrandize the damage by filling the cracks with gold. They believe that when something's suffered damage and has a history, it becomes more beautiful.*
> - Billie Mobayed -

The gold is not meant to fix us. It is meant to add a new dimension to our being, much like when we are forced, by change or circumstance, to create a life in the "new normal." By doing so, our understanding is broadened and deepened, and we become more beautiful.

> *What seems nasty, painful, or evil can become a source of beauty, joy, and strength if faced with an open mind. Every moment is a golden one for him who has the vision to recognize it as such.*
> - Henry Miller –

Post Traumatic Growth[1-4]

We often hear the term Post Traumatic Stress Disorder (PTSD), a psychological health condition triggered by a traumatic event. PTSD is commonly used in the context of military personnel returning from active duty, but it applies to anyone who has faced traumatic events such as sexual or physical assault, an acute or chronic health condition, natural disasters, the unexpected death of a loved one, or an accident. Families of victims can also develop PTSD, as can emergency personnel and rescue workers. Symptoms may include flashbacks, nightmares, and severe anxiety, as well as uncontrollable thoughts about the event.

Most people who experience a traumatic event will have reactions that may include shock, anger, nervousness, fear, and even guilt. These reactions are common and for most people, go away over time. For a person with PTSD, feelings of intense fear, helplessness, or horror continue and may even increase, becoming so strong that they keep the person from living a normal life.

A term we hear far less about, if at all, is called Post Traumatic Growth (PTG). PTG refers to people who become stronger and create a more meaningful life in the wake of tragedy or trauma. They don't just bounce back, which is resilience; they bounce higher than they ever did before.

This concept is not new. For centuries people believed that suffering and distress can yield positive changes. It wasn't until 1995 that the term Post Traumatic Growth was coined by Richard Tedeschi, Ph.D., and Lawrence Calhoun, Ph.D., psychologists at the University of North Carolina, Charlotte.

PTG is characterized by people changing their views of themselves, such as an increased sense of strength; "if I lived through that, I can face anything." They tend to show more gratitude and have greater acceptance of their vulnerabilities and limitations, and also develop a sense that new opportunities have emerged from their struggle. Relationships are enhanced; people come to value their friends and family more, feel an increased sense of compassion for others and a longing for more intimate relationships.

They can also experience an increased sense of connection to others who suffer. They gain a greater appreciation for life in general, finding a fresh, positive outlook each day; they re-evaluate what really matters in life, become less materialistic, and are better able to live in the present. Another common feature is a change or deepening in spiritual beliefs.

I was never diagnosed with PTSD, but I lived through periods of intense fear, anger, desperation, and hopelessness after experiencing a dramatic shift in my life due to dystonia, chronic pain, and other events. Having worked through a lot of these emotions over the years and letting go of my attachment to many of the things that cause them, I have seen a significant amount of growth.

For example, I appreciate many things I once took for granted. I realize how fragile life is and how it should be honored by treating ourselves and others with love and respect. I have a much deeper appreciation for people who struggle with life challenges. I have come to better understand the meaning of loss, which has increased my ability to live in gratitude. I have also found greater meaning in my life and feel a deeper spiritual connection.

Adversity can truly be a source of growth for all of us in ways we probably never imagined, and research has shown that in the face of great challenges, significant human and spiritual growth can occur. For it to take place, it is crucial that we are open to the possibilities that lie within our "misfortune."

We must abandon hatred and anger, for it will only worsen the pain we feel, preventing us from any kind of growth. Every experience in life is a gift. There is something to be learned from everything to help catapult us to a higher level of being, if we choose to embrace this belief.

A healthy way to deal with problems is to look at them as opportunities for growth.
- C Norman Sheely, MD, PhD -

References
1) www.ptgi.uncc.edu, Retrieved August 23, 2014 from: https://ptgi.uncc.edu/what-is-ptg/
2) Stephen, J. What Doesn't Kill Us: The new psychology of posttraumatic growth, Retrieved on August 23, 2014 from: http://www.psychologytoday.com/blog/what-doesnt-kill-us/201402/posttraumatic-growth
3) www.livehappy.com, Retrieved August 23, 2014 from: http://www.livehappy.com/science/positive-psychology/science-post-traumatic-growth
4) www.webmd.com, Retrieved August 23, 2014 from: http://www.webmd.com/anxiety-panic/guide/post-traumatic-stress-disorder

Chapter 19
Self acceptance

Most of us are our own worst enemy and have a knack for beating ourselves up way too often about way too many things, such as different body features we don't like or how we said or did something in a work or social situation, or critiquing a meal we made, a do-it-yourself home project, or something similar. An example I would like to share about myself is the way I process certain experiences. Not only do I have a certain way that I process things, but I sometimes beat myself up for the way I process them. I know others do the same, so I hope this is relatable.

We all have a unique way that we process life events and none of them are right or wrong. Judging our process is where we need to be careful. The process for me tends to be exhausting because I can play events and interactions over and over in my head, often questioning my perspective, thoughts, comments, judgments, etc., as well as all the same things about the other people involved. Did I come off okay? Did I say the right thing? Was I kind or did I maybe offend someone? What are they saying about me?? Why did they say this when I said that? I could go on, but I think you get the point that my overthinking brain can get a little out of control. Not always, but it happens from time to time.

I can go through this in a few minutes or as long as a couple of days. This is the case for all things; not just painful times. Even the fun times I might process in a similar way. In a nutshell, I can be an overthinker, sometimes to my benefit and sometimes to my detriment. When it is to my detriment, I have to talk myself down because it can be so painfully exhausting.

Eventually during my processing, I reach a point where I almost feel like I am torturing myself and I get angry that I do this to myself. I then shift my thoughts and talk to myself in a loving, rational way, saying something like the following: "Tom, this is how you process things. It is who you are and how you are. It's okay to be this way. Allow yourself to process things the way you are wired to process things. There is nothing wrong with it or you. Stop fighting who you are. A big part of the reason you process things this way is because you are sensitive, caring, fair, and kind. You want to make sure you did and said things that were thoughtful. Take yourself off the hook. This is who you are and how you are, and there is nothing wrong with it. Honor yourself for these qualities rather than tear yourself down."

Since I began saying this, I don't process things as intensely anymore, and if I do, it is not so exhausting. I'm just a person who feels things very deeply, which can be painful at times, but I am okay with who I am and telling myself what I said above is a way of forgiving myself when I start to beat myself up over being me.

When we think bad things about ourselves, we can fool ourselves into thinking that others might judge us the same way, which I think is rarely the case. Most people don't even notice our insecurities and we tend to forget or ignore our good qualities because we often only see what we view as flaws. Most others do not see those so-called flaws and value who we are more than we are often aware.

I want to share two short stories that have powerful lessons about how much we make a difference.

The Cracked Pot

A water bearer had two large pots, each hung on the ends of a pole which he carried across his neck. One of the pots had a crack in it, while the other pot was perfect and always delivered a full portion of water. At the end of the long walk from the stream to the house, the cracked pot arrived only half full.

For a full two years this went on daily, with the bearer delivering only one and a half pots of water to his house. Of course, the perfect pot was proud of its accomplishments, perfect for which it was made. The cracked pot was ashamed of its imperfection and miserable that it was only able to accomplish half of what it had been made to do.

After 2 years of what it perceived to be a bitter failure, it spoke to the water bearer one day by the stream. "I am ashamed of myself because this crack in my side causes water to leak all the way back to your house."

The water bearer said to the pot, "did you notice that there are flowers on your side of the path, but not on the other pot's side? That's because I have always known about your flaw and I planted flower seeds on your side of the path. Every day while we walk back, you've watered them. For two years I have been able to pick these beautiful flowers to decorate the table. Without you being just the way you are, there would not be this beauty to grace the house."

The pencil maker

A pencil maker told the pencil five important lessons just before putting it in the box:

1) Everything you do will leave a mark.
2) You can always correct the mistakes you made.
3) What is important is what is inside you.
4) You will undergo painful sharpenings which will only make you better.
5) To be the best pencil, you must allow yourself to be held and guided by the hand that holds you.

This story should remind you that you are a special person with unique talents and abilities. Only you can fulfill the purpose for which you were born. Never allow yourself to think that your life is insignificant. Like the pencil, always remember that the most important part of who you are is what's inside of you.

The most beautiful people we have known are those who have known defeat, known suffering, known struggle, known loss, and have found their way out of the depths. These persons have an appreciation, a sensitivity, and an understanding of life that fills them with compassion gentleness, and a deep loving concern.
Beautiful people do not just happen.
- Elisabeth Kubler-Ross –

Accepting our challenges with compassion

We all must understand that in a moment's notice, life can change on a dime from subtle to dramatic ways, but the circumstance need not be how we define ourselves. It is learning to be okay with what we, at the moment, do not view as okay. This is an important perspective shift.

Reaching the point where we can be at peace with all challenges is one of the hardest things we will ever do, but the key to a joyful life. Everything that happens in life is just one chapter among many other chapters. It is not the book of our life.

Work hard every day to think about your life right now and not the life you once had. The past is over and as much as you may miss parts of your former self, you must let go and live in the present, accepting the new you with compassion and understanding.

Focus on things just as they are; not the way you think they should be. The changes that can come out of this acceptance are incredible. Take each day one at a time and fully embrace even the most seemingly minor accomplishments. If you have any kind of challenge, the things you do now are much greater accomplishments than before when everything was much easier. Honor yourself for this! With some of the intense things many of you have to deal with, sometimes just getting out of bed is an accomplishment. Please acknowledge this.

Saying how much we hate anything in life will not make it go away. I promise. Unless we take action to change what we hate that is in our power to change, just saying how much we hate something with no action is pointless. I mention this many times in this book because it is something we must never forget.

Instead, find a way to cohabitate with all adverse conditions because no amount of anger will ever take anything away. This has been one of the most important things I have learned (still learning) to better manage all the symptoms that come with dystonia, both physical and emotional/mental. I had to learn to live with it rather than fight with it. The more I do this, the less power it has over me. This might sound counterintuitive, but it might be the best way for us to find peace and healing. Stop waging war on your health problem or any other problem. You will only get worse. The stress of it all will break you down.

As I have mentioned several times. I had years of ruthless symptoms where I could barely speak sometimes because of the breathtaking pain, to starting a business, becoming a life coach, and writing a book that was recognized by the Michael J Fox Foundation (*Diagnosis Dystonia: Navigating the Journey*). I still deal with some pretty rough symptoms, but my mind is in a better place where I am more at peace with how things are. This leads to greater acceptance and a greater ability to be more productive.

I am not nearly as productive as I once was but beating myself up over this is a complete waste of time and energy. I would rather focus what energy I have on my abilities, rather than all that is wrong with me. I invite you to do more of the same. Accept what is by learning to deal with it, rather than dwell in the past or on everything you can't do. Focus on your abilities that exist now. I know most of you do more during your day than you give yourself credit. Please shift your mindset and celebrate yourself. Although I am not as productive as I once was, I honor myself every day for what I accomplish, which is a lot given some of my challenges. I prefer to call them challenges instead of limitations because "limitations" creates a limited mindset that I want to avoid. An exercise you can do is to write down 5 things you acknowledge about yourself at the end of every day. This shifts our focus away from all that is wrong with us and trains the mind to see our lives differently.

You need not feel any shame for anything that gets tough and for how you are dealing with it. Life gets messy. Simple as that. Take control and do what is best for you so you can better manage today, and just today. Tomorrow will take care of itself, and please always remember that it is not what happens to us in life that defines us. It is what we do with it that defines us.

We all have periods when we feel overmatched and not up to the challenges, but we always get through the day. If you have a racing mind full of questions and concerns, please reach out to the many support services in your area and groups online so you can talk with others who can relate. Life can get very distressing and exhausting. Share what you are thinking and feeling. Listen to what others are saying. You will find that you are far from alone.

There's nothing wrong with being open about struggling with our faults or venting or complaining every now and then. We must, however, accept the fact that our thoughts and actions are the foundation by which we live our lives, which can be to our benefit or detriment depending on our patterns of thought, so please be very careful.

The biggest and most complex obstacle we will ever have to overcome is our own mind. We are not responsible for everything that happens to us in life, but we are responsible for undoing the self-defeating thinking patterns that undesirable outcomes create. Thinking better takes discipline and practice. This is what I love about life coaching. Not only do I help my clients think better and live better, I learn more about the importance of this every day, and it holds me accountable to do the same.

Life's challenges are not supposed to paralyze you.
They're supposed to help you discover who you are.
- Bernice Johnson Reagon -

Chapter 20
Compassion and understanding

I think a safe assumption to make is that we all desire is to be understood by the people in our lives. Everyone is dealing with something and we all need a shoulder to lean on, which can be hard if the ones we love most and need most cannot relate to or understand our challenges.

I have a coaching client who lives with chronic pain. She has a close friend who does not understand why she has to spend so much time lying down or use ice and heat and do other self-care activities. She says things like, "well if you can work then you should be able to do x, y, z." What this person fails to understand, even though she has been told, is that 4 hours of work means that she needs about 2-3 hours of recovery time, if not more some days. It's also a part time job where she works two to four days a week because that is all she can handle. She loves her job and it gives her identity, but it is extremely painful most days. She endures the pain, which means she has to sacrifice time and energy in other areas. Not having her friend understand this is very frustrating.

However, my client's friend also has a difficult, hectic life. My client does not fully understand what that is like, so she is judgmental of her. It works both ways. While both desire a better relationship, they pick fights with each other, rather than work to accept and understand the other person. It is a war of egos.

I suggested she stop challenging her friend anytime she comments about the struggles in her life and instead acknowledge her and try to understand. Better yet, just be understanding that she also has issues to deal with. My message to her was, "treat your friend and talk to your friend when she is having a tough time the way that you want her to treat and talk to you." Since she began doing this, the stress of the relationship has been reduced. It even reduced her husband's stress.

For those who are wondering what it is like to live with chronic pain like my client (and me)… it is exhausting! It is like a full-time job so anything we do above and beyond what we need to do to get through the day takes extraordinary effort sometimes. Not only are we physically and mentally tired from battling our symptoms all day, we are also tired of explaining why we cannot join in activities; recreational, social, work, or otherwise. Sadly, because it is hard to understand, some people can be quite harsh with their judgments. Perhaps better words are indifferent and dismissive. Some of the things I have heard people say include:

"You'll just have to tough it out."
"It's all in your head."
"You're just having a bad day."
"Everybody gets tired and has pain."
"Get over it already!"
"If you would just get out more."
"It can't be that bad."
"There are people worse off than you."
"If you would just exercise more."
And one of my personal favorites: "You STILL have that??"

While I value the opinions of people in my life, these totally miss the mark when it comes to a chronic health condition, or a short-term health condition or other challenge a person is working through. It can be applied to anything and anyone. For my own sanity, I have had to learn to be independent of the opinion of others and live my life the best way I know how so I am most comfortable, regardless of what others think.

Someone's opinion of us does not have to become our reality. Finding comfort should be our number one priority, or at least at the very top of our list; not pleasing others. Hopefully, family, friends, and co-workers will respect us for this. For those who don't, perhaps the following list will help them better understand your reality... and this is the short list! Let them know that these are things that may happen because of your situation, particularly if it is related to your physical or mental health:

- We may not reply to messages right away or answer the phone.
- Some days we can easily do certain things that we are unable to do the next day. Every day is a mystery to us. Some days, it is hour to hour not knowing how we will feel, which can cause anxiety and depression. The persistent, nagging feeling of not knowing from moment to moment how we will feel and what we can do is agonizing for us.
- It might take a while for us to recover from what seems to others as the most mundane or easiest of daily tasks. On a personal note, this is my reality every day. Generally speaking, for pretty much every hour of work, especially physical, I need a minimum of 1-4 hours

recovery time. Some days, just a tiny bit is all I can do for that day. Other days I can do a lot more. I NEVER know.

- We might cancel plans, maybe even at the last minute.
- We might leave a party or other social gathering unexpectedly or earlier than planned.
- Sometimes we might suddenly need to lie down and rest, and maybe need to use ice, heat, a massage machine, trigger point tool, or something similar.
- Our level of energy might change at a moment's notice and we can be exhausted. In addition, many of us also have a racing mind so it is hard to rest when we need it most. Sometimes we need to isolate ourselves to tune out the world for a little while so we can recharge.

This list is brief, but I think it sums things up well for a lot of us. We must be honest with others and also respect that what we go through is not always easy for them either.

When you are faced with people who are tough to be around that do not try to understand, it might be helpful to follow the advice of Marc and Angel Chernoff who have a blog called, *Marc and Angel Hack Life*.

- Breathe deeply and often.
- Remind yourself that we can't control other people.
- Do not take other's behavior personally. Choose to see the good in them.
- Let go of the ideals and expectations you have about others that causes unnecessary frustration, arguments, and bouts of anger.
- Remember that when others are being difficult, they are often going through a difficult time we may know nothing about, so give them empathy, love, and space.
- There is one I would like to add to Marc and Angel's list which is, "always live in a place of gratitude and forgiveness." This sets us free from the pain we allow others to inflict upon us. The key word is "allow" because no one can make us feel a certain way unless we let them. People will be how they will be and there is little we can do about that, except how we react or respond to their behavior.

We need to put ourselves in a position of power and not accept labels that may be put upon us such as lazy, mental, apathetic, sympathy seeking, hypochondriac, or any other thoughtless label. This is especially relevant to a chronic health condition. We need to be careful not to label or judge ourselves either. Honor yourself for the efforts you make every day to live the highest quality life possible.

Lastly, pace yourself and ask others for their patience. Most importantly, be patient with yourself. Take responsibility for your challenges in life so you can make the best decisions. This is your life. Own it and live it how you choose, independent of what others think.

While it is not possible for anyone to truly understand what someone else is going through in life, and it can be about anything, it is comforting to know that those closest to us have some idea or at least make us feel like they do. They may not fully understand what we are experiencing and feeling, but acknowledging our challenges goes a long way. It makes us feel less alone.

The one thing most people close to me have come to understand over the years is that they don't understand. What they do understand and accept is that there are times when dystonia and pain get the better of me and I need to take time to care for myself. This understanding helps me tremendously. Being open with them about my symptoms has helped a lot. I don't mind if people don't understand how it is to live this way. I just ask that they be understandING and compassionate, and make sure I be the same for them. Everyone is going through something so compassion is as necessary as air.

I am much better at accepting the fact that life has changed and I may never again be able to do some of the things I used to, but the daily grind is what is most difficult. Dystonia and pain are draining, both physically and mentally, and then certain activities, or sometimes just sleeping wrong, can worsen symptoms even more.

Many people do not understand this reality. Not knowing from day to day how functional I will be can feel unsettling. This is my biggest challenge because I am always doing a balancing act.

Some people become upset when they have an acute injury or illness that sidelines them from a favorite activity or hobby for only a few days or weeks. Imagine if a few weeks turned into a few years or even a lifetime. This is how it is for many of us with chronic health conditions.

I know that my life with dystonia and pain, particularly the mental side, is very hard to understand, so I don't expect people to get it. I also don't want anyone to feel sorry for me. We all have challenging things to deal with in our lives.

What would be helpful, and this goes for every single person alive today, is if we asked each other more often how we are feeling and how we are managing with everything going on in our lives. This form of acknowledgement reminds us that we are not alone and that we matter. It is also important that we answer honestly.

We can get empathy from others, but a complete understanding is probably out of reach and something we have to acknowledge and accept. This being the case, embrace that you may not get the understanding you desire so you don't beat yourself up over something which you have little to no control.

Life is deep and simple. What our society gives us is shallow and complicated. Be a first rate version of yourself. Not a second rate version of someone else.

Asking for help is good for us and also helps others

For more than half of the 20 years I have had dystonia, I had a hard time asking for help. I was certainly helped significantly by my loved ones, but it came with guilt, until I put myself in their shoes. They wanted to help. They just didn't always know how to help, and I didn't know how to ask because I struggled with the reality that I needed a lot of help.

As a competitive athlete, private business owner, traveler, go getter, nothing stands in my way kind of person, my life became the total opposite of that independent, self-sufficient person when dystonia hit and the severe pain took over. I needed help big time, but I still fought for my independence. Wow, did it wear me out trying to do it on my own!

One of my emotional barriers asking for help was feeling guilty for having a condition where I needed help. I was living in shame and thought I could still do everything on my own, which was silly because I was literally barely able to get off my living room floor, where I spent most of the day because sitting or standing for any period of time caused screaming pain that made it near impossible to even prepare a quick meal, let alone drive, work, grocery shop, clean my house, do laundry, etc.

I was also negligent asking for help because I felt like a burden to others. Interestingly, those closest to me often felt guilty and a burden because they didn't know how to help and thought they were making my situation worse by not doing more. Little did we know, we all felt helpless and guilty... for no reason. This is where clear communication is vital by letting others know what we need and letting them know that we are here for them as well. Even just saying that you don't know what to do or what kind of help to ask for can be helpful and open the door to mutual understanding.

When I surrendered to the fact that I needed help to do pretty much everything, I knew I had to break down my wall and ask for it. When I finally let others in, negative feelings about myself and my sense of helplessness and unworthiness dissipated. When I finally began to share my feelings and what kind of help I needed, the isolation and shame began to lift. When I finally realized that it was okay to ask for and accept help, and that I was not being a burden, my life and those around me began to change. Life became much lighter for all of us and to my surprise, others began to open up about their struggles which made me feel less alone. It also put me in a place to be helpful, which took some of the focus off me and my problems.

A couple years ago, my sister had foot surgery and developed an infection that complicated the issue. She was in great pain and had difficulty walking, so she needed to rely on her family and friends to do a lot of things for her. She felt bad for having to lean on everyone so much. One, because she hated being in this situation (which we can all relate to) and two, she felt like she was being an inconvenience. The reality of the situation is that none of us thought twice about coming to her assistance any time of day. We love her and care about her so we will do all we can to help her, just as she has done for all of us and will again in the future. It makes us feel good to know that we can be there for her.

Asking for help and relying on other people when necessary does not indicate weakness or failure. It is a sign of strength. It takes courage and humility to admit we need help. It is also a gift we give to others. This is the part we often don't think about. Most people who care about us want to help, and it feels good to help, but they don't know how until we tell them what we need. Sharing our feelings with others so they can be there for us is a gift for everyone.

What I also learned is that by sharing what I was struggling with and asking for help gave other people permission to open up about things that were bothering them that they were uncomfortable talking about. So, we are not only doing ourselves a favor. We open the door for others to work through their problems as well. The other cool thing from a biological perspective is that there is an increase in serotonin when people are on the giving or receiving end of help or a kind deed. Thus, helping others is a very healthy activity! Many helping hands are there. We just need to reach out.

While there are relationships that have been ruined because of many different life challenges, I have seen many that have become stronger. It is all a matter of how we deal with it individually and collectively. We need to listen just as much as we talk, if not more. Mutual sharing is the best way for us to help one another and strengthen our relationships.

Understand that some people have a strong desire to fix us. When they realize that they are unable to, some will retreat and then less of our needs are met. It is our responsibility to let our spouses, parents, kids, siblings, and friends know that it is okay that they cannot fix us and that we don't expect them to.

Sometimes we just need to talk. We need to just have people listen to us without trying to fix us or change anything. We need to feel that they are here for us and the best way they can do that is to just listen, open their arms and hearts, and simply acknowledge our feelings. Not change our feelings. Acknowledge our feelings to let us know that we matter and how we feel matters. It is important that they remind us that we are loved and not alone. Sometimes all we need is a hug.

Comparison is not a compassionate activity

Theodore Roosevelt said, "comparison is the thief of joy." What an insightful comment. Anytime we compare our lives with someone else or how our lives were before whatever circumstance caused it to change, we reject who we are right now, which will always leave us feeling empty. We know all the dirty details of our situation and only the surface information about others. It is self-punishment to hold ourselves up to some outside vague standard. We should measure the value of our lives by our principles.

Just because someone may be able to do things you can't or find difficult does not make you any better or worse. There may very well be things you can do with ease where others struggle. Either way, it doesn't matter. You and everyone in your life should focus on the strengths that exist and the accomplishments achieved. Put away the measuring stick unless you are using it to measure and compare ONLY YOUR growth from one day to the next.

The only people we should compare ourselves to, if we do any comparing at all, is ourselves because there's no way we can ever accurately measure our progress based on someone else's life.
- Tom Seaman -

Simplify your life
Today's world is so chaotic that it is hard to sit in peace and focus our attention on one thing. It demands so much effort and practice, but that's okay. The troubles can be minimized if we break them into smaller pieces. Practice not worrying about the big, busy day you have to get through. Just get through the morning. Just get through the first item on your to-do list and go from there. BE in the moment. Tell yourself, out loud, to STOP or SLOW DOWN. Count to ten if you have to. Whatever needs to be done to slow down, do it. Simplify your time and it will simplify your life, bringing you peace you may have never experienced before. What a feeling it is to give ourselves a break and live with love and compassion for ourselves.

You can't kiss your own elbow
This is another way of saying, "it is what it is." Some things simply are what they are and there is nothing we can do about it other than accept it. For a long time, I very much disliked the statement, "it is what it is." I thought it was a copout. I always thought another line should be added that says, "but it doesn't have to be."

For much of my life, I believed that nothing had to be how it was if we didn't want it to be. When I realized there are some things we can't do much or anything about, my attitude changed. This made a very positive impact on my ability to cope with life challenges. The only thing we can really change about most things is how we respond to them.

When we are able to let go of what can't be changed, we are challenged to change ourselves; to grow beyond the unchangeable, and that transforms our life if we accept the challenge. When I think about life from this perspective, I really like the saying, "it is what it is" because "it" (life events/circumstances) can't be anything else, so "it" truly "is what it is." "It" can't be anything else. How we deal with "it" is what matters. This is why I named this section, "you can't kiss your own elbow," because some things are the way they are and there is nothing we can do about them - how many of you are trying to kiss your elbow right now? ☺

That said, I am not at all resigned to think that I can't change things about myself or the circumstances of my life, and that you can't either. I have busted my tail to better accept the challenges placed before me and I work to improve things all the time. When I approach challenges in a proactive instead of reactive fashion, it is easier to find ways to make the best of difficult situations.

By working to find peace of mind in the present moment, no matter what I am going through, it helps me better roll with the punches day in and day out. Every night I go to bed praying that I wake up with an easier day than the last one. If this does not happen, I am better at not fighting what I can't change in the moment. I can only change how I respond to how I feel and be grateful for what I am able to do on that given day. This eases my emotional tension which reduces the physical tension I feel. This is self-compassion in action.

Chapter 21
Perception means everything

I want to begin this chapter with a short story about perception:

A married couple moves into a new neighborhood. The next morning while they are eating breakfast, the woman sees her new neighbors hanging the washing outside.
"That laundry is not very clean," she said. "The new neighbors don't know how to wash correctly. Perhaps they need better laundry soap."
Her husband looked on and remained silent.
Every time her neighbors would hang their wash to dry, the woman would make the same comments.
About one month later, the woman was surprised to see a nice clean wash on the line and said to her husband:
"Look, they learned how to wash correctly. I wonder who taught them this."
The husband said, "I got up early this morning and cleaned our windows."
And so it is with life. What we see depends on the purity of the window through which we look!

Perception is reality - Be realistic about your pain and suffering
When you look very closely at life events and really think about the outcomes they produce, there is no such thing as a "big" or "small" thing. Everything makes a difference in our lives. I think all of life is a tapestry, where events occur and the people we meet along the way are meant to be there for a reason, and the decisions we make help steer the direction our lives take. I also believe that life always has a way of working out. Sometimes we may not like our current circumstance, but each is a doorway to another chapter in our lives if we choose to view it this way. This is my ongoing perception about everything and everyone.

Several years ago, my town and home were hit extremely hard by a hurricane. The outside of my house was covered in trees and one tree limb pierced through the roof into my living room (while I was sleeping), causing water damage, mold, and other issues. Seven months later, my roof was finally replaced, and the interior ceiling, walls, flooring, and windows were repaired from the water damage.

The hurricane was a major inconvenience with many days without power and limited water and food. With flooding and trees down everywhere, it was a mess in and around the house. The crazy thing is that the hole in my roof was not much bigger than my hand. The small size of the tree limb that created this hole to make its way into my house is an indication of how powerful the storm was. Although it was a little hole, it set so many things into motion.

This is what I mean by "big" and "small" things in life. Size is irrelevant. The hurricane was huge and the hole was tiny in comparison, each providing a different, yet equally challenging, set of circumstances. If this tree limb did not pierce through my roof into my living room, my life would have gone on as normal. I would not have had to temporarily move out, repair or replace damaged household items, or spend weeks cleaning mold and other damage to make the house safe to live.

I also would not have been as motivated to get the new roof that I needed, new flooring that I also needed, and a new paint job that was overdue in that part of the house...all because of a hole no bigger than my hand! This is what hit me as I saw all the work being done. To get everything done, it took 4 teams of workers and me having to move out twice, along with days of cleaning and putting the house back together after all the work was done.

Some people may look at the hurricane and see it as a tragedy, and in some ways it most certainly was. From my perspective, I believe events like this can either bring us down or make us stronger. It did a little of both for me, but it mostly made me stronger and more resilient. To add even more opportunity for resiliency, during the writing of this chapter, another hurricane came through my area and a tree fell on my car causing significant damage. No one was hurt and the car was repaired, but it was a tough blow to see my relatively new car covered by a tree at 11pm at night. I am still amazed I was able to sleep.

As I have shared many times, for 20 years I have lived with severe chronic pain from a neurological movement disorder called dystonia. For me, it was a massive obstacle which led to severe anxiety, depression, and isolation for many years. I eventually learned that I needed to change my perspective about the cards I was dealt (the metaphorical "hole in my roof" and "tree on my car") if I wanted to work out of the painfully lonely place I was in, and it was a very dark one in many ways.

I believe I had to go through all of it to get to a better place, but I could have gotten there sooner had I made the conscious decision to view my circumstances as a lesson and make different choices. When I began to do this, my life changed for the better and I found meaning and purpose again; in many ways, more meaning and purpose than I had before developing this life altering health condition.

But no one told me any of this was possible or to look at my situation in a different way with a more open mind to see the opportunities it might present, which is why I am sharing this message with you. I very well might not have listened given the grief I was going through at the time, along with the severe physical and mental pain, so I totally understand if this is not hitting home for some of you, but it sure would have been good for me to hear a different perspective than the negative broken record playing over and over in my mind.

I have learned many things from pain and dystonia and all other challenges in my life. They include perseverance, patience, gratitude, courage, compassion, strength, humility, resilience, and a never give up attitude. What I have also learned is that whenever an obstacle gets in our way, if we don't look for the opportunity it might be presenting, it creates more suffering and we remain stuck. To prevent this from happening, my ongoing thought is, "how do I make the best out of a difficult situation." This keeps me in a proactive state of mind so I can see my options. I shared this mindset a couple times previously and I feel it is worth mentioning again.

I was the total opposite for a very long time where life to me seemed like it was over and I would never have the chance to enjoy anything ever again. My ongoing thought back then was, "everything in life completely stinks and I don't want to live." This is why it was so hard to see a way out and why I wrote this section (and book), because I know so many people who are suffering the very same way.

Perhaps your life needs to go in a different direction for reasons unbeknownst to you at the moment. Do not resist it and you will begin to see doors open that will lead you to a better place. No problem (or hole in the roof) is too small or too big to change the course of our lives in negative or positive ways. How we respond to problems is what determines the direction life takes and what defines our character. Not the problem, unless we let it.

The following is a wise quotation attributed to Abraham Lincoln about perspective: "We can complain because rose bushes have thorns or rejoice because thorn bushes have roses." As with life, the outcome of all experiences in all situations depends on our perspective. We can allow obstacles to tear us down or lift us up. It is all about how we think and the lens through which we choose to see things. People and events around us may not change. They may always be the same. It is when we change our perspective that everything looks different and how we relate to the world changes in positive, productive, and exciting ways.

The power of perspective when living with pain and adversity

People often tell me how upbeat and positive I am, despite pain from dystonia all day, every day, for the last 20 years. I would say this is accurate most of the time nowadays, but I wasn't always this way. For years, I denied, I resisted, and I ran from my suffering. I did everything I could think of to avoid the physical and emotional pain, anxiety, and depression. In retrospect, it was the running from the emotional pain from my life changing disorder that fueled the anxiety and depression. I continue to be a work in progress, but for those who know me, you know that I have come a long way from some very dark places, and you can too.

For those of you who are deeply suffering, encouraging you to shift your thoughts and perspective to foster acceptance may anger you, and I completely understand. There was a time when it would infuriate me also. What I have learned over time though, is that this is the way to live well with any life challenge, but we can only embrace this mindset when we are ready. Take your time. Allow the grief process to play out (read more about the stages of grief in Chapter 10), understanding that there will hopefully come a time when we realize that "going into" our suffering rather than running from it or denying it is the way to transcend it.

Look for what lessons the suffering might be teaching you. Find a way to be grateful for it if possible, without forgetting to be grateful for all the other blessings in your life. Without pain, we would never know what joy and pleasure feel like. Everything in life has its opposite. Everything has a silver lining if we look for it. I know what suffering is like, so I am not putting a fluffy spin on things. Bottom line…life is hard!

The important thing is what we do when life kicks us extra hard in the gut. It is called the "decision point." Some people feign happiness and a positive outlook, while others live it head on. Living it, no matter what is going on in our lives, is the key, because when we look for the opportunity in an obstacle, it brings hope and optimism into our lives.

There is a popular saying, "attitude determines altitude," and this is the truth in my opinion. I lived in a very pain filled, depressed and anxiety ridden world for a long time, but I chose to not let myself be that person anymore. I was living the life of a victim, which I want to describe/clarify. Events and people can victimize us, but we choose whether or not to become a victim of that event or circumstance. It is our choice, and for the first 5 or so years after developing dystonia, I chose the victim route and was miserable (see more about victim mentality in Chapter 6).

It took me a while, but I realized that there is no way for me to live and battle successfully with anything if I wallow in misery. Instead of fighting those really tough days, I try to flow with them. One of my favorite affirmations when it feels like life is running out of control is, "I relax into the flow of life and life flows through me with ease."

Forget about yesterday. Forget about tomorrow.
Just get through this moment right now
and tomorrow will take care of itself.

Learning to be okay with what we view as not okay
Confronting our suffering can be a monumental task. We prefer to shield ourselves from pain and trauma, which I did for many years to my detriment. I had to take a different approach. I had to learn to be okay with everything I viewed as not okay. The main thing of course being the complete life change when I was hit with very severe symptoms of dystonia.

As mentioned a few times, one of the most popular self-help books of all time is called, *The Road Less Travelled*, by M. Scott Peck. It documents how confronting and solving problems is a painful process, which most of us attempt to avoid. This avoidance results in pain and the hampered ability to grow both emotionally and spiritually. Dr. Peck provides strategies for confronting and resolving our problems, and how suffering through changes can enable us to reach a higher level of self-understanding.

Even though we may be suffering with something, no matter how big or small, we can still have a fulfilling life if we are open to something new, and if we choose to face the pain rather than hide from it. Life always has options if we choose to see the options, versus seeing a wall in front of us.

Our health and other circumstances do not have to rule our lives unless we let them define who we are. As is often heard and mentioned several times in this book, it is not what happens to us in life that matters. It is what we do with it that matters. I didn't respond well to different situations in my life, especially when I got sick with dystonia. I no longer kick myself for this. I accept that I am human and this is what happens. We make mistakes and that is totally okay. If we use the outcome of these choices to make better choices going forward, then we are growing. This is how we find meaning and purpose in our lives.

I am not saying that this shift in thinking can change overnight or will change who we are overnight. It is a lifelong practice. Acknowledging the so called "baby steps," which to me are giant leaps given some of the very tough circumstances people live with, is critical for us to see that our efforts are paying off.

When trauma occurs, we all need time to grieve and vent, so allow yourself to go through this process. Just be careful about anything becoming all-consuming where grief and other emotions rule your life.

I want to make a special mention about emotions, especially anger because it is so easy to be angry when life doesn't go as planned. If we live in a place of anger all the time, our mind and body are physiologically incapable of healing or finding peace. When the stress factory is working at high capacity, which is created by emotions, it compromises every system within the body.

As lonely as life can sometimes feel when we are hit with any kind of adversity, please understand that you are not alone. There are people all over the world who are living with the same struggles. Reach out to them. Don't be afraid to share your story. Educate yourself and educate others. Helping others is also a big part of helping ourselves. Do not lose contact with the outside world. If you are physically unable to get out, use social media to communicate.

Please also refrain from comparing your life now to how it was before it changed. Compare your life now with you at your darkest time in life. This is a very important strategy. Many of us compare our lives to who we were before life changed. This is a mistake. One, it neglects who we are today and the efforts we make, and two, the true measurement of who we are is how far we have come from our toughest struggles; not when life was easy. If your darkest time is right now, measure your progress day to day or week to week. Break things way down so they are within your current potential of progress.

Be kind to yourself. Self-care is critical to our well-being. When looking for outside help, do not leave any stone unturned because anything and everything, or anyone, could possibly change your life for the better. Most people I know who do well living with physical or emotional pain utilize a variety of lifestyle management protocols. Sometimes minor changes are necessary and sometimes major changes need to happen. Be willing and open to all things.

Focus on the emotional pain you are experiencing just as much, if not more, as the physical trauma you may be experiencing. The mind-body connection is very powerful and it needs to be addressed for us to be as healthy as possible. Emotional trauma feeds off physical trauma and vice versa.

As M. Scott Peck also says in his book, "until you value yourself, you won't value your time. Until you value your time, you will not do anything with it." I did not value my time for years because I did not value myself. When I became sick I felt like a failure, so I didn't do anything of value with my life.

When I chose to value myself, my time became precious and I took better care of myself. This was the clincher for me. I had to learn to value who I was, no matter what was right or wrong, for my time to be greater utilized. I now use this precious time to make myself the best version of me I possibly can. This is the opportunity we all have every day. The only thing that matters is the first step we take out of bed in the morning. Then the next step and so on. Our days, weeks, and years are all built on moments. BE in the moment! THIS very moment is your life!

One final thought about self-growth that is so important. True nobility is not being better than anyone else. It is about being better than the person we were yesterday and all the days before, regardless of our struggle. It is the effort that matters. Acknowledge your efforts!

Replacement activities when living with pain

Prior to developing my current health condition, I was very active in private business, social events, athletics, travelling, and pretty much anything else a healthy person would do. I was involved in many physical activities such as baseball, golf, hiking, swimming, tennis, martial arts...you name it. I derived great pleasure from these activities. When I could no longer do them, I felt worthless. I felt a deep sense of loss. Basically, I had an identity crisis for about the next 5 years. Although I have improved a lot with my health, I am still not involved in some of the activities mentioned, which is where I excelled the most and where I really got the endorphins flowing and felt the most joy.

I have since replaced many of those old activities with new activities where I derive just as much pleasure. These are things such as writing, gardening, and photography to name just a few. I was not all that interested in these things before and I began to wonder what it is about them that gives me so much joy. What I realized is that I approach these new activities the same way I approached previous activities, and as a result, achieve the same outcome.

Take sports for example, where I excelled at a high level. Along with the physical activity of playing, what I really enjoyed most was the mental game. I thrived on the challenges that sports presented, and the need to be creative and strategic to better my skill set against an opponent. As much as I enjoyed the physical sports themselves, what I really loved most was the thinking aspect of them, similar to a chess match. For anyone familiar with sports like golf or baseball, it takes a tremendous amount of thinking, strategy, and concentration prior to the event or game itself, as well as during the event or game. This is what I loved most.

For many years after developing dystonia, I did not do anything that challenged my strategic, creative mind. After years of sitting around bored to tears living with so much pain, I began doing some creative writing. From there, things steamrolled into other creative outlets. I now take on projects and hobbies that challenge me and make me think, and I do things that stimulate my creativity and mental edge to improve; the exact same things I did with sports and other activities I am not involved with anymore. Now I get the dopamine, serotonin, and endorphin rush from my new activities and every day I feel joy, excitement, and motivation again.

If you are in a similar situation where you are physically unable to do activities you once could, what is it that you enjoyed so much about doing those things? How can you achieve the same outcome doing new things? What are you able to do now where you can be just as enthusiastic and passionate as those previous activities?

I didn't think like this right away. It took a while to get there. Honestly, I never previously thought about what I was even getting out of my activities or what I was missing so much. I just loved them and was so upset I couldn't do them anymore. That was my only focus. I couldn't wrap my head around the fact that I was so disabled. All I kept asking was, "why me?" and "how did this happen?!?" What I didn't realize was that I could look at these things differently and replace my old activities with other things and feel joy again. It never even occurred to me because those things were so much a part of my identity that I avoided trying anything new to create a new identity. I just wallowed in misery which didn't open my mind to other options. Since having changed my perspective, my life has been completely transformed.

Just because life might be different now does not mean that we can't find things to make our lives very fulfilling. Although I was an avid golfer, very much into martial arts, and almost a professional baseball and football player, I don't miss any of those things. I couldn't care less if I ever play those sports again. It's just not who I am anymore, and for those who know me, this would sound shocking because I was always playing something. But I have become a different person who does different things, and by accepting the new me, I have been able to replace the old me with new things to enjoy and look forward to doing.

The important questions to ask ourselves are: "what are things I can no longer do because of my problem/situation (whatever it is) and what was it that I got out of those things that fulfilled me?" And... "what can I do right now within my physical abilities where I can get the same positive feelings from these new things?" Then, do your best to replace your old activities with new ones where you achieve the fulfillment you desire. In other words, instead of trying to bring back the old you, create a new you. Choose one thing, no matter its size, that you can get excited about. Then just go with it and see where it takes you.

Perception about the past

I often hear people say how much they miss the person they were before they developed a particular problem and they want that person back; or that old life back. I can totally relate to this mindset because I grieved the loss of many things after developing dystonia. So much of my life fizzled away... friends, work, money, traveling, playing sports... I had no identity and my only "friends" were pain, anger, debt, anxiety, and depression. It took me years to find my bearings and see life from a different perspective.

Many of us intensely focus on the person we once were, but in what way does this serve us? This is a somewhat rhetorical question because I understand why we think this way, so I don't mean to sound aloof. I know we need to grieve and it is a process that takes time, but for how long do we allow ourselves to suffer more than we might have to by always living in the past? At some point or another, we must let it go and focus on now. At some point we must stop looking back in despair and look forward and prepare.

Focus on the problem at hand, whether it be a health problem, relationship issue, financial debacle, or anything at all, and use the lessons they teach us to become a better person than we were before the problem began. At least please be open to this possibility.

My way of thinking now versus when I was suffering with blinding, persistent pain, immobilizing anxiety, panic attacks, and depression, is like night and day. I wish I thought more like I do now back then. I didn't because I didn't have the information and the tools to do it, which is why I am sharing this with all of you who may be in the same boat as me. I don't want you to go down the same dark paths I did. They are so easy to get into and so hard to get out.

Years ago, I heard a quote by Wayne Dyer that helped change my life: "When we change the way we look at things, the things we look at change." When I began to look at things differently, my life improved and being sick and having lost so much didn't matter as much anymore. My perception about the life I had and the life I could potentially create totally changed, which was critical for my healing journey. Our perception and how much we believe in that perception (about anything), are powerful beyond our wildest imaginations. The perception we choose to embrace, and the strength with which we embrace it, will dictate the path our lives take.

I deeply embraced this quote, which really helped me see things differently and create a new life. Opening my mind to new possibilities has opened new doors, and what I do with my life NOW is what matters most. Past experiences have helped me work through today's problems, but I don't live in the past in a mournful way. When I focus on the past like this, the worse my health becomes and the more I reject the evolving person I am today.

This is what I am stressing to you. Use your current problem/challenge as an opportunity to become a better version of yourself and create a better life for yourself than the one you had before. I believe that with any challenge, when we embrace it, we erase it, creating a whole new outlook where life takes on a fresh new meaning with purpose; perhaps a purpose even greater than we had before.

No matter what we decide, life is going to move on. We can move on with it and look for the joy and the opportunities, or we can stay stuck in the past where we hold onto pain that impedes our progress. The choice is ours.

Chapter 22
The power of conviction

As mentioned several times, our mind is a powerful weapon. It can bring us down or be our best ally. The way we think can open doors or it can turn impediments into permanent obstacles. Our belief in our ability to accomplish a task will determine how well we are able to do it as well as our level of commitment. For example, if we want to learn a new task and don't believe we are smart enough, our chances of learning are reduced. Also, how much we value what we want to learn helps or keeps us from doing a certain behavior.

The quote under my senior picture in my high school yearbook is, "Never try. Do or do not. There is no try." Yoda said this to Luke Skywalker in the movie, *The Empire Strikes Back*. The exact quote is: "Always with you what cannot be done. Hear you nothing that I say? You must unlearn what you have learned. Try not. Do. Or do not. There is no try."

Yoda was training Luke to be a Jedi Knight and Luke kept saying how hard everything was and how things could NOT be done. He did not believe in "The Force" or himself and was therefore unable to accomplish certain tasks, so he gave up. Yoda did believe and used his power of belief and conviction to do things that marveled Luke.

Withholding any philosophical or spiritual reference, I am sharing this example to illustrate the power of belief in ourselves and how the words we use shape our thoughts which determine our attitude which determines our dedication to accomplishing anything in life.

The statement, "do or do not, there is not try," is absolutely true. We can't really "try" anything. We either do it or we don't. If I ask you to *try* and pick up a pencil from the table, you either do it or you don't. You don't try. With this in mind, doing or not doing something is a choice. That being said, there are certain things we are unable to do because we lack the skill set, but it still follows that we either do it or don't do it. And it is important to "try/do" because whether we fail or succeed, we are going to learn something, and learning is always valuable.

Not to split hairs or make more of this than need be, the point I want to stress is that our mindset often determines the outcome in most everything we do. If you believe strongly in something or have limiting beliefs about something, find evidence that either supports or disproves your belief. Many of us believe things without even knowing why. Most of it comes from conditioning from family, friends, and society/culture.

Challenge your thoughts and beliefs by asking this simple question: "Is it true?" Often, we believe something simply because we have heard it over and over and over, without ever investigating its truth or merit. This is the meaning of the word meme, which is discussed in great detail in the book, *Virus of the Mind: The new Science of the Meme*, by Richard Brodie.

What do you want to do with your life and how convicted are you to achieve it? If your beliefs conflict with your behavior, it will keep you from getting it. This is why challenging our beliefs and opinions is so important.

Think of all of life as an egg. If you break it from the outside, life ends. When it is broken from the inside, life begins. Just like the egg, all great things begin inside us.

As a final note to end this book, I want to share a story I included in the beginning of my first book. It speaks to the power of conviction and how seeing the opportunity in an obstacle can make great things happen.

"Great moments are born from great opportunity"
I first heard this quote watching one of my favorite movies called, *Miracle*. It is based on the true story about how the 1980 United States Olympic hockey team was able to defeat the Soviet Union in the semi-finals before going on to win the gold medal against Finland.

Not only were the United States and the Soviet Union in the midst of a cold war and for all intents and purposes, enemies, the Soviet national team was comprised of well-seasoned players and considered the most dominant team in the world. It won four straight gold medals from 1964 to 1976, almost every world championship since 1954, nearly defeated a team of Canada's top professional players in 1972, and beat several NHL teams in exhibition games during the 1970's.

Many of the players on the 1980 Soviet team were members of the Red Army, though they had few military responsibilities. The government allowed them to devote their lives to hockey, training together year-round while retaining their amateur status. Although they were considered amateurs, the government was paying them to primarily play hockey, technically making them professional athletes. This was a loophole the Soviet government used to boost the prowess of their athletes, prior to the current rule which allows professionals to compete.

In contrast, the Americans were a collection of college students with little history of playing together. In fact, prior to becoming part of the United States hockey team, many played against each other for colleges that were bitter rivals. They now had to put their rivalries aside and become teammates.

Putting aside their personal rivalries to come together as a team and then the overwhelming odds against them to beat the Soviets was a feat that no one in the world thought was remotely possible, except the players on that team and their coach Herb Brooks. "Great moments are born from great opportunity" is what Brooks said to his team in the locker room prior to the game against the Soviets. In an unforgettable, exciting game, the United States beat the Soviet Union that evening, something the world never remotely expected.

People who never watched hockey before or had any interest in hockey were glued to their televisions watching a game that rivals most any single sporting event in history. At the final buzzer, broadcaster Al Michaels yelled, "Do you believe in miracles?!?" Having watched this game live on television as a little kid, it is a moment that still brings me chills.

So, I ask you…do you believe that great moments are born from great opportunity as Herb Brooks said to his team before the David and Goliath battle took place? Do you see adversity as opportunity, or do you see it as an obstacle? If you see it as an obstacle, is it one that you can climb over or one that you allow to stand in your way and keep your life from moving forward? While you may feel that you have lost a lot because of the challenges you are facing, what have you gained? Can you become an ally with your challenges that you view as a rival like those college kids did? Can you live beyond your pain and suffering?

While I hope you are able to see your life challenges and any adversity that comes your way as things that provide you with new opportunities, as does any event or circumstance, I also acknowledge the very hard times in life that seem insurmountable. I lived in a place in my mind and body for many years where I didn't feel any reason to go on, so I understand where some of you are right now and hope that my words have inspired you.

Whenever I doubt my ability to accomplish anything and/or lose trust in the power of conviction and commitment, I recite the following words that I put to memory many years ago. It reminds me that all we need to do is take one convicted step to get ourselves on track towards where we want to go, and the rest falls into place.

> *Until one is committed there is hesitancy,*
> *the chance to draw back; always ineffectiveness.*
> *Concerning all acts of initiative there is one elementary truth,*
> *The ignorance of which kills countless ideas and splendid plans:*
> *That the moment one definitely commits oneself, then Providence moves too.*
> *All sorts of things occur to help one that would never otherwise have occurred.*
> *A whole stream of events issues from the decision,*
> *Raising in one's favor all manner of unforeseen incidents and meetings and*
> *material assistance, which no man could have dreamt would have come his way.*
> *Whatever you can do or dream you can, begin it.*
> *Boldness has genius, power and magic in it.*
> - William Hutchison Murray -

Summary

This book was an honest account of the light and dark side of pain, suffering, and adversity, with the intent to acknowledge you, offer understanding, provide hope, and help you find meaning in your life that transcends your suffering.

Life always throws us curveballs, so we must learn to adapt to changes. If we are being honest, we have no other choice if we want to live as well as possible, and it is often during these times when the greatest learning in our lives takes place. We can look for this opportunity or we can close our eyes and be angry, keeping us imprisoned. The greatest teacher in my life has been adversity, and I suspect that if you look closely, you will find that your challenges are your greatest teachers as well.

Don't avoid or distract yourself. Stand tall in your pain and suffering to get through it. Ask yourself what the lessons and purposes are for your suffering. That is the answer we need to seek and find to get past our pain. Too often we look at difficult times with a closed mind. This, to me, is when we need to be the most open-minded because this is when our lives can change in the most monumental ways.

Surrender to the event or circumstance. Go into the pain. If you truly allow yourself to let go and be led by it, you will see incredible lessons that will transform your life for the better.

A question to ask ourselves is, "what can I do on a daily basis that puts me in a position to make a difference about my situation?" This is a far more productive use of our time than being angry about our current situation. We never reach a point of acceptance and peace with this mindset.

To find peace, we must deal with our truth every step of the way and learn the lessons. Everyone is flawed and those who can be vulnerable become strong, powerful, and inspirational. As the famous quote goes, "the most beautiful stones have been tossed by the wind and washed by the waters and polished to brilliance by life's strongest storms."

Use your life experiences as lessons to help you grow and help others grow along the way. Become a student of life with humility, grace, and gratitude, for this is the way to make adversity your ally to help transcend any form of pain and suffering.

I would like to end this book with my wishes for you, in the words of Bob Perks:

I wish you enough sun to keep your attitude bright no matter how gray the day may appear.

I wish you enough rain to appreciate the sun even more.

I wish you enough happiness to keep your spirit alive and everlasting.

I wish you enough pain so that even the smallest of joys in life may appear bigger.

I wish you enough gain to satisfy your wanting.

I wish you enough loss to appreciate all that you possess.

I wish you enough hellos to get you through the final good-bye.

Made in the USA
Las Vegas, NV
14 November 2023

80828422R00142